ƒP

WHEN THE MISSISSIPPI RAN BACKWARDS

Empire, Intrigue, Murder,

and the

New Madrid Earthquakes

JAY FELDMAN

FREE PRESS

NEW YORK · LONDON · TORONTO · SYDNEY

FREE PRESS
A Division of Simon & Schuster, Inc.
1230 Avenue of the Americas
New York, NY 10020

FREE PRESS and colophon are trademarks
of Simon & Schuster, Inc.

For information about special discounts for bulk purchases, please contact Simon & Schuster
Special Sales: 1-800-456-6798 or business@simonandschuster.com

Designed by Dana Sloan

Manufactured in the United States of America

1314 QVS 15 14 13 12 11 10

Maps and figure illustrations
by Meg Hehner

Library of Congress Cataloging-in-Publication Data
Feldman, Jay.
When the Mississippi ran backwards: empire, intrigue, murder, and the new Madrid earth-
quakes/Jay Feldman.
p. cm.
Includes bibliographical references and index.
1. Earthquakes —Missouri—New Madrid Region. 2. Mississippi River—History—19th century. 3. Indians of North America—Missouri—History—19th century. 4. Mississippi River
Valley—History—19th century. I. Title.
QE535.2.U6F45 2005
551.22'09778'985—dc22
2004057537
ISBN 978- 0-7432-4279-0

*To my wife Marti
and my parents Ben and Edna
for all their love and support*

Contents

Part IV: AFTERSHOCKS ·

The night has been unruly: where we lay,
Our chimneys were blown down; and, as they say,
Lamentings heard i' the air; strange screams of death,
And prophesying with accents terrible
Of dire combustion and confused events
New hatch'd to the woeful time. The obscure bird
Clamour'd the livelong night: some say, the earth
Was feverous and did shake.

WILLIAM SHAKESPEARE, *Macbeth*

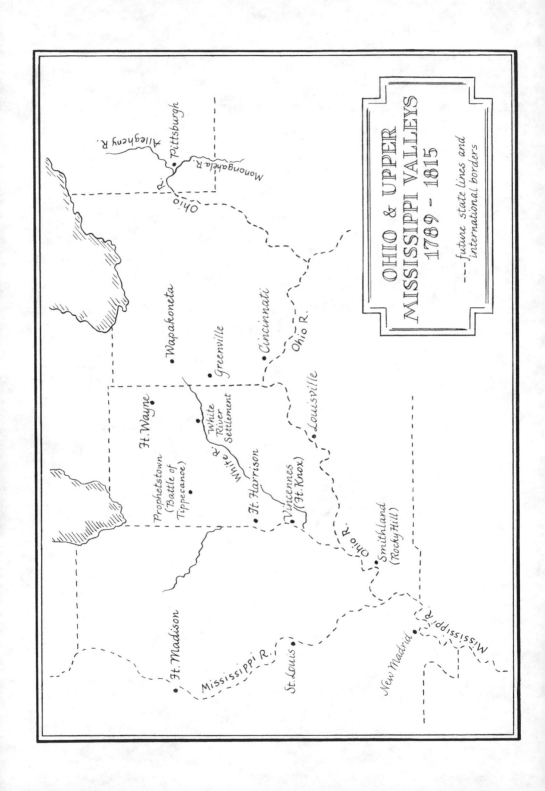

OHIO & UPPER
MISSISSIPPI VALLEYS
1789 – 1815
-- future state lines and
international borders

Allegheny R.
Pittsburgh
Monongahela R.
Ohio R.

Wapakoneta
Greenville
Cincinnati
Ohio R.

Ft. Wayne
White River Settlement
White R.
Louisville

Prophetstown
(Battle of
Tippecanoe)
Ft. Harrison
Vincennes
(Ft. Knox)

Ohio R.
Smithland
(Rocky Hill)

Ft. Madison
Mississippi R.
St. Louis
New Madrid
Mississippi R.

When the Mississippi
Ran Backwards

———

Part One

PORTENTS

——

Chapter One

A TIME OF
EXTRAORDINARIES

Accompanied by an entourage of Shawnee, Kickapoo, and Winnebago warriors, the Shawnee chief strode decisively through the Creek village of Tuckhabatchee. He was a striking figure: five-feet, ten-inches tall, handsome, straight-backed, with a slight limp. As he and his warriors made their way through the village, word spread quickly among the Creeks: Tecumseh has arrived.

The great Shawnee leader was on the last leg of a mission that had taken him three thousand miles in six months. Beginning in the summer of 1811, he traveled south from Indiana to spread his message of intertribal unity. Night after night, the powerful orator stood before the council fires, exhorting the southern nations to bury their various and long-standing grudges and divisions, and prepare for a collective war against the whites to defend what remained of tribal lands, which were being lost to the United States government at an alarming rate as the young republic pushed westward.

Twenty years earlier, a decade and a half after the United States declared its independence from Great Britain, the new nation was already bursting at the seams, and westward expansion had become a deeply embedded tenet of the republic. After the Revolution, the process of acquiring Indian land accelerated as settlers streamed beyond rapidly widening national boundaries. Waves of settlers poured over the Appalachian and Allegheny mountains into Kentucky (then part of Virginia), Tennessee (then part of North Carolina), and the Old Northwest Territory, which included the future states of Wisconsin, Michigan, Indiana, Illinois, and Ohio.

The migrations inevitably led to confrontations with the indigenous tribes of these regions. Between 1790 and 1795, native resistance escalated on the "frontier"—a fluid boundary that in the late eighteenth and early nineteenth centuries included the Ohio and Mississippi valleys, Georgia, the future states of Alabama and Florida, and the area around the Great Lakes. Much of this territory remained unstable throughout this period, as a result both of Indian conflicts and of great-power rivalries among Spain, Britain, and France, and the upstart United States of America. Beginning with the Treaty of Greenville in 1795, the U.S. government embarked upon an aggressive course of acquiring tribal lands in the Old Northwest, while simultaneously juggling its relationships with the European colonial powers.

In the decade that followed the Treaty of Greenville, the tribes of the Old Northwest Territory ceded a staggering amount of land to the federal government, giving up millions upon millions of acres. The devious methods used to obtain these cessions included bribing tribal leaders and/or plying them with liquor, exploiting tribal poverty with promises of annuities and/or threatening to cut off previously guaranteed annuities, striking deals with individuals who had no authority to represent their tribes, and accepting grants of one tribe's land from individuals of another tribe. By 1805, the entire north bank of the Ohio River had been cleared of Indian title.

Tecumseh saw the handwriting on the wall. Counting on the British to help him resist the U.S. land grab and defend what was left of the natives' ancestral homelands, he had set out to form a military confederation of northern and southern nations. The British, who obtained Canada from France in 1763 as part of the settlement that ended the French and Indian War, had been watching with alarm as the U.S. encroached on the Canadian border. The American government, on the other hand, was apprehensive about both the confederation of Indian tribes and the natives' alliance with the British.

Uniting the tribes against European and Euro-American invaders had been attempted before by leaders like the Ottawa warrior Pontiac, the Mohawk organizer Joseph Brant, and the Creek chief Alexander McGillivray. It was a daunting task, considering the fractured, tense relations among and within some of the nations. Yet by 1811, Tecumseh had met with a considerable degree of success in the north, claiming substantial support among the Potawatomi, Kickapoo, and Winnebago tribes, and a lesser degree among the Shawnees, Miamis, Wyandots, Weas, Piankeshaws, and others. In August 1811 he headed south, traveling with his retinue to the Choctaw, Chickasaw, Creek, Seminole, and Cherokee nations.

The trip had not started well. The Chickasaws and Choctaws were not responsive to Tecumseh's call for unity against the whites. Frustrated, he and his followers continued on to the Creeks, his mother's people.

Tecumseh's band made their visit to Tuckhabatchee, in what is now Alabama, in late September, timing their appearance to coincide with the annual council of the Creek Confederacy, an amalgamation of about fifteen different Creek groups, at which Chickasaws, Choctaws, and Cherokees were also in attendance. The thousands of people who were gathered in Tuckhabatchee, the largest town of the Upper Creeks, included tribesmen, their families, white traders, and government officials. Arriving a few days after the conference had begun, Tecumseh and his entourage electrified the gathering by making a stunning entrance.

"Tecumseh, at the head of his . . . party, marched into the square," wrote one early chronicler. "They were entirely naked, except their flaps [breechcloths] and ornaments. Their faces were painted black, and their heads adorned with eagle plumes, while buffalo tails dragged from behind, suspended by bands which went around their waists. Buffalo tails were also attached to their arms, and made to stand out, by means of bands. Their appearance was hideous, and their bearing pompous and ceremonious." After marching around the square several times, they finally approached the assembled chiefs and presented them with tobacco, a common gesture of friendship.

As the council progressed, Tecumseh would come to the meetings in the square each day, but with U.S. Indian agent Benjamin Hawkins present, he refused to speak. "The sun has gone too far today," he would say every evening. "I will make my talk tomorrow." Finally, after more than a week, Hawkins concluded his business with the Creeks and left.

That night, before hundreds assembled in the council house, Tecumseh rose to deliver an impassioned recruitment talk, "full of fire and vengeance," urging the southerners to take up the cause of a pan-tribal confederation. No U.S. agents were allowed into the council house, so there is no direct transcription of the speech, but it was a talk Tecumseh had given before and would give again. A reasonable record of a version given a few months later suggests the power of his words on this night.

He stood for several minutes before beginning, surveying the assembled warriors "in a very dignified though respectfully complaisant and sympathizing manner." Then he began, his persuasive, evocative rhetoric punctuated by his manly, athletic gracefulness.

"*Brothers* — We all belong to one family; we are all children of the Great Spirit; we walk in the same path; slake our thirst at the same spring; and now affairs of the greatest concern lead us to smoke the pipe around the same council fire!

"*Brothers* — We are friends; we must assist each other to bear our burdens. The blood of many of our fathers and brothers has run like water on the ground, to satisfy the avarice of the white men. We, ourselves, are threatened with a great evil; nothing will pacify them but the destruction of all the red men."

Looking around at his audience, Tecumseh no doubt reminded the assembly of his familial connection with Tuckhabatchee—his mother and father had lived in the village, and he still had relatives there. He continued:

"*Brothers* — When the white men first set foot on our grounds, they were hungry; they had no place on which to spread their blankets, or to kindle their fires. They were feeble; they could do nothing for themselves. Our fathers commiserated their distress, and shared freely with them whatever the Great Spirit had given his red children. They gave them food when hungry, medicine when sick, spread skins for them to sleep on, and gave them grounds, that they might hunt and raise corn.

"*Brothers* — The white people are like poisonous serpents: when chilled, they are feeble and harmless; but invigorate them with warmth, and they sting their benefactors to death. The white people came to us feeble; and now we have made them strong, they wish to kill us, or drive us back, as they would wolves and panthers.

"*Brothers* — The white men are not friends to the Indians: at first they only asked for land sufficient for a wigwam; now, nothing will satisfy them but the whole of our hunting grounds, from the rising to the setting sun.

"*Brothers* — The white men want more than our hunting grounds; they wish to kill our warriors; they would even kill our old men, women, and little ones."

Tecumseh spoke for hours, delivering a "vehement narration of the wrongs imposed by the white people on the Indians, and an exhortation for the latter to resist them."

But it was not only military resistance that the Shawnee chief counseled. He also implored his listeners to return to their traditional ways, and to abandon the farming and weaving that had been put on them by white men. He warned them that after the whites had turned all the forests and hunting grounds into farms they would enslave the red man, just as they had the black man. He urged them to employ none of the white man's weapons, but to use instead only the tomahawk, knife, and bow. He pressed them to likewise spurn all the white man's clothing, and to dress themselves in the skins of the animals the Great Spirit had provided for them. His message was, in short, one of religious fundamentalism, which gave his rhetoric that much more power even as it made his plan far less practical.

Tecumseh further beseeched the assembled warriors to stand firm against any more land cessions, to replace weak-willed chiefs who would give away the land, and to prepare for battle. He advised them to be outwardly friendly toward whites, to neither steal from them nor fight with them, but to mask their real intentions until the right moment arrived for an all-out war, which he promised would be supported by the British and, more important, by the Great Spirit, who had sent him on this journey.

The Great Spirit, Tecumseh told the warriors, had shown his approval of this plan by sending a sign. After all, had his arrival in Tuckhabatchee not been accompanied by the great comet that now blazed in the northern sky each night? (The Great Comet of 1811, with its 15,000,000-mile-wide head and 100,000,000-mile-long tail, was visible for 260 days.) And had that comet not increased in brightness during his stay here? And was his name not Tecumseh—Shooting Star? This was clearly a sign sent by the Great Spirit to bestow his blessing on Tecumseh's mission.

He finished up his talk with a fervent call for unity:

"*Brothers* — My people are brave and numerous; but the white people are too strong for them alone. I wish you to take up the tomahawk with them. If we all unite, we will cause the rivers to stain the great waters with their blood.

"*Brothers* — If you do not unite with us, they will first destroy us, and then you will fall an easy prey to them. They have destroyed many nations of red men because they were not united, because they were not friends to each other.

"*Brothers* — We must be united; we must smoke the same pipe; we must fight each other's battles; and more than all, we must love the Great Spirit; he is for us; he will destroy our enemies, and make all his red children happy."

For all its passion and power, Tecumseh's talk met with only mixed success. Certain Creeks, like the well-regarded warrior Menawa and the medicine man Josiah Francis, were swayed, but others, like Big Warrior, the head civil chief of Tuckhabatchee, remained aloof. Tecumseh needed Big Warrior's support to offset the weak response he had received from the Chickasaws and Choctaws. If he could get a commitment from Big Warrior, it might persuade some of the fence-sitters to join the confederation.

In the Creek chief's lodge, with others present, the Shawnee leader offered gifts and once again gave his talk, but Big Warrior, a mixed-blood, remained noncommittal. Frustrated by the indifferent reaction, Tecumseh stood up to leave. He gave Big Warrior a withering look, and then, according to a legend that would soon spread across the frontier like wildfire and convince many Creeks to join him, Tecumseh uttered a prophetic pronouncement.

"Your blood is white," he disdainfully told Big Warrior. "You have taken my talk and the sticks and the wampum and the hatchet, but you do not mean to fight. I know the reason. You do not believe the Great Spirit has sent me. You shall know. I leave Tuckhabatchee directly and shall go straight to Detroit. When I arrive there, I will stamp my foot on the ground and shake down every house in Tuckhabatchee." Then he turned and left.

As the legend has it the Creeks began counting the days, reckoning the time it should take the Shawnee chief to reach Detroit. Early on the morning of December 16, the day of his calculated arrival, Tecumseh's prophecy was fulfilled. The earth began to tremble violently. The Creek village was leveled.

The upheaval that shook down every house in Tuckhabatchee was the first of the New Madrid earthquakes—the most powerful series of quakes ever to hit the United States.

ON DECEMBER 15, the night of the first quake, Lilburne Lewis summoned his slaves to the kitchen cabin of his property, Rocky Hill, in the western Kentucky county of Livingston. The slaves came quickly, not wishing to anger their owner, who, together with his younger brother, Isham, had been drinking heavily all evening. The slaves knew only too well the rages to which Lilburne was prone when he was drunk.

When the six slaves entered the cabin, they saw the seventh of their number—George, a seventeen-year-old who served as errand boy, house servant, and general handyman—chained to the floor, face down in a spread-eagle position. The fearful slaves huddled together, not knowing what to expect. Whatever they might have been imagining, however, could not have been as ghastly as what was about to take place.

Like many thousands of the settlers who invaded aboriginal lands in Kentucky, the Lewis brothers were émigrés from Virginia. They were nephews of Thomas Jefferson and scions of a branch of one of the founding families of Virginia. Through a century and a half of exploitive farming practices, generations of Lewises, like so many other Virginia farmers, had laid waste to what had once been the fertile, productive soil of Virginia. Seeking a fresh start on the frontier, Lilburne Lewis, together with his brother Randolph, their father, Charles, and their three families, set out for Kentucky in late 1807.

Things did not go well for the Lewises in Kentucky; despite their hopes for a new life, their fortunes deteriorated rapidly. In 1809, when his wife died, leaving him, at age thirty-two, with five children, Lilburne was already deeply in debt. Early the following year, Lucy Jefferson Lewis—mother of Lilburne, Isham, and Randolph, and sister of Thomas Jefferson—passed away, and in February 1811, Randolph died, leaving Lilburne with the additional responsibility of caring for his brother's eight children. Lilburne's new marriage, to a daughter of one of western Kentucky's most powerful families, was not a happy one, and it became just one more disaster in an accumulated series.

The arrival of Lilburne's ne'er-do-well younger brother, Isham, in the fall of 1811 did nothing to help the situation. As he saw his own life and the Lewis dynasty unraveling, Lilburne, on a downward spiral of wrecked fortune, began drinking heavily. By the end of 1811, his slaves knew enough to steer clear of him when he was under the influence.

On the evening of December 15, Lilburne and Isham had already started their nightly bout of debauchery when Lilburne gave the seventeen-year-old George—whose cheek was disfigured by a large and distinctive scar—a pitcher and sent him to fetch water from a spring on the property. Somewhere along the way, George—who had a history of talking back to Lilburne and had recently gone missing from the plantation for a short time—broke the pitcher. By the time he returned to the house, the two brothers were roaring drunk, and when George showed them the broken piece of pottery, Lilburne flew into a wild rage. He and Isham dragged the unfortunate young man out to the kitchen cabin, threw him to the floor, and chained him.

Lilburne then summoned the rest of the slaves. When they were assembled in the cabin, he commanded them to build a blazing fire in the kitchen fireplace. After the fire was built up, Lilburne bolted the door and bellowed that he was going to teach them all a lesson about disobeying him.

He picked up an axe and began moving ominously about the crowded room, alternately muttering under his breath and shouting profane threats, finally coming to rest over the prone body of George. From his face-down position on the floor, George pleaded with Lilburne, as the other slaves joined him in a wailing chorus. But with Isham egging him on, Lilburne was past the point of reasoning. As the six slaves watched in horrified disbelief, he raised the axe above his head and swung it down on George's neck, severing the young man's spine and slicing his jugular vein and carotid artery with one chop.

As the cries and wailing of the slaves filled the night air of Rocky Hill, the Lewis brothers forced one of the men to take the axe, hack up George's body into pieces and throw the pieces onto the fire. Lilburne then told the terrified slaves that if they ever revealed the murder to anyone they would suffer the same treatment as George.

It was well past midnight when the slaves finished scrubbing the cabin clean of George's blood and bits of flesh and bone. Then, with another warning, they were sent back to their quarters. Before Lilburne and Isham retired, the brothers heaped wood into the fireplace, priming the fire to burn for the rest of the night and consume all evidence of the crime.

Less than an hour later, however, the first of the New Madrid earthquakes would cause the chimney to collapse, extinguishing the fire, preserving George's remains, and, in due course, bringing the murder to light.

TECUMSEH's legendary prophecy and the Lewis brothers' barbaric act were not the only portents. From events both local and distant, a superstitious observer might almost have predicted the New Madrid earthquakes or some comparable set of catastrophes.

In 1811, the planet was in turmoil, and ominous signs were everywhere to be seen. International or civil wars were being fought throughout Asia, Africa, the Middle East, and Central and South America. Europe was locked in the grip of the Napoleonic wars, and in an extension of the broader hostilities, the British defeated the Dutch in Java and the French in Madagascar.

Internally, England was in convulsion, the war with France having taken a heavy toll on the nation's economy. In March, the Luddite rebellion began in the county of Nottinghamshire as angry workers smashed machinery in protest against the growing mechanization of the knitting industry.

In North America, 1811 was an annus mirabilis, a year of wonders filled with a daunting proliferation of natural phenomena and catastrophic disasters. The year was ushered in by a small earthquake that jostled the cities of Columbia, South Carolina, and Augusta, Georgia, on the 13th of January.

During the summer, the Ohio and Mississippi valleys were inundated by massive flooding, which led to widespread, unparalleled illness. "Between St. Louis and New Madrid," wrote Daniel Drake, a Cincinnati physician, "many parts of the valley were overflown extensively. This was followed, in autumn, by the bilious unremitting fever, which prevailed in that quarter to a great extent. . . . [T]his was clearly referable to the vegetable putrefaction which was the consequence of that flood."

Where it was not raining, it was stifling. "In the summer months the heat was, in many places, the most intense that was ever known," reported one newspaper. "The crops in many parts of the United States were destroyed by drought."

In the fall, hurricanes and tornadoes slammed the eastern U.S. from Georgia to Maine. On the 10th of September, a devastating twister struck Charleston, South Carolina, killing more than a dozen people and causing extensive damage to structures.

Nashville, Tennessee, was hit by another tornado in late October, reported in the *Lexington* (Kentucky) *American Statesman* as having been "more violent and destructive than is often heard of. . . . The damage sustained by the citizens of this town cannot . . . have been less than 10,000 dollars." Many longtime residents of the area stated that they had "never witnessed such a scene of destruction in this country before."

In early September the Great Comet appeared, with a head 15,000,000 miles wide and a tail 100,000,000 miles long, and it was visible to the naked eye for the remainder of the year. As in the case of other comets throughout history, many people took it as a foreshadowing of catastrophe. An article in the *Kentucky Gazette* tried to assuage people's fears. "Anciently these sideral erratics were held to be precursors of great calamities—revolutions, pestilence and wars. But philosophers of later years have ascertained their nature to be like that of the planets, *'parts of one harmonious whole.'*"

On September 17, there was a near-total eclipse of the sun. "The day was remarkably serene, and the skies entirely clear of clouds," read one account, "so that its appearance was the most solemn and impressive that we could conceive."

Animals exhibited strange behavior. "A spirit of change and a restlessness seemed to pervade the very inhabitants of the forest," wrote English tourist Charles J. Latrobe. "A countless multitude of squirrels, obeying some great and universal impulse, which none can know but the Spirit that gave them being, left their reckless and gambolling life, and their ancient places of retreat in the north, and were seen pressing forward by tens of thousands in a deep and sober phalanx to the South. No obstacles seemed to check this extraordinary and concerted movement; the word had been given them to go forth, and they obeyed it, though multitudes perished in the broad Ohio, which lay in their path."

In retrospect, some of these portents appear to have been directly connected to the impending earthquakes. William Leigh Pierce, a traveler on the Mississippi, observed, "On the 30th of November, 1811 about one half hour before sun-rise, two vast electrical columns shot up from the eastern horizon, until their heads reached the zenith"; he went on to note that from then until the first earthquake on December 16, "there was a continued want of perfect transparency in the atmosphere, and wherever the sun was even partially visible, it exhibited a dull and fiery redness."

The onslaught of unsettling phenomena caused understandably

widespread trepidation about what might be coming next. "These are no common events," said one newspaper article in a reflection of the general apprehension, "and without incurring the charge of superstition, they may be deemed portentous of still greater events.

"Surely so many occurrences in the course of a few months ought to excite something of meditation and reflection."

The moralists seized upon the occasion as an opportunity to issue remonstrances. "The great scale upon which Nature is operating," warned an editorial in the *Lexington American Statesman*, "should be a solemn admonition to men, (or those animals in the shape of men) to abandon their pitiful grovelling, schemes of venality and corruption in the prosecution of which they are so ardently engaged. An *honest heart*, alone, can view those great events, with composure. The political *swindler* the *assassin of reputation*, must feel severely, the visitations of conscience, at such momentous periods, when Nature appears, in spasmodic fury, no longer to tolerate the moral turpitude of man."

Others registered the amazing string of events without drawing conclusions. "Whether these things are ominous or not," wrote the Reverend John Carrigan, "one thing is certain, this is a time of extraordinaries."

THIS IS the story of the greatest series of earthquakes in the history of this country, of the people caught up in them, of the extraordinary confluence of forces and events leading up to them, and of the upheaval they caused. The United States was at a turning point, one of those defining moments in history when forces converge so powerfully that something has to give. This was true geologically as well as historically—it was almost as if the earthquakes were a symbol of the turmoil of the times.

This is the story of the New Madrid (pronounced new MAD-rid) earthquakes, but it is equally a story about America, and while it describes events that happened two hundred years ago, it is replete with themes and issues that reverberate down to the present day and continue to bedevil our nation: expansion, conquest, violence, corruption, greed, race relations, environmental degradation.

Between December 16, 1811, and late April 1812, the Mississippi River Valley was rocked by a chain of catastrophic earthquakes. Of the more than two thousand tremors that hit during this time, three would have measured near or over 8.0 on the later-devised magnitude scales, ranking them among the severest earthquakes to hit the contiguous United States in recorded history, about as powerful as the shock that devastated San Francisco in 1906. At least six others were in the 7.0–7.5 range. Yet today, curiously enough, the New Madrid earthquakes have been all but forgotten except by residents of the area and a handful of earthquake scientists.

The New Madrid quakes, centered in what is now the bootheel region of Missouri, were felt as far away as Mexico, Canada, Boston, New Orleans, and the Rocky Mountains. A million and a half square miles were affected, and the earth was in constant movement for nearly four months. Towns were destroyed, an eighteen-mile-long by five-mile-wide lake was created, and the Mississippi temporarily ran backwards. The quakes spawned an intense albeit short-lived religious revival, and the first federal disaster relief act in U.S. history was enacted by Congress to aid the victims of the quakes but unintentionally led to a colossal land fraud scandal.

The New Madrid earthquakes came on the eve of the War of 1812 and helped shape the direction of the war. When the dust cleared, the course of westward expansion was firmly set; the tribes of the Old Northwest and, with one exception, the south were decisively defeated; and British attempts to regain land south of the Canadian border were finally put to rest.

Because the surrounding area was sparsely populated at the time of the quakes, the death toll was not notably high, but the New Madrid Seismic Zone is still considered the area of greatest seismic risk east of the Rocky Mountains—if a comparable series of quakes, or even one major quake, were to occur today, the death toll would be staggering—tens, perhaps even hundreds of thousands of people would be killed. Two centuries after the 1811–12 sequence, minor earthquakes continue to occur on a frequent basis in the New Madrid fault zone, and while seismologists differ on many details about the 1811–12 earthquakes, they agree on one thing—it is only a matter of time until the New Madrid fault once again asserts itself in a catastrophic way.

THE STORIES of Tecumseh and the Lewis brothers touch on two of the driving engines of early U.S. history: Indian relations and slavery. Along with the country's shifting and dangerous relations with Britain and Spain, these two issues combined, on the Mississippi and Ohio valleys' frontier, to create an exceedingly combustible era. The period between the end of the American Revolution and the War of 1812 has been generally overlooked, but in the west, those years were a perilous time that would determine the future direction of the nation.

But slavery, Indians, and great-power politics were not the only driving forces. There was also the relentless, very American push for technological development.

TWO MONTHS before the dreadful events of the night of December 15, an extraordinary boat left Pittsburgh bound for New Orleans, the city for which she was named. It was a historic sailing, for not only was this the maiden voyage of the *New Orleans,* it was also the first steamboat trip ever on the Ohio and Mississippi rivers. The *New Orleans* represented the wave of the future—the strength of steam power would make upriver traffic practical. The boat would also prove to be one of the only structures on land or water strong enough to survive the earthquakes.

On board the *New Orleans* as she set out on October 20, 1811, were the boat's builder and one-third owner Nicholas Roosevelt, his eight-months-pregnant wife, Lydia, their two-year-old daughter, Rosetta, the family's huge Newfoundland dog, Tiger, and the boat's crew. The big boat—148 feet long and 32 feet wide—had cost $38,000 to build and had been two years in the making. Roosevelt had set out to prove to his partners, Robert Fulton and Robert Livingston, that a steamboat could handle the Ohio and the Mississippi, which were much wilder and far more hazardous than the placid Hudson with its easier current, where Fulton's *Clermont* had been so successful four years earlier.

Hundreds of cheering though skeptical spectators lined the east bank of the Monongahela River to see the *New Orleans* off on a voyage that would radically accelerate the development of the west. The success of the voyage would be a singular moment in westward expansion, opening up transportation and commerce, and creating a major impetus for settlement, which would in turn encroach yet further on the lands of the native tribes.

At first glance, Nicholas and Lydia Roosevelt (great-grand-uncle and great-grand-aunt of Theodore) were an unlikely couple. She was twenty, he forty-four. They had met eleven years earlier, when Roosevelt had been a business associate of Lydia's father, the renowned architect Benjamin Henry Latrobe. Over the objections of Latrobe, they were engaged when Lydia was thirteen and married four years later. Modern sensibilities will recoil at such a match, yet all the evidence indicates they were extremely well suited for each other and a very devoted couple. In fact, as marriage partners, they enjoyed a degree of companionship and equality rarely seen in the early nineteenth century.

Nicholas Roosevelt was a maverick and a man of many skills— mechanic, metallurgist, machinist, civil engineer, and builder of steam engines. At age thirty, he had been recognized as the only engine maker of any importance in the United States. Lydia Roosevelt was an adventurous iconoclast at a time when a lady of her class was expected to act with a stupefying degree of decorum. A woman of remarkably advanced attitudes, she was bright, assertive, artistic, and, above all, fearless.

This was not the Roosevelts' first trip down the Ohio and Mississippi. Two years earlier, while Lydia was pregnant with Rosetta, they had made a six-month voyage by flatboat in order to survey the western rivers and ascertain the feasibility of steamboat travel on them, a prospect about which there was great skepticism. Lydia had undertaken the flatboat voyage against all advice, and now, two years later, once more pregnant, Lydia was again strongly counseled not to make the steamboat trip. The perils of such a voyage were numerous enough—the Falls of the Ohio, which had claimed many a fine boat; the possibility of the steam engine's exploding; the increasingly hostile Indians—not to mention that she was eight months along. Not only did she disdain this advice, she took her two-year-old daughter along with her.

All along the banks of the Ohio, people turned out to watch the *New Orleans* steam deafeningly by. With the slow communications of the age, particularly on the frontier, many people in the west had not yet heard of the *Clermont*. "The novel appearance of the vessel," according to Englishman Charles J. Latrobe (a cousin to Lydia), "and the fearful rapidity with which it made its passage over the broad reaches of the river, excited a mixture of terror and surprise among many of the settlers on the banks, whom the rumour of such an invention had never reached."

In Wheeling, a huge crowd awaited the arrival of the *New Orleans,* and Roosevelt invited the public to board the boat for a 25-cent tour. The multitudes—including hundreds who had made a special trip in from the surrounding countryside—willingly paid their quarter and came aboard, where they saw the lavish living cabins, the crew's quarters, and the massive engine with its thirty-four-inch cylinder.

A week out of Pittsburgh, Lydia felt close to delivery. Forgoing the opportunity to make a similar promotional stop at Cincinnati, the *New Orleans* forged ahead for Louisville, where Lydia knew a midwife. As a disappointed crowd of well-wishers stood by on the bank, the boat cruised by Cincinnati at somewhere around twelve miles per hour.

The 1,500 residents of Louisville were safely asleep in their warm beds when the *New Orleans* steamed into the town's harbor at about midnight on October 28, having made the seven-hundred-plus river miles from Pittsburgh in eight days. The ship's earsplitting din was like nothing ever heard in those parts before. Awakened from their peaceful slumber, many of the inhabitants went running out into the streets in their nightclothes. In the dark, one panic-stricken person opined that such a fearsome racket could only be caused by one thing—the Great Comet had fallen into the river.

The following day, Roosevelt donned the uniform—complete with ceremonial sword—that he had brought along for "official" occasions, and opened the boat up for tours. The people of Louisville flocked aboard. On October 30, Lydia gave birth to a boy, named Henry Latrobe Roosevelt, after his grandfather.

It was more than a month before the *New Orleans* could continue downriver because the Falls of the Ohio, a treacherous, two-mile stretch of rapids just below Louisville, was not yet swelled enough by seasonal rains to allow the boat, with its twelve-foot hull, to proceed safely. To make good use of the time, Roosevelt, ever the promoter, began offering upriver boat trips for one dollar, the novelty of which turned out to be so lucrative that he ordered the boat to return to Cincinnati, where he put the scheme into operation and once again cleared a handsome profit.

Finally, on December 8, the river had risen to where the *New Orleans* could proceed. A week later, the boat stopped at Yellow Bank, where it was stocked up with coal, a good load of which would mean fewer delays on the four-hundred-mile haul between the town of New Madrid, just below the mouth of the Ohio, and Natchez, a stretch of the Mississippi with no sizable settlements.

Yellow Bank was over three hundred river miles from New Madrid but less than two hundred miles as the crow flies. On the evening of December 15, the passengers and crew of the *New Orleans* retired early, planning to start out promptly at dawn the following morning. They would be up earlier than they expected.

IN THE POPULAR imagination, the American frontier is commonly associated with the territory around present-day Kansas, Nebraska, and the Dakotas and the time period of the mid- to late nineteenth century. At the beginning of the nineteenth century, however, the Mississippi River was the western edge of the frontier, and that frontier was every bit as wild and woolly as the later frontier that we know as the Wild West.

In American mythology, the frontier is glorified as a magnificent adventure, but our pop culture concept of the frontier is a distilled and sanitized version that we view through the filter of entertaining movies and books. The reality of frontier life was something very different.

New Madrid was a favorite stopping-off place for river boatmen bound in both directions, and on any given day, the boats would arrive by the dozen. Timothy Flint, a frontier missionary who once counted a hundred vessels in New Madrid's harbor, recorded his impressions of "the boisterous gaiety of the hands, the congratulations, the moving picture of life on board the boats, in the numerous animals, large and small, which they carry, their different loads, the evidence of the increasing agriculture of the country above, and more than all, the immense distances which they have already come. . . . You can name no point from the numerous rivers of the Ohio and Mississippi, from which some of these boats have not come."

There were boats loaded with planks from New York; dry goods from Ohio; pork, flour, whiskey, hemp, tobacco, bagging, and bale rope from Kentucky; similar items plus cotton from Tennessee; peltry and lead from Missouri; and cattle and horses from Missouri, Illinois, and Ohio. There were boats carrying corn, apples, potatoes, cider, dried fruit, and various kinds of spirits—"in short, the products of the ingenuity and agriculture of the whole upper country of the west." Some boats were floating mercantile establishments, among which was a vessel whose crew crafted, sold, and mended tinware, another that featured manufactured iron tools and included a blacksmith's shop, and another that carried a complete dry goods store "with its articles very handsomely arranged on shelves."

When the boatmen pulled into port, fiddle music filled the air, accompanied by a veritable barnyard symphony of roosters, pigs, cattle, horses, and turkeys, as the boatmen leaped from one boat to the next, meeting and greeting, renewing old acquaintances, forging new ones, dancing, gambling, and drinking. As a class, the boatmen were a rough-hewn lot—tough, wild, profane, and prone to violence. Each barge carried between thirty and forty men and, as one contemporary writer noted, "The arrival of such a squadron at a small town was the certain forerunner of riot. The boatmen, proverbially lawless and dissolute, were often more numerous than the citizens, and indulged, without restraint, in every species of debauchery, outrage, and mischief."

Before long this cauldron of testosterone would inevitably boil over. One western traveler witnessed such an incident when an argument over a woman broke out between two drunken boatmen. They began trading boasts, and the dispute escalated. "I am a man; I am a horse; I am a team," declared one of the belligerents. "I can whip any man *in all Kentucky*, by God."

The other was uncowed, replying, "I am an alligator; half man, half horse; can whip any *on the Mississippi* by God."

By now, a good-sized crowd had gathered, and the spectators began egging on the contestants. The first one shot back: "I am a man; have the best horse, best dog, best gun, and handsomest wife in all Kentucky, by God."

The second boatman hissed, "I am a Mississippi snapping turtle: have bear's claws, alligator's teeth, and the devil's tail; can whip *any man*, by God."

Soon they were at it, pummeling each other, butting heads, biting, scratching, kicking, tearing each other's hair out, as the crowd cheered and yelled encouragement. The fight went on for a good half-hour, until the Mississippi snapping turtle had no bite left in him, and the man-horse team was proclaimed the winner.

One of the boatmen's favorite amusements was called "sweeping." Taking a rope from one of the boats, a gang of rowdies would go ashore. One half of the bunch took one side of the street and the other half went across. With the rope stretched taut between them, the two groups advanced up the road, bringing down whoever and whatever was unfortunate enough to be in their path. Men, women, children, carts, horses, and cattle went sprawling to the ground, while the boatmen laughed uproariously at the chaos they had created.

After enough of these incidents, townspeople began to fight back, unwilling to just stand quietly by and let their villages be left in a shambles. As an English traveler wrote, "the citizens, roused to indignation, attempted to enforce the laws; the attempt was regarded as a declaration of war, which arrayed the offenders and their allies in hostility; the inhabitants were obliged to unite in the defence of each other."

Faced with this hooliganism, the residents of towns like New Madrid fought for their settlements, for they were only too aware that if the boatmen prevailed, their victory would be accompanied by the destruction of furniture, fences, signs, and sheds. Beating the invaders back, the townspeople felt well within their rights in meting out a good dose of frontier justice, not hesitating to administer a vigilante-type drubbing in putting an end to the carousing and street brawling.

THE MONTH of December 1811 was rainy in New Madrid. Sunday the 15th was a peaceful enough sabbath, with no man-made disturbances recorded. In the evening, the ethnic French population enjoyed their customary Sunday night dance. Christmas was just ten days away.

Part Two

RUMBLINGS

Chapter Two

———

A COUNTRY EQUAL
TO OUR MOST
SANGUINE WISHES

T HE NAMING of New Madrid is a reminder that Spain once
owned the Louisiana Territory, and that the Mississippi River was
once the western boundary of the United States. The Spanish acquired
Louisiana in 1762, when King Louis XIV of France secretly ceded it to
his cousin, King Charles III of Spain, in order to avoid being forced to
hand it over to England as part of the settlement ending the French and
Indian War. And although Spain continued to rule Louisiana for the
next thirty-eight years, New Madrid, founded in 1789, was named not
by a Spaniard, but by George Morgan, an American—which serves as a
further reminder that loyalties were highly negotiable on the early frontier, where fealty was an item of exchange, and an oath of allegiance to
one nation meant little in the way of a lasting commitment. As Spain
and the United States faced each other across the Mississippi River at
the end of the American Revolution, a struggle for control of the river
ensued, and both sides of the Mississippi became places where everything was up for grabs.

George Morgan expended a tremendous amount of energy in the

founding of New Madrid, and his covert rival James Wilkinson made an equally strenuous attempt to undermine his plans. Ironically, less than twenty-five years later, all their efforts and machinations would be wiped out by the earthquakes.

ON JANUARY 3, 1789, a convoy of four armed flatboats with seventy men aboard pushed out into the icy current of the Monongahela River at Fort Pitt. Two hundred yards downstream, the turbid roil of the Monongahela united with the clear water and unbroken surface of the Allegheny to form the great Ohio. Led by Colonel George Morgan of New Jersey, the purpose of the expedition was to locate a site and establish a new colony in Spanish Louisiana.

As the forty-five-year-old Morgan stood on the deck of the lead boat, the sharp winter wind that laced his face could hardly chill his optimism. Having twice been frustrated by the fledgling U.S. government in large land deals, Morgan was now looking to cash in on his scheme with Spain, hoping it would bring him the fortune and status that had previously eluded him.

George Morgan was a distinguished patriot of the American Revolution, a member of America's ruling class who counted George Washington, Thomas Jefferson, John Hancock, Samuel Adams, Patrick Henry, and Benjamin Franklin among his many correspondents. Morgan was, as one of his contemporaries characterized him, "a man of education and refinement . . . in addition to liberal hospitality."

Morgan was not a large man, but he was endowed with tremendous physical energy and endurance. In the course of his long and varied career, he had been a merchant, an Indian agent, and a scientific farmer—"the first in America in the knowledge of agriculture," as another acquaintance wrote of him. Morgan had spent more than a decade on the western frontier, where he learned to deal with the native tribes of the region and came to be regarded by them as a trusted friend and ally.

Perhaps most important, George Morgan was a land speculator who had been stymied by the federal government in two grand colonizing schemes in the west. The first involved approximately 1.8 million acres in what is now northern West Virginia, the other a two-million-acre tract on the east bank of the Mississippi opposite the mouth of the Missouri, with roughly the same boundaries as the present state of Illinois.

Land speculation was the main investment scheme of the age. It had been carried out with great appetite in colonial America, where large grants of land, often hundreds of thousand of acres, could be obtained from the Crown or from the colonial governments for a pittance. In 1748, for example, a group of influential Virginians formed the Ohio Company and secured half a million western acres; the following year, the Loyal Company, also composed of leading Virginians, acquired 800,000 acres. With a minimal investment, speculators could turn an exorbitant profit reselling land parcels to settlers. George Washington, Benjamin Franklin, Patrick Henry, and other founding fathers were all land speculators on a grand scale.

In the summer of 1788, while Morgan's second land deal was being held up in Congress, he was approached by the Spanish ambassador Don Diego de Gardoqui. Gardoqui was the consummate diplomat—a businessman turned king's servant, a charming, self-assured gentleman who easily made friends and put people at their ease. He was fluent in English, having studied in London for several years, and had been a key player in negotiations with American representatives in Spain during the War of Independence.

Gardoqui had been dispatched to New York in an attempt to counter America's westward expansion. As settlers streamed to the frontier in the land rush that followed the Revolution, Spanish officials in Louisiana had grown increasingly apprehensive about the empire taking shape at their eastern border. The Spaniards were alarmed by the ferocity with which the Americans moved west. "Grimly," as one historian has written, "they drove the Indians out before them, and exploited natural resources, slaves and public office, trampling down with pitiless determination every obstacle to prosperity."

Spain's fear was that sooner or later the U.S. would cross the Mississippi and invade Louisiana. In an attempt to foment the alienation of western Americans from their government and build a buffer zone on the west bank to discourage U.S. expansion, Gardoqui encouraged American citizens to colonize the west side of the river by offering them free land and free trade.

He let it be known in influential circles that the Spanish Crown would look favorably on proposals from prominent U.S. citizens to establish colonies west of the Mississippi. All that would be required of immigrants would be an oath of allegiance to Spain. Before long, Gardoqui in New York and Louisiana governor Esteban Miró in New Orleans received dozens of proposals from ambitious Americans seeking to take advantage of this liberal immigration policy.

But Gardoqui was not interested in just anyone. He knew of George Morgan by reputation, and the reports he had of this man's character intrigued him; he also knew about Morgan's anger with the U.S. government. With Morgan now in New York for the congressional hearings on his current land development proposal, Gardoqui took the opportunity to contact him, through intermediaries, about the possibility of applying for a colony grant in Louisiana.

Like so many others, George Morgan was disenchanted with the ineffectual, crisis-ridden U.S. government. Formed seven years earlier under the Articles of Confederation, the government had only one branch, Congress, which had no real power; it could make recommendations, but it had no mechanism in place for enforcing them.

Morgan resented Congress for thwarting his land grabs; he was offended that his part in the struggle for independence should be so lightly regarded. In Morgan's mind, his patriotism entitled him to a nice chunk of property that, properly developed, could set him up comfortably for the rest of his life. Now, as Congress debated his future, Morgan was forced to consider Gardoqui's overture.

Deciding he had nothing to lose, Morgan sat down to write Gardoqui a letter and feel the Spaniard out. "Would it be consistent with the Policy of Spain," Morgan asked, "to admit an accession of several thousand Subjects in America from the United States, & to grant a free toleration of Religion? Men born and inured to Habits of Industry? excellent Farmers & Mechanics?"

The more he thought about the possibility, the better Morgan liked it. He remembered full well the breathtaking land he had seen twenty years earlier, in the fall of 1767, when he had descended the Kaskaskia River and become the first white American to make the voyage down the Mississippi River to New Orleans.

He described for Gardoqui the borders of his proposed colony—the verdant country he had seen opposite the mouth of the Ohio River had made such an impression on him that two decades later he could pinpoint it from memory as the ideal location for a settlement: from Cape Cinque Homme west two degrees longitude, south to the St. Francis River and down the St. Francis to the Mississippi. "I fix on these Limits," he pointed out, "from my knowledge of the Lands they contain, & because they interfere with no Indian Settlements. Should it be consistent with the Policy of the Nation, I could make such a settlement on the Premises myself as would induce several thousands to join me & to take the oaths of Allegiance to the King of Spain."

He closed his letter by telling Gardoqui that, should his proposals "be accepted or not, you are at Liberty to make what use you please of them as I do not mean to make a secret of them, nor my intentions."

Gardoqui was delighted with Morgan's inquiry. The minister had led the horse to water; with the proper encouragement, he could surely be induced to drink. On September 2, Gardoqui responded. "Permit me . . . to mention that your plan, far exceeds in solid prospects to any of the many lately proposed," wrote the ambassador, and continued his sales pitch to assure Morgan that "from the moment that you become a Spanish Subject you will enjoy the free & unmolested navigation of that River to find a market free *from duties* for the produce of your lands & . . . even a purchaser in his Majesty who pays in ready Mexican dollars. . . . Add to the above as a Spanish Subject you will be entitled to all the comercial privileges that the Citizens of New-Orleans enjoy with any other of his Majesty's rich dominions . . . so that if you enter into a comparative view of the matter, you will find fresh advantages springing up in every line. . . . [F]rom your known respectable character I am very willing to give you the prefferance to others who have applied about it." Gardoqui went on to express hope that "his Majesty will be pleased to approve it."

For the next month, Morgan's frustration with Congress mounted, as the legislature continued to delay giving him the go-ahead on his land proposal. Morgan could not stop thinking about the opportunity Gardoqui had offered him. It was the prize that had eluded him for twenty years. Since Congress was dragging its feet in deciding whether he could have two million acres on the east side of the Mississippi, why not simply cross the river, get the land from the Spaniards, and gain access to the Spanish-controlled port of New Orleans in the bargain? Finally, at the end of September, disgusted by his dealings with Congress, Morgan submitted a detailed proposal to the Spanish ambassador.

Morgan crafted his application carefully, making certain to offer concessions as well as to state his requirements. He asked the Spanish Crown for a grant of about two million acres opposite the mouth of the Ohio. There he would establish a colony that would allow the Spanish to control all commerce west of the Alleghenies. In exchange for this land, Morgan would take an oath of allegiance to the Spanish king and would recruit a large number of American families to emigrate with him. The immigrants—who would be permitted to bring with them, duty-free, their slaves, livestock, farming and household implements, and two years' worth of provisions—would likewise swear loyalty to Spain.

But Morgan insisted that the inhabitants of his colony be allowed freedom of religion and self-government, including the right to form a representative body with the power to draft its own laws. Morgan himself would be in command of the new colony, subject to the governor of Louisiana's orders, with the authority to appoint officials. As head of the colony, he would be paid a salary and be granted the same rank in the Spanish military as he held in the United States army. Morgan, his wife, and each of his five children would receive one thousand acres. Finally, and perhaps most important, he would be allowed to profit from the sale of land to the new settlers.

Gardoqui gave Morgan's proposal his endorsement—subject to the final approval of the king, of course, which the minister assured Morgan would be forthcoming. "As you seem anxious not to lose any time," wrote Gardoqui, "I forthwith transmit a passport and letters for the Spanish authorities, so that you may go at once, examine the territory in which you contemplate making your settlement."

Morgan was elated, and in his euphoria, he had a brainstorm: as a way of both honoring and flattering his Spanish patrons, he would name his colony after their own capital. Supremely confident now that his application would be ultimately accepted, he impetuously plunged ahead without waiting for the royal imprimatur. He printed and distributed handbills dated October 3, 1788, announcing an expedition down the Ohio and Mississippi Rivers for the purpose of establishing "Settlements in the Western Country."

The broadside read, "All Farmers, Tradesmen, &c. of good Characters, who wish to unite in this Scheme, and to visit the Country under my Direction, shall be provided with Boats and Provisions for the Purpose, free of Expence. . . . Every Person who accompanies me in this Undertaking, shall be entitled to 320 Acres of land, at one eighth of a Dollar per Acre. . . .

"All Persons who settle with me at New-Madrid, and their Posterity, will have the free Navigation of the Mississippi, and a Market at New-Orleans, free from Duties, for all the Produce of their Lands. . . .

"This new City is proposed to be built on a high Bank of the Mississippi River, near the Mouth of the Ohio, in the richest and most healthful Part of the Western Country, about the Latitude of 37°."

The handbill also promised, "All persons will be assisted in building a House, clearing a Spot of Ground, and in getting in their first Crops. Horned Cattle, Horses, and Swine, will be delivered to the Settlers at New-Madrid in such Quantities as they stand in Need of at first, at very reasonable Rates, for Cash or future Produce."

From the hundreds who applied to join his party, Morgan chose seventy men to accompany him on the western excursion. The group included surveyors, artisans, farmers, merchants, and Morgan's two sons. On January 3, 1789, the expedition embarked down the Ohio from Fort Pitt in four armed flatboats.

*   *   *

THE RIVERS dominated life in the west, being the main avenue for trade, transportation, and news. Commerce on the Mississippi was particularly vital to the prosperity of the western settlements. On the Mississippi, westerners could efficiently ship produce to New Orleans, where it could be sold or shipped on to cities on the east coast; otherwise, merchandise had to be carried over the mountains, a tedious and unprofitable proposition.

But in the late eighteenth century, navigating the Ohio and Mississippi rivers was a painstaking and potentially deadly enterprise. Even today, when large boats are made of steel and equipped with engines and radar, certain perils remain (and new ones exist—no boat pilot in George Morgan's day had to worry about locks, dams, bridge piers, pleasure craft, or Jet Skiers). But when boats were built of wood and powered by oars, they were far more vulnerable. The Mississippi, especially, was swift and treacherous; one French traveler wrote that a "voyage on the Mississippi is more dangerous than a passage across the ocean; I do not mean merely from the United States to Europe, but from Europe to China."

Grounding, still a danger today, was a constant risk, particularly when the rivers were low. Running aground always meant the loss of time and money. In the winter of 1790–91, one ill-fated boat carrying flour for the Philadelphia firm of Reed and Forde lost twelve days to grounding, not to mention the £99 it cost to hire a crew from forty miles downriver to get her going again.

Traveling in the winter, Morgan's boats had to be on constant alert for ice, another threat that still menaces riverboats. In *The Navigator*, the indispensable and comprehensive guide to travel on the Ohio and Mississippi first published in 1801, author Zadok Cramer wrote, "To be sure, of all enemies we meet with on the Ohio, the ice is the most formidable and dangerous." Besides the large chunks that floated down on the current, "There are many places where the shore, projecting to a point, throws off the cakes of ice towards the middle of the river." Johann Heckewälder, a Moravian missionary, wrote of seeing five boats loaded with 1,500 bushels of corn destroyed by ice in January 1793; the loss—boats and cargo—was calculated at more than £400.

There was the Falls of the Ohio, just below Louisville, where many a staunch boat ended its trip—or even its life. The Falls, somewhat misnamed, was a stretch of rapids that dropped twenty-six feet in about three miles. When the water level was high, the Falls was easily navigated, but when the water dropped, the exposed rocks formed a perilous gauntlet. Boats could be delayed in Louisville for weeks or even months awaiting a rise in the river.

Wood was another serious threat. The riverbanks were constantly caving in, taking large numbers of trees with them. Driftwood logs, propelled swiftly and unpredictably downriver by the current, could cause serious harm to the sturdiest of boats. In some places, these would clump together in "wooden islands" or "rafts," which were especially dangerous because, unlike true islands which split the current and carried the boat safely around the landmass, wooden islands had nothing below the surface to divert the flow of water, and a boat could be propelled headlong into the mass of logs.

The worst of the wooden hazards were the snags, which came in two types. "Sawyers" were so named because they resembled a mill saw in their up-and-down bobbing motion. The most treacherous were the "sleeping sawyers," whose tops never broke the surface of the water but instead lurked submerged, silently waiting to slash the hull of an unsuspecting craft. "Planters," like sawyers, were tree trunks rooted in the river bottom and often hidden below the surface. Unlike sawyers, planters were immobile and so firmly planted that, running into one, a boat could become impaled or even overturned. If the top of a sleeping sawyer or planter lay just below the surface, an experienced pilot might be able to read the water and avoid the peril, but any deeper and the danger was all but invisible.

Weather was often a factor. Violent storms were capable of dismembering stout vessels and placing the crew at the mercy of the raging waters. On George Morgan's first trip down the Mississippi in 1767, he was delayed several days by fog, once making a journal entry about fog "so heavy that we could not see the boat's length." (Even now, depending on its density and the boat's location, pilots will sometimes stop for fog.)

Eddies, formed where the current hollowed out the river bottom, could be up to two miles in circumference. A boat that got sucked into one of these whirlpools could easily be several hours in escaping the vortex—if it were not entirely destroyed by the force of the whirlpool. As recently as 1996, a shipping company barge sank when it was pulled into an eddy.

Even if a boat successfully navigated the many hazards of nature, there were the human-induced disasters. Hostile Indians were a constant concern, as were river pirates. There were boat-wrecking crews, whose specialty was hiring on to pilot the boat of an unsuspecting crew and passengers and then running the boat into the rocks, whereupon it would be plundered by the rest of the gang. These crews were also known to steal aboard a boat after dark and drill holes in the hull, causing it to sink, after which it would be similarly looted.

The most dangerous of the man-made hazards was shoddy boat-building. Zadok Cramer estimated that three-quarters of all river disasters could be attributed to poor construction. Cramer told of one man whose boat was lost when it hit a rock just below Pittsburgh. The owner sued the pilot for damages, but the riverman brought the rotten bottom plank to court and showed the board to the judge, who acquitted him of liability.

Finally, there were the foolish, self-inflicted mistakes, like the one committed by the inexperienced crew that, attempting to tie up on its first night out, threw anchor and cable overboard and "tore away all the frame-work around the deck."

The dangers of river travel were summed up in a letter written en route in the course of a flatboat trip by the merchant John Bower to his wife. "I think Jonas will have a second time to go down this river Before he learns every manouvre of Boating—that is Before he learns not to scratch the Shore fifteen or twenty miles before he can get the boat Stopped and then to run night and day in the most eminent danger and the weather most excessive Cold—when the Boats will run above 100 miles in 24 hours and the nights so dark that the Shores Cannot be known from the water any other way than by throwing Stone or Coal out from the sides and hearing where they light—when his rest cannot

exceed 4 hours out of 24, and all the rest be watching and fatigue—
when running on an Island how to Carry his boat in the river again—
when thrown on land by the ice his Oars run in the earth almost to the
handle how to get her afloat again and how to run into a harbour for
Safety and live in the boat when it is cold enough to freeze a dog to
death."

THESE, then, were the many perils that George Morgan's party had to
avoid on its voyage downriver. There are no specifics of the trip, but the
boat crews apparently observed every safeguard and stopped whenever
necessary, for it was a full six weeks—twice the normal time it should
have taken—until the company navigated the 1,132½ river miles and
finally reached the mouth of the Ohio on February 14. "The inclemency
of the season, and the precautions necessary for the advantage and security of our party and enterprize, rendered our voyage down the Ohio
long, though not a disagreeable one," said an April 14 letter from several
of the men to friends in Pittsburgh.

When they reached the Mississippi, Morgan went north to present
his passport to the Spanish commandant at St. Louis. From his days as
an Indian agent, Morgan enjoyed a sterling reputation among the
Delaware and other native tribes of the region. Now, as a gesture of
goodwill, he asked that an intertribal delegation accompany him to St.
Louis, an act that undoubtedly put his project on the right footing with
them. The rest of Morgan's group proceeded south, where their leader
rejoined them three weeks later, after his meeting with the Spanish
commandant.

When he climbed ashore and looked out at the future town site
that would be the center of his colony, George Morgan beheld a prairie
of fertile beauty. Thick, six-foot-high grasses swayed lazily in the
breeze. A small, clear lake could be seen in the near distance. Ancient,
majestic oaks dotted the flat landscape, and walnut, pecan, wild grape,
and mulberry all flourished effortlessly in the rich soil. Game was pro-
lific, with abundant populations of deer, bear, buffalo, pheasant, and
wild turkey.

Morgan had not the slightest idea, of course, that the coming tem-blors would take this paradisiacal setting and violently shake it, as a dog would a rat, permanently scarring the idyllic landscape.

ALTHOUGH there had initially been some differences of opinion about where to situate the town site that would be the center of the new colony, "after maturely considering every circumstance, and examining the country in this neighborhood fully," Morgan and his compatriots finally unanimously decided to establish their new city "about twelve leagues below the Ohio." The site had first been settled by white men in 1783, when two French-Canadian trappers, François and Joseph LeSieur, started downriver from St. Louis looking for a location closer to New Orleans where they could establish a trading post. They named the place L'Anse à la Graisse, or Cove of Grease, presumably for the profusion of bear and buffalo meat to be had in the area.

The site was strategically located on the north bank of a twenty-five-mile, south–north–south bend in the river—the largest such bend on the Mississippi. The north bank (actually the west side of the river, but the north bank of the bend) was the first high ground below the mouth of the Ohio; elevated twelve feet above the water, it appeared to be immune from flooding and held a commanding view of the river for six miles upstream and ten miles downstream. A fortified settlement here, Morgan believed, would control river traffic between St. Louis and Natchez and be the gateway for all trade west of the Alleghenies.

But it was the quality of the soil and the climate that Morgan's companions found so congenial. "The country rises gradually from the Mississippi," read the letter to Pittsburgh, "into fine, dry, pleasant and healthful grounds, superior, we believe, in beauty and in quality, to every other part of America.

" . . . We are pleased with the climate, and have reason to flatter our-selves that we have at last found a country equal to our most sanguine wishes."

After the land had been surveyed and cleared, Morgan laid out plots of 320 acres, and individuals made applications for particular parcels at the price of 48 Mexican dollars per farm. By the time of the emigrants' April 14 letter to Pittsburgh, the group had "built cabins, and a magazine for provisions, &c.," and were "proceeding to make gardens, and to plough and plant 100 acres of the finest prairie land in the world with Indian corn, some hemp, flax, cotton, tobacco, and potatoes."

In many ways, George Morgan was a man of great elegance and style. Two decades of frustrated planning had given him plenty of time to consider his ideal community and over the years contemplate the features he would incorporate. In his planning of the colony and the city of New Madrid, Morgan showed himself to be far ahead of his time, with remarkably modern sensibilities in the areas of environmental conservation, public land use, urban planning, and religious and cultural tolerance.

In his "General Directions for Settlement at New Madrid," Morgan laid the foundation for the modern system of rectangular survey of public lands. His directions to surveyors also included instructions to record, in their field books, all "mountains, hills, valleys, bottom-lands, timber trees, quality of the soil, for what best adapted, rivers, brooks and springs, salt, fresh or mineral; salt licks, minerals of iron, copper, lead or coal, and all appearances of rock and stone, and the quality thereof, whether free stone, lime stone, flint, marble, or other nature." Each surveyor was further "requested to preserve or make a drawing of every kind of beast, bird, fish or insect, he may kill or see in the country; and to note the kind of tree, shrubs, vines, plants, &c, &c, which may come under his view; and make a drawing of all those which are not common in Pennsylvania, noting the dimensions, flower, foliage, bark, fruit, &c, and their qualities."

The city of New Madrid was to extend four miles south along the river bank and two miles west from it, having at its center "a beautiful deep lake, of the purest spring water, 100 yards wide, and several leagues in length." The lake, called St. Ann's, fed a stream that meandered through the city. The lake water was "deep, clear, and sweet, the bottom a clean sand, free from wood, shrubs, or other vegetables, and well stored with fish." Morgan saw the lake as not only the physical but the spiritual center of the city. "On each side of this delightful lake, streets are to be laid out 100 feet wide, and a road to be continued round it of the same breadth, and the trees are directed to be preserved for ever, for the health and pleasure of its citizens."

Throughout the "General Directions," Morgan stressed the importance of safeguarding as many trees as possible. "No trees in any street of the city, nor in any road throughout the country, shall be injured or cut down, but under the direction of the magistrates of the police . . . and no timber injured or cut down in any street or road, shall be applied to private uses."

As an urban planner, George Morgan was akin to Pierre L'Enfant, who would lay out Washington, D.C., in 1791, and Gouverneur Morris, whose Manhattan street grid would be approved in 1811. Morgan laid out the city with all the streets at right angles. There were ten east–west streets parallel to the river and eighteen north–south streets perpendicular, with a 120-foot-wide, tree-lined boulevard fronting the water, "to be kept open for the security, pleasure and health of the city, and its inhabitants."

Certain lots were designated for schools, others were earmarked for churches of all denominations, and a number of blocks were given to the people for marketplaces. In keeping with his egalitarian vision, Morgan set aside a large number of common areas: "Forty lots of half an acre each shall be reserved for public uses, and shall be applied to such purposes as the citizens shall from time to time recommend, or the chief magistrate appoint; taking care that the same be so distributed in the different parts of the city that their uses may be general, and as equal as possible. . . . So soon as these lots shall be laid off, the timber, trees and shrubs, now growing thereon, shall be religiously preserved as sacred."

In his original letter to Gardoqui, Morgan specifically mentioned that the land he chose would "intefere with no Indian Settlements," demonstrating a sensitivity that certainly helped his cause among the area's tribes. According to the emigrants' April 14 letter, "Even the neighboring Indians have expressed the greatest pleasure on our arrival, and intentions of settlement.

"There is not a single nation or tribe of indians who claims or pretend to claim, a foot of land granted to Colonel Morgan. This is a grand matter in favour of our settlement."

Morgan's provisions, as set forth in the "General Directions," for relations with Native Americans show why, when he served as the Indian agent at Fort Pitt in the late 1770s, the Delaware named him Tamanend—The Affable One—after one of their revered legendary chiefs, an honor that conveyed the highest degree of respect. The directions stipulate that, "No white person shall be admitted to reside in this territory who shall declare himself to be a hunter by profession, or who shall make a practice of killing buffaloes or deer without bringing all the flesh of every carcass to his own family, or to New Madrid, or carrying it to some other market. This regulation is intended for the preservation of those animals, and for the benefit of neighboring Indians, whose dependence is on hunting principally—this settlement being wholly agricultural and commercial, no encouragement shall be given to white men hunters."

NEW MADRID was a planned utopia, an idealized land of plenty that George Morgan envisioned growing into a great metropolis, the key to controlling river traffic on the lower Mississippi. He had no reason to believe that his project would be anything other than a ringing success.

Yet even before Morgan's utopia could meet with natural disaster in the earthquakes' upheaval, it would encounter man-made upheaval in the form of a human disaster named James Wilkinson, one of the boldest scoundrels in American history.

Chapter Three

———

DISAPPOINTMENTS AND SUFFERINGS

THE DECADES following the American Revolution were a wild and unstable time, particularly in the west. The frontier was teeming with intrigues and conspiracies, a place where almost anything could and did happen. It was a time when the frontier appeared to stretch endlessly westward and white Americans recognized no limits. Land seemed inexhaustible, and the pursuit of it was all-consuming.

In the last decade of the eighteenth century, the threat of Kentucky's secession from the Union was one of the most volatile issues on the frontier. (At the time of George Morgan's trip to New Madrid, Kentucky had been part of Virginia and would not be granted statehood until 1792.) During this period, Kentuckians were especially incensed over two issues. The first was the failure of Virginia and later the federal government to protect Kentucky's isolated settlers from increasingly intensifying Indian attacks. The second was the struggle with Spain over control of the Mississippi River and the government's failure to protect Kentucky's interests, since her economic survival depended on being able to ship produce and receive goods via the river. Agents of both Great Britain and Spain fanned the flames of discontent in Kentucky, offering encouragement and assistance to Kentuckians in an attempt to undermine the stability of the Union. The turmoil in Kentucky would have a direct effect on George Morgan's plans for New Madrid.

ENTER James Wilkinson, an audacious and unscrupulous schemer who, a few short years later, would secretly be on the payroll of the king of Spain at the same time he was commanding general of the western army of the United States, and who would also, in the course of his career, be twice court-martialed and acquitted. One of his contemporaries wrote that Wilkinson was the only man he "ever saw who was from the bark to the very core a villain"; another referred to him as an "unprincipled imbecile"; a third called him "the worst of all bad men."

From an early age, Wilkinson had shown a keen interest in military affairs. In March 1776, as a teenager, he was among the American troops who watched British general William Howe evacuate Boston in a retreat by sea. That same month, Wilkinson made captain. He quickly established himself as an aspiring young officer, manifesting an uncanny, chameleon-like ability to size up situations and adapt to them and to cultivate the right relationships that would afford him continued, rapid advancement. Nothing was beneath Wilkinson when it came to achieving his goals. This was the man who, later in life, would write, "Some men are sordid, some vain, others ambitious. To detect the predominant passion, to lay hold of it, and to derive advantages from it, is the most profound part of political science."

In May 1777, Wilkinson was promoted to deputy adjutant general, and on October 17, the twenty-year-old boy wonder was designated to negotiate the surrender of General John Burgoyne at Saratoga. Three weeks later, he was given the brevet rank of brigadier general; the following March he was appointed secretary of the board of war.

Wilkinson's army service was not without its dark side, however. He was a protégé first of General Benedict Arnold and later of General Horatio Gates but ultimately lost the patronage of both, and wound up twice challenging Gates to duel. The first contest, scheduled for February 24, 1778, was triggered by Wilkinson's disclosure, while tipsy, of the

1777 Conway Cabal, a sinister conspiracy to remove George Washington from his post as commander-in-chief of the Continental Army and replace him with Gates, the disgrace of which caused Wilkinson to resign his position with the Board of War. Just before the scheduled duel, however, Gates forgave Wilkinson, and it was called off. The second duel, six months later, was an outgrowth of the original incident. Traded insults led to a challenge, and this time the duel went ahead. Three rounds were fired without either man making a serious attempt to injure the other. "Honor" was satisfied, and both Gates and Wilkinson survived with their mutual enmity intact.

More than a year after resigning his office as war board secretary, Wilkinson was appointed clothier general to the army. In March 1781, after a year and a half at the job, he resigned that commission as well after being accused of corruption over irregularities in the department's account books.

After two years in which he made a modestly successful foray into Pennsylvania politics but also acquired a significant number of debts (mostly due to his habit of entertaining lavishly), Wilkinson, like so many others, saw a chance to make a new start in the west, and at the end of 1783, he moved his family to Kentucky, where he became a salesman of general merchandise. Wilkinson traveled the countryside, peddling his wares, looking for real estate, and engaging in the talk of the frontier. What he learned from these conversations was that Kentuckians were up in arms.

The growing sentiment was for separation from Virginia and statehood. Kentucky County had been annexed by Virginia in 1776, when a group of Kentucky settlers, alarmed at the Indian threat, delegated George Rogers Clark and Gabriel Jones to petition the Virginia legislature for protection and incorporation. Between 1784 and 1792, Kentuckians held ten constitutional conventions in the Danville courthouse for the purpose of breaking away from Virginia and becoming a separate state. Using his natural abilities to speak and charm, Wilkinson quickly insinuated himself into the forefront of the autonomy movement, drafting the call for the 1786 convention and winning election as a delegate. The autonomy/statehood process would drag on for another six years, during which time Wilkinson would become involved in some of the most brazen and cunning double-dealing ever contrived and carried out in the early republic.

IN THE SPRING of 1787, Wilkinson hatched a daring plan. Loading a barge with a cargo of Kentucky produce, including tobacco, flour, butter, and bacon, he boldly set out for New Orleans. Three years earlier, Spain had closed the Mississippi to all but Spanish vessels, creating a distinct hardship for Kentuckians. Now, in direct violation of Spanish law, Wilkinson floated down the river without a Spanish passport. At every outpost along the way, he presented himself as a brigadier general, glad-handing the Crown's officials and showering them with expensive gifts—bribes, in exchange for his passage. Word of this high-flying American traveled downriver, and by the time Wilkinson arrived in New Orleans in early July, Louisiana governor Esteban Miró was already wondering who this brash interloper could possibly be and what business he had in New Orleans.

Soon after his arrival in port, Wilkinson called on Miró at the governor's headquarters, and as was his wont, he charmed the man who could advance his cause. The following day, Wilkinson sent a seventy-page letter to Miró, stating everything he had discussed in their meeting.

In the seventy-page document that has come to be known as Wilkinson's "First Memorial," he provided Miró with a long-winded appraisal of the situation in Kentucky, slanted in such a way as to lay the groundwork for a scheme by which, if the governor approved, Wilkinson would profit handsomely. After discussing the disaffection of Kentuckians for the eastern states, he stressed the need for Spain to court the frontiersmen's favor lest, by aligning themselves with Great Britain, they would become a dire threat to Louisiana, just across the river. Near the end of the document, Wilkinson made clear the "grounds and objects" of his coming to see Miró.

"Know then," he wrote in his trademark, convoluted prose, "that the leading characters of Kentucky, the place of my residence, impatient under the inconveniences and destress which they suffer from the restraints on their commerce, urged and intreated my voyage hither, in order to develop if possible the disposition of Spain towards their Country, and to discover, if practicable, whether she would be willing to open a negociation for admission *to her protection as subjects.* . . . I shall take much pleasure in employing all my faculties to compass this desireable event, and for such consideration, as my services may be deemed to merit."

Wilkinson then slipped in, almost as an afterthought, the real reason for his trip to New Orleans. "I hope, however, that I shall not [be] condemned for attempting *at the same time that I am labouring to advance a Worck, which may lead to the aggrandizment of Spain and the prosperity of thousands,* to provide for the safety and happiness of my own Family. For this purpose, and to give the strongest assurance of the sincerity of my professions I humbly pray that I may be permitted to transmit to an Agent in this City in Negroes, live Stock, tobacco, Flour, Bacon, Lard, Butter, Cheese tallow, Apples the amount of fifty or sixty thousand Dollars, cost of Kentucky, which articles may be sold for my account, and the proceeds held by his Excellency the Governor, as a pledge for my good conduct until the issue of our plans is known, or I have fixed my residence in Louisiana."

In plain terms, Wilkinson was offering Miró a deal: in exchange for a monopoly on Kentucky produce sold at New Orleans, Wilkinson would use his influence—which, of course, he had greatly exaggerated—to steer Kentucky toward separating from the United States and joining Spain.

Wilkinson concluded his memorial with a warning about the need for "the most inviolable secrecy both as to the plan, and my name, which is well known to Mr. Carmichael, the American charge d'affaires, at the Court of Madrid. . . . To you . . . I have committed secrets of an important nature, such as would, were they divulged, destroy my fame and fortune forever. But I feel the strongest confidence in your silence and discretion, and if the plan should eventually be rejected by the Court, I must rely on the candor and high honor of a dignified Minister to bury these communications in eternal oblivion."

In addition to the memorial, Wilkinson also submitted to Miró a

"Declaration" proclaiming his expatriation. This document, in which he changed his "allegiance from the United States of America to His most Catholic Majesty," prominently displays Wilkinson's Machiavellian approach to politics. "Interest is the ruling Passion of Nations, as well as of Individuals," he wrote, "and He who imputes a different motive to human conduct either decieves Himself, or means to deceive others."

Miró was a diplomat; he understood quid pro quo. He wrote the Spanish court suggesting that not only should Wilkinson be given the monopoly on trade, he should also be granted a pension of $2,000 per year—a not inconsiderable sum when compared to Miró's annual salary of $4,000. Thus was born what history knows as the "Spanish Conspiracy," which might have more aptly been called the "Wilkinson Conspiracy," since it was entirely conceived and initiated by him. In addition to exaggerating his own influence, Wilkinson also greatly overstated the willingness of his fellow Kentuckians to abandon the U.S. for allegiance with Spain. But such were his gifts of persuasion and charm that Miró was taken in. Besides, Miró had ambitions of his own, and what could possibly provide a greater boost to his career than delivering Kentucky to the Crown?

IT DID NOT take very long before a number of Kentuckians and others came to suspect Wilkinson and even accuse him of treason, but because the "Memorial" and "Declaration," as well as the rest of his extensive correspondence with Spanish officials, were kept secret by the Spanish for more than a century, the suspicions about Wilkinson's conduct in this affair could not actually be proven.

The depths of Wilkinson's treachery and his lack of fealty to any but himself make it almost impossible to definitively ascertain his true motives, but it would appear that he never did in fact intend to work at moving Kentucky toward Spain. (This is not to say that if, in the course of events, it became advantageous to him to undertake such action, he would have hesitated—Wilkinson was clearly willing to do whatever necessary for his own benefit.) Ever in need of money, his most likely motive was to gain the trade monopoly and other advantages, and if it took promising to bring about the alignment of Kentucky with the Spanish Crown, he was only too willing to do that.

As far as Wilkinson's declaration of expatriation goes, it was certainly in keeping with the spirit of the times in the west. After all, American patriots such as George Morgan, George Rogers Clark, and others were ready to renounce their U.S. citizenship and swear loyalty to Spain. Furthermore, as one merchant's description of trips from Pittsburgh to New Orleans informs us, the "Declaration" need not be taken all that seriously: "It was the usual practice upon their arrival at Natchez for owners and Boat crews, to take the Oath of Allegiance to the King of Spain; It was practiced by those who went to that Country at the time . . . to induce the Spanish officers to believe, that it was their intention to become subjects & as preparatory to this step & previous to obtaining a passport to proceed, the Oath of Allegiance was administered, upon which a passport was granted, or permission to sell at Natchez was procured. Americans who migrated to that Colony were permitted to sell their property free of duty."

There are significant differences, however, between the offers of allegiance proffered to Spain by Morgan and Wilkinson. First, Morgan's was made openly—"I do not," he wrote Gardoqui, "mean to make a secret of . . . my intentions"—whereas Wilkinson insisted on "the most inviolable secrecy." Moreover, Morgan was utterly committed to carrying out his plan of becoming a Spanish subject, while Wilkinson was simply using his declaration of expatriation as part of his ruse to land the monopoly on trade.

AFTER his return to Kentucky, Wilkinson began his commercial venture—shipping produce to New Orleans—and carried on a copious correspondence with Miró, some of it in cipher or code, keeping the governor abreast of developments in the territory, where conditions continued to be volatile. "I must proceed with caution & carefully avoid every circumstance which could excite surprize or alarm," Wilkinson wrote, playing up the undercover nature of his endeavor. In his letters, he did not hesitate to exaggerate freely and even lie outright where it served his purpose of creating the impression for Miró that Kentucky was all but ready to join Spain. "I can solemnly assure you," he informed the governor, "that I found every eminent Character in the District, except a Col. Marshall, a Land Surveyor, & a Col. Muter one of our Judges, dicided in favor of a Secession from the United States & an appeal to Spain." At the same time, he hedged his bets, saying that "the Idea of *subjection* to Spain, must for the present be kept out of sight, and that the most politic ground I could take, would be . . . a Secession from the United States, & a connection with Spain . . . without defining the precise conditions of such connection."

For the next half-decade, Wilkinson would walk a precarious tightrope, as he balanced efforts to keep Kentuckians in a froth over Congress's injustices toward the district (which allowed him to claim with at least a grain of truth, in his progress reports to Miró, that Kentucky was on the verge of separating from the U.S. in favor of Spain) with restraining his fellows from becoming so enraged that they might actually secede (which would make Wilkinson's trade monopoly worthless). As one historian has written, "The traitor's scheme was certainly a most daring one, but he planned it with consummate skill, laid its foundations with elaborate care, was quick to see and utilize every agency and event which might contribute to its success, and—amazing to record—he carried it out precisely as planned."

WILKINSON was more than a year into his devious scheme when George Morgan issued the handbill advertising his expedition to Louisiana. In November 1788, Wilkinson's old friend and business associate Isaac Dunn got wind of the New Madrid project and wrote him that George Morgan "goes north of the Ohio on the Spanish side of the Mississippi with intention of settling a Spanish colony, having obtained a grant from Gardoqui to that effect with liberal and extraordinary indulgences such as will alarm you." Dunn's letter went on to say that there were other proposals "of the same nature before Gardoqui . . . which I have read. All the Atlantic world are in treaty with the Spaniard, we have no time to lose."

When Wilkinson received Dunn's letter, he was indeed alarmed. Morgan's proposed colony put Wilkinson's scheme in jeopardy; if New Madrid were to become a port where Kentuckians could trade their produce, his New Orleans monopoly would be worthless. This upstart Morgan would have to be stopped.

Shaken, Wilkinson penned a letter, tinged with hysteria, warning Miró that Gardoqui "has hurried . . . into confidential communications with Persons undeserving of trust & even with Strangers, as will appear to you from the extracts of his Letters to Col. Morgan." Wilkinson also indirectly cast aspersions on Morgan's venture, cautioning the governor that those migrating to Louisiana "are generally Debtors & fugitives from Justice—poor & without principle, such men are not only worthless, but are dangerous subjects and ought to be guarded against." This charge, as much of Wilkinson's propaganda, was made of whole cloth; in fact, the men in Morgan's party were all merchants, farmers, tradesmen, and professionals. Wilkinson ended his screed by telling Miró that he would not write again for several months, "unless some unexpected Event should render it necessary."

Two days later, consumed with anxiety, Wilkinson scribbled another tirade to the governor in which he denounced Morgan's character and intentions. "This Colonel Morgan . . . is a man of education and understanding, but a deep speculator. He has been bankrupt twice, and finds himself at the present moment in extreme necessity. He was sent to New York by a company of New Jersey gentlemen to negotiate with Congress the purchase of a vast parcel of land. . . . But while this business was pending, he . . . found it advantageous to change his negotiation from America to Spain." Wilkinson then informed Miró that he had a spy follow Morgan down the river, whereby he learned the details of Morgan's planned colony, which he went on to describe, including Morgan's intent to make New Madrid a "free port." He cautioned the governor that Morgan's colony would be nothing but a liability to Spain because the Americans who settled there would remain an insulated pocket, and by retaining "their old prejudices and feelings," would "continue to be Americans as if they were on the banks of the Ohio."

After urging Miró to fortify the Spanish side of the river, Wilkinson once again laid into Morgan, with unfounded and defamatory attacks on his character and motives. "I am informed that Morgan intends visiting you, as soon as he shall have finished the survey of the lands conceded to him. Permit me to suplicate you, my most esteemed of friends, not to give him any knowledge of my plans, sentiments or designs. He has long been jealous of me, and you may rest assured that, in reality, he is not well affected towards our cause, but that he allows himself to be entirely ruled by motives of the vilest self interest, and therefore that he will not scruple, on his return to New York, to destroy me."

Wilkinson also maligned Gardoqui for his folly in endorsing Morgan's plan and advised the governor that he, Miró, and not Gardoqui should be in charge of dealing with issues concerning Kentucky and the river. Clearly, Miró must see that the situation was unacceptable.

MEANWHILE, at New Madrid, the Morgan party was hard at work. Confident with the start they'd made, Morgan wrote to Miró in mid-April, informing the governor of his plans and of their approval by Gardoqui, and of his intention to call upon Miró shortly.

When he arrived in New Orleans the following month, however, Morgan was shocked to find Miró dismissive of both him and his project. At the top of Miró's list of objections was the idea of Morgan's selling land for his own profit. If he wanted to continue with his colony, the governor informed him, land would be distributed free. In addition, while immigrants could practice their own religions, the only public worship permitted would be Roman Catholic. The following day, Miró wrote Morgan a devastating letter, reiterating those points. He went on:

> Now you will see how much this differs from what you have proposed: Indeed I am very sorry that there would be such a wide disparity, for by the information I had from Dn. Diego Gardoqui of your respectable character and enviable character I expected your arrival with impatience confident that your plan would be adaptable to the King's interest. I find myself under the necessity of disapproving it, being entirely against the political welfare of the King's dominions to encourage the erection of a

Republick in their center, for indeed it is in this light that I construe the form of Government that you project though with a shadow of subordination.

I find myself equally disappointed by your conduct in surpassing the project of your voyage to the country in question exceeding yourself beyond all expectation, for the letter wrote by your Committee to the Gentlemen in Fort Pitt has caused a wrong impression in the minds of all the Inhabitants of the Ohio giving for granted an extensive conception of lands in your favour. This report is likewise publick in Kentucky from whence copys of the same letter are sent to me, & seem confirmed by your drawing out the city, giving it a name only right of a sovereign, & tartly calling it in the said letter our city when Dn. Diego Gardoqui authorized you only to examine the country. What a difference there is from this to what you have done?

Nevertheless, despite Wilkinson's defamation of Morgan's character, the American apparently made a favorable impression in his meeting with Miró, for in closing the governor wrote, "I am now . . . personally acquainted with your good qualitys [which] makes me consider your behaviour in a favourable light being persuaded that it was the effect of an extraordinary eagerness of promoting the emigration into this province." As a final gesture of goodwill, Miró bestowed grants of one thousand acres upon Morgan and each of his sons.

The following day, Morgan answered, apologizing for his excess of zeal in granting land and naming the city without the king's approval. "The name given to the Settlement: so far from being offensive in our Ideas, was intended to shew our Devotion, Respect, and attachment to his Majesty, & to Spanish Nation." Morgan ended his letter by accepting the restrictions set down by Miró.

In his reply, the governor gave Morgan authority under the terms allowed to proceed with his project. He informed Morgan that the Crown would import English-speaking Irish priests, but that nobody would be molested for not becoming a Catholic. Finally, the immigrants would be given a free market to New Orleans exempt from taxes or duties.

Morgan agreed and left New Orleans. In spite of the setbacks, he seemed still to be willing to move ahead with the venture. When he returned home to New Jersey in August, he wrote a long letter to Gardoqui, describing his trip and his negotiations with Miró, deriding the governor and his association with Wilkinson. "I do not believe his Excellency, Governor Miró, is possessed of the necessary ideas respecting the object his Majesty has in view, and his warmth of temper and passions prevent his obtaining the knowledge and information requisite to his station. His copartnership with Genl. Wilkinson has been exceedingly injurious to his Majesty's colony, and will, I fear, be attended with more very inconvenient consequences. . . . It is scarcely possible for you to conceive the warmth of resentment with which he expressed himself on your having listened to my propositions."

Nevertheless, in closing, Morgan seemed to be committed to continuing. "I have now only to add, that I hold myself ready to proceed in this business, with your approbation, upon Governor Miró's plan, until his Majesty may be graciously pleased to give further instructions; or, if you have no objection, I will repair to [New] Madrid to wait such orders as his Majesty may think proper to give."

JUST ABOUT the time Morgan was leaving New Orleans in 1789, James Wilkinson arrived with twenty-five boatloads of Kentucky produce, making an impressive entry into the city, but the Kentuckian was greeted with disappointing news. Nearly two years after Wilkinson had submitted his original proposal, the king's response had arrived, and it contained several provisions that all but ended Wilkinson's hopes for making a big killing in his dealings with Spain. First, the Spanish monarch refused to finance any espionage efforts aimed at separating Kentucky from the United States. Moreover, he opened the Mississippi to all American citizens on the condition they pay a 15 percent duty on goods transported. The king had originally closed the river in hopes of controlling settlement patterns. Now, recognizing the inevitable, he opened it in hopes of reaping a profit. Finally, settlers who pledged fealty to Spain were granted land, commercial privileges, and freedom of religion. It was a great victory for the town of New Madrid.

George Morgan had been both right and wrong about the location he chose for his settlement. His evaluation of its strategic position in controlling river traffic between St. Louis and Natchez was entirely correct; as he had foreseen, the town soon became the commercial center of the frontier.

Encouraged by Morgan's glowing portrait of New Madrid and by the Spaniards' liberal immigration policy, settlers made their way to the area, and the colony grew apace, although Morgan's plan for the layout of the city was quickly discarded. As shown on the earliest surviving map of New Madrid, drawn in 1794, the town was centered around Fort Celeste, built by the Spanish-appointed commandant, Pierre Foucher, and named for Miró's wife. The fort stood about a third of a mile from the riverbank; the streets were arranged around it, and the town contained none of the parks, greenbelts, or other amenities that Morgan had so carefully delineated.

By 1791, there were nearly two hundred new settlers in New Madrid, the majority of whom were ethnic French from the Illinois Territory, attracted by Spain's generous land grants. In 1793, a private school was operating. Three years later, English traveler Francis Baily recorded that the town was composed of "two or three hundred houses, scattered about at unequal distances within a mile of the fort, which stands in the center of a square in the middle of the town."

In 1796, an eight-page promotional tract in English written by Charles de Hault Delassus, civil and military commandant of Upper Louisiana, attracted more English-speaking settlers to the town. The brochure extolled the virtues of "that part of Louisiana, which lies between the mouth of the Missouri and New Madrid," lauding the bounty of land and pasturage, the fertile soil, the diversity of crops and fruit trees, the mild climate, and the abundance of water, wood, and minerals, all of which, wrote Delassus, "I have verified with my own eyes and in person." If all those inducements were not enough, Delassus also declared, in a grandiose bit of frontier hyperbole, that "this country is so far blessed, as to be exempt from chicanery & lawyers."

In 1797, a census put the population of New Madrid at over six hundred, including slaves, an increase of more than a hundred from the previous year. By 1799, a flour mill had been built—in 1803, traveler Paul Alliot noted that New Madrid's "inhabitants were the first along the river to engage in the cultivation of wheat"—and the town boasted nearly seven hundred residents.

In 1795, the Spanish opened the Mississippi to American citizens under the Treaty of San Lorenzo, also known as Pinckney's Treaty, for Thomas Pinckney, the U.S. envoy to Spain who negotiated it. The treaty was Spain's attempt to gain the United States as an ally against a projected British attack on Spain's North American colonies. Boats that had come down the Ohio were now required to stop at New Madrid for inspection and to pay the duty on their cargo. With its critical location, New Madrid continued to be a vital center of commerce; by the end of the eighteenth century, it was the key point for all trade between New Orleans and the Allegheny region.

In his assessment of New Madrid's location as the ideal site for a city, however, George Morgan could not have been more mistaken. The difficulties began the first summer, as Indian agent Benjamin Hawkins noted in a letter to James Madison: "Col. Morgans settlement on the mississippi is come to nothing the land they settled on, overflowed amazingly, and numbers of the adventurers are returned to Kentuckey very Much disgusted."

The flatness of the prairie, lacking drainage, caused rainwater to collect in stagnant ponds. As French traveler Georges-Henri-Victor Collot wrote, "putrid fevers and agues are very prevalent from the month of June till November." Also, the original plan for the town extended two miles back from the river, but a mile from the water's edge, there was a swamp, which the Morgan party had managed to overlook in their initial enthusiasm.

Worse still, the relentless effects of the river began to take their toll on the settlement. The problem was that the high north bank, which Morgan saw as the site's chief asset was, in fact, also its greatest liability. Every year, the river, swollen by melting ice and spring rains, tore away dozens of yards of riverbank, taking with it sizable pieces of the town. Whole blocks of New Madrid were washed downstream as the raging current cut and sliced its way along the bend in the river. In 1796,

Collot observed, "Nothing can hinder this destructive effect. . . . Every annual revolution carries off from one to two hundred yards of this bank; so that the fort, built five years since at six hundred yards from the side of the river, has already lost all its covered way; and at the time we passed, the commander had given orders to empty the magazines and dislodge the artillery, having no doubt but that in the course of the winter the rest of the fort would be destroyed."

In an 1810 map of New Madrid, Fort Celeste and two entire rows of streets are no longer part of the town. In 1811, Henry Brackenridge, a writer, preacher, lawyer, and later a judge on the Pennsylvania Supreme Court, observed that "at least three hundred yards have disappeared. Three forts, and a number of large and spacious streets have been taken away, within these fifteen years."

After New Madrid's heyday at the turn of the nineteenth century, the population began a steady decline. With the Louisiana Purchase in 1803, both sides of the river now belonged to the U.S., and the city lost its strategic value.

For some, New Madrid still held a certain charm. S. P. Hildreth, an 1805 river voyager, wrote of "the cheerful little town" where "many of the houses were painted white, with wide verandas or piazzas," and pointed out that after coming through the wilderness region below the Falls of the Ohio, "the first view of this smiling village was animating and delightful." At the time of Hildreth's visit, the population had stabilized at about four hundred, "amongst which were a number of genteel families, noted for their hospitality."

Others found New Madrid to be the most repulsive kind of frontier settlement. "I must give you an unfavorable account of the inhabitants," wrote Englishman Thomas Ashe in an 1806 letter. "A stupid insensibility makes the foundation of their character. Averse to labor, indifferent to any motive of honor, occupied by mean associations, without any solicitude for the future, and incapable of foresight or reflection, they pass their lives without thinking, and are growing old without getting out of their infancy, all the faults of which they studiously attain. Gaming and drinking at times rouze them from this supine state into a depravation of manners, which debase still more the distorted features of their mind. They are composed of the dregs of Kentucky, France and Spain, and subsist by hunting and trading with the Indians, who exchange with them rich furs for whiskey, blankets, ammunition and arms."

In all likelihood, the reality of New Madrid lay somewhere between the two accounts, as Brackenridge's description indicates: "It is the residence of several amicable and genteel families, from whom I acknowledge with pleasure, to have received much kindness and hospitality. There is, however, a due proportion of the worthless and despicable part of society."

The New Madrid area actually had two distinct groups of white immigrants—ethnic French and Anglo-American—and they could not have been more dissimilar in their habits and lifestyles. (Despite their nearly four decades of governance, the Spanish were never more than a ruling minority in the territory.)

The French were easygoing—some considered them indolent—and social people who tended to clump together in settlements. They loved community celebrations, and dancing was a favorite pastime. They preferred hunting, trapping, and trading with the Indians for their sustenance, leaving agriculture for the most part to the more industrious Anglo-Americans. Theirs was a barter economy; when currency was needed—in buying cloth, for example—pelts served the purpose. Known for their culinary talents, the French served a varied menu that included salads, vegetables, and soups, as well as breads and meats.

The Anglo-Americans, on the other hand, were farmers, whose mission was to conquer the backcountry. They were individualistic and enterprising. Accustomed to the wilderness and having little need for social activity, they were content to live on remote, isolated homesteads. They spun their own cloth, rather than importing it as the French did, and unlike the French, they had little sympathy for the Indians. Their diet, unimaginative and unchanging, consisted of meat, variously prepared, and cornbread.

Whatever their origins or social class, the early settlers all shared the difficulties of frontier life. "I have heard particulars . . ." wrote the missionary Timothy Flint, "in the disappointments and sufferings of these original adventurers, enticed away by coloured descriptions, which represented these countries as terrestrial paradises. Many of the families were respectable, and had been reared in all the tenderness of opulence and plenty. There were highly cultivated and distinguished French families,—and here, among the bears and Indians, and in a sickly climate, and in a boundless forest, surrounded by a swamp, . . . they found the difference between an Arcadian residence in the descriptions of romance, and actual existence in the wild woods."

AFTER leaving New Orleans in 1789, George Morgan never returned to New Madrid. Despite his seeming willingness to pursue the project under Miró's terms, a number of circumstances soon combined to kill his interest in the undertaking. To begin with, when his right to sell land had been denied, it meant his profit from the venture would be limited to trade, i.e., the sale of his produce at New Orleans. Furthermore, he knew that Spain's opening the river to Americans would cut down sharply on the number of people who would be motivated to move to Louisiana. In addition, he learned that Miró had appointed Foucher as commandant of New Madrid, and Morgan was not inclined to take a subservient position to a Spanish-appointed commander. Also, in the eight months since Morgan had left Fort Pitt, the unstable Continental Congress had been replaced by a new government, and Morgan believed—erroneously as it turned out—that he could reverse his earlier disappointment in the second land deal by appealing the decision to the newly created United States Supreme Court. Finally, just after Morgan reached Philadelphia, his brother John suddenly died, leaving Morgan the bulk of his estate, which included a large holding of land in western Pennsylvania that would require Morgan's full-time attention.

For a third time, George Morgan had been defeated in his ambitious land speculation plans. He lived the rest of his life at Morganza, the domain he inherited from his brother. He died in early 1810, spared the further pain of learning about the destruction of New Madrid in the earthquakes less than two years later.

*   *   *

IN 1811, with its quarter-century anniversary in view, New Madrid was far from Morgan's dream of a great utopian metropolis, but at least it was on the map, one of the favorite stopping-off places for Mississippi crews on their way up- and downriver.

In choosing the site for his city, Morgan had made several mistakes in judgment. The lack of drainage, the swamp, and the eroding bank were the obvious drawbacks he had failed to perceive. The most insidious feature of the location, however, and the one that Morgan could not possibly have known about, lay hidden: New Madrid, it turns out, sat directly above an active seismic fault zone situated deep in the earth. Three miles below the earth's surface lay a massive rift valley measuring 100 miles wide and 350 miles long.

And it was getting ready to shift.

CANADA

LOUISIANA TERRITORY

Mississippi R.

Ohio R.

Greenville Treaty Line

• Pittsburgh

OLD NORTHWEST
TERRITORY
ca. 1800

--- future state lines and
international borders

Chapter Four

———

ONE OF THOSE
UNCOMMON GENIUSES

T HE GEOLOGICAL shift was a counterpoint to the political and
military changes that were taking place. All through the years that
James Wilkinson conspired with Governor Miró over Kentucky, Native
Americans throughout the Ohio Valley were waging a desperate battle
for survival as, outnumbered and overpowered, their hunting grounds
continued to shrink and the available game dwindled drastically.

For the white settlers, life on the frontier was difficult enough without the need to be on constant alert against the possibility of a surprise
attack by Indians. To the pioneers, Indians were nothing more than savages who were capable of committing the worst depredations imagina-
ble. Settlers demanded more and more land and a removal of all
Indians. Clashes between the natives and the settlers resulted in atrocities on both sides. The tension was constant and mounting.

In response to the never-ending U.S. land grab, Tecumseh worked
tirelessly to rally the tribes. His message, which echoed the program put
forth by earlier pan-tribalists, was that in order to protect their lands,
the tribes had to agree to common ownership of all remaining land and
to unite in a political-military confederation. As long as they stood
united, the government could not take advantage of them, as it had all

too often in the past by negotiating treaties with individual tribes and by pitting one tribe against another. Tecumseh promised that under his leadership such a confederation would be capable of resisting further U.S. encroachment.

IN AUGUST 1810, a landmark council was held in the town of Vincennes (Fort Knox) in Indiana Territory. The conference included a number of territorial officials and a dozen chiefs of the northwest tribes, and it brought together for the first time the two men who had become the principal adversaries in the U.S.-Indian struggle for control of the frontier—Shawnee chief Tecumseh and Indiana Territory governor William Henry Harrison.

The meetings were held at a fenced-off, grassy area in a grove near the governor's home. As agreed upon beforehand, Tecumseh left behind most of the seventy-five warriors who had accompanied him to Vincennes, arriving at the clearing with an escort of only a dozen chiefs. Also by agreement, Tecumseh and his party left their firearms at their camp, bringing only tomahawks and war clubs to the council.

Arriving at the meeting ground, they found the governor seated on a platform with several other Indiana officials. Nearby, a small guard of a dozen soldiers from Fort Knox stood nervously by. Also present were several pro-government chiefs, including Harrison's Potawatomi sycophant Winamek, whom Tecumseh had already threatened to kill for his part in the signing of the Treaty of Fort Wayne, which had transferred three million acres of tribal lands in Indiana to the United States a year earlier.

Harrison sat stiffly in his chair, awaiting the arrival of his opponent. He had prepared a chair for Tecumseh next to his own on the platform. When the Shawnee chief entered the council area, Harrison beckoned him to come and take the seat that had been reserved for him. "Your father invites you to be seated," said the governor in a patronizing tone, gesturing toward the empty chair.

Solemnly and defiantly, Tecumseh pointed at the sky. He paused for emphasis and said, "Governor Harrison is not my father—the Great

Spirit is my father." He pointed at the ground, saying, "The Earth is my mother, and I will repose upon her bosom." Then he sat on the grass.

Following Tecumseh's lead, the rest of his party took their seats on the ground. "The effect . . . ," wrote one chronicler of the council, "was electrical, and for some moments there was a perfect silence." The meeting had gotten off on a note of friction, and the tension would build steadily over the next few days.

At thirty-seven, Harrison was five years younger than Tecumseh. The governor, who had many years of experience intimidating defeated and accommodationist chiefs, was taken aback by the Shawnee's boldness. It was he, after all, not this savage, who was in charge.

Harrison was a hard-liner. When it came to acquiring Indian lands for the federal government, few men could match the ruthless and heartless zeal of William Henry Harrison. Between 1802 and 1805 alone, employing trickery, bribery, cajolery, threats, and whiskey, the governor had signed seven treaties with various tribes, giving the United States title to vast areas of present-day Indiana, Missouri, Wisconsin, and Illinois. The tribes were compensated at the rate of 2 cents an acre.

Harrison began by telling Tecumseh he understood that the chief had issues to raise and promised to listen fairly. But diplomacy was not Harrison's long suit. He insisted that he had always treated the Indians honorably and justly, and that Tecumseh was the first to accuse him of acting otherwise. Harrison also stated that he had heard reports blaming Tecumseh for stirring up trouble between the northwestern tribes and the United States by claiming that the chiefs who sold the lands in the Fort Wayne treaty had no right to do so. He challenged the Shawnee to declare "under a clear sky, and in an open path" whether these reports were true.

Tecumseh slowly rose to his feet. In his compelling style, the chief began by putting forth the position that tribal lands were held in common and declared that the treaties had been negotiated deceitfully and were therefore null and void. He spoke scornfully of the Indians who sat near Harrison, heaping abuse on Winamek and promising the accommodationist chiefs that they would be punished for their betrayal, which so unnerved the Potawatomi that he began loading the pearl-handled pistol he had received as a gift from Harrison. Finally, Tecumseh acknowledged that he had organized a confederation to resist further encroachments by the government but insisted he did not want war. If the government would return the land of the Fort Wayne treaty, there would be no hostilities.

John Badollet of the Vincennes land office, an outspoken critic of Harrison's, wrote his friend Albert Gallatin, the secretary of the treasury, that Tecumseh spoke to the governor "with a freedom and sense which excited surprise, he reproached him in the face of day, with having bought the land from tribes which had no right to it, or from persons whom he himself had made chiefs. . . . It is my opinion that Government ought to look closer into this business, and rather to cherish than exasperate that man, that the indians want nothing but good treatment to become well disposed to the United States."

That day and the next, as had come to be expected of him, Tecumseh delivered a series of long, powerful speeches in which he chronicled the past injustices of the United States government toward Native Americans. The litany of wrongs went back decades and covered a great deal of ground—"There are unfortunately too many of them," wrote Harrison to Secretary of War William Eustis in his account of the proceedings.

Harrison's answers to Tecumseh's charges were vague and evasive. He was offended by Tecumseh's lack of deference, later writing to Eustis that while Tecumseh was obviously "the great man of the party . . . his speeches the first two days were sufficiently insolent and his pretensions arrogant."

After several days, frustrated by the sense that he was getting nowhere with Harrison, Tecumseh looked the governor in the eye and told him earnestly, *"Brother,* I wish you to listen to me well. . . . As I think you do not clearly understand what I before said to you, I shall explain it again." He once again enumerated a lengthy list of atrocities committed by the whites against Native Americans, including the 1782 massacre of ninety-six peaceful Christian Delawares at the Moravian mission at Gnadenhutten by U.S. soldiers. How, Tecumseh pressed

Harrison, "after this conduct can you blame me for placing little confidence in the promises of our fathers the Americans. . . . How can we have confidence in the white people? When Jesus Christ came upon the earth you kill'd and nail'd him on a cross."

Tecumseh concluded his talk with a typical flourish. *"Brother.* Since the peace was made you have kill'd some of the Shawanese, Winebagoes, Delawares and Miamies and you have taken our lands from us, and I do not see how we can remain at peace with you if you continue to do so."

Tecumseh's plea fell on deaf ears. In answer to the chief's accusations, Harrison denied that the government had ever acted in bad faith and asserted that the U.S. had always treated the Indians fairly. He disputed Tecumseh's contention that the tribes were one nation, citing as evidence the fact that the Great Spirit had given them many different tongues. He chastised the Shawnee leader, telling him that the Fort Wayne treaty lands had been purchased from the Miami tribe, and that Tecumseh had no right to come from a foreign land and tell the Miamis what they could and could not do with their own lands.

The speech was first translated into Shawnee. Then, as the interpreter began to explain Harrison's double-talk to the Potawatomis, Tecumseh lost his temper and leapt to his feet. Using emphatic and uncharacteristically violent gestures, he interrupted the translator and angrily accused Harrison of lying.

The interpreter quickly turned to the governor and informed him that the Shawnee chief had called him a liar. Harrison's face flushed with anger, and he jumped up out of his chair. Immediately, everyone else on the platform followed suit. Seeing this, Tecumseh's entourage sprang to their feet. In a flash, the thin facade of civility had crumbled, exposing the animosity that lay just below the surface.

Territorial secretary John Gibson, who understood Shawnee, urgently told Harrison, "Those fellows intend mischief. You had better bring up the guard." Harrison signaled for the guard to move in, and Winamek once again charged his pistol and primed it for firing. Tecumseh's men crouched, prepared to do battle, as the soldiers stepped forward, bayonets at the ready. The warriors brandished their war clubs; the troops cocked their rifles. Tecumseh raised his tomahawk; Harrison drew his sword. For one interminable, heart-stopping minute, the threat of violence hung over the council, as thick as the humid Indiana summer air.

But everyone froze in place, and when nobody made the first move, the governor lowered his sword and ordered the soldiers to let down their rifles. Sheathing his weapon, Harrison declared the council over, telling Tecumseh that he would respond to the chief's charges in writing, and that if Tecumseh ever again wanted to speak to him, he should do it through an intermediary. Tecumseh's party left the meeting ground and returned to their camp.

That night, while Harrison was assembling three companies of militia to protect the town, Tecumseh was regretting his impetuous words. The next morning, he sent a message of apology, which was accepted. The council resumed later that day.

At the final meeting, Tecumseh spoke calmly and politely but firmly, still defiant. He warned Harrison not to interfere in intertribal affairs, and stated, "I am alone the acknowledged head of all the Indians." As he finished, he made one last poignant plea: *"Brother.* They want to save that piece of land. We do not wish you to take it. It is small enough for our purposes. . . . I want the present boundary to continue. Should you cross it, I assure you it will be productive of bad consequences."

After Tecumseh, chiefs from several of the other tribes spoke, affirming what the Shawnee had said and acknowledging him as their leader. At the end of the meetings, Tecumseh asked Harrison to send his remarks to the Great Chief, President James Madison. Harrison agreed but cautioned that there was little chance Madison would approve of them. Hearing this, Tecumseh shook his head sadly. "Well," he said, "as the Great Chief is to determine the matter, I hope the Great Spirit will put sense enough into his head, to induce him to direct you to give up this land. It is true, he is so far off, he will not be injured by the war; he may still sit in his town and drink his wine, whilst you and I will have to fight it out."

*   *   *

By all accounts, Tecumseh was an impressive-looking man. Captain George Rogers Clark Floyd, commandant of Fort Knox, referred to him as "one of the finest looking men I ever saw—about six feet high, straight, with large, fine features, and altogether a daring bold-looking fellow."

But it was the nobility of Tecumseh's character, more than his looks, that set him apart. "This great chief was a man of wonderful intellect, brave, fearless, and of pure integrity," said a white settler who had dealings with him. "He would do nothing but what was right, and would submit to nothing that was wrong."

His hospitality and generosity were legendary. According to Anthony Shane, a mixed-blood who married one of Tecumseh's relatives, "His house was always supplied with the best provisions, and all persons were welcome and received with attention. He was particularly attentive to the aged and infirm . . . and he made it his particular business to search out objects of charity and extend the hand of relief."

He was an enormously charismatic figure who elicited reverence from friends and respect from foes. As Stephen Ruddell, a white captive who had been Tecumseh's close friend as a child and young warrior, related, "Tecumtheth was always remarkable from his boyhood up for the dignity and rectitude of his deportment. There was a certain something in his countenance and manner that always commanded respect, and at the same time made those about him love him."

Even his enemies regarded him with esteem. Harrison wrote, "The implicit obedience and respect which the followers of Tecumseh pay to him is really astonishing and more than any other circumstance bespeaks him one of those uncommon geniuses, which spring up occasionally to produce revolutions and overturn the established order of things. If it were not for the vicinity of the United States, he would perhaps be the founder of an Empire that would rival in glory that of Mexico or Peru."

Another distinguishing aspect of Tecumseh's moral fiber was his aversion to the mistreatment of prisoners of war. In a culture that regularly practiced the torture and burning alive of captives as a religious rite, he was outspoken in his opposition to such barbarity. According to Ruddell, "when prisoners fell into his hands he always treated them with as much humanity as if they had been in the hands of civilized people. No burning—no torturing."

He had a playful sense of humor that easily manifested itself, as on the evening when he visited the Ohio cabin of Captain Abner Barrett in 1802 or 1803. Tecumseh was an occasional and welcome visitor at Barrett's and according to one of those present, "About dark, the door of the worthy Captains house, was suddenly opened without any previous knocking, according to Indian custom, and Tecumthe entered with his usual stately air." His gaze swept across the assembled group and settled on a brawny Kentucky man who had just recently arrived in the area and had already expressed apprehension upon learning that there were Indians camped in the vicinity. He was "much alarmed and could not look the stern savage in the face." Immediately sensing the man's disquiet, the Shawnee pointed at the Kentuckian and said to Barrett, "A big baby! A big baby!" He then walked over to the man and, cuffing him lightly and good-naturedly on the shoulders, repeated, "big baby, big baby" several times, as the newcomer grew increasingly anxious and the other settlers roared with laughter.

Finally, there was Tecumseh's skill as an orator. Shawnee Indian agent John Johnston referred to him as "a great publick speaker," and Ruddell said he was "naturally eloquent very fluent, graceful in his gesticulation. . . . He always made a great impression on his audience."

He was not without faults, of course, but they were considerably outweighed by his strengths. As one recent biographer has written, "Arrogance, impulsiveness, and a haughty pride and capacity for ruthlessness were all part of his makeup, but it was his virtues that were remembered."

THE EVENTS that led to the 1810 council at Vincennes were set in motion in 1805, when Tecumseh was in his late thirties, the head—both civil and war chief—of one of a series of villages on the White River, near current-day Anderson, Indiana. In the spring of that year, Tecumseh's younger brother Tenskwatawa experienced a life-transforming vision that became the inspiration for a new religion. The new faith was based on the twin tenets of a return to traditional native ways and pan-tribal unity.

Tenskwatawa, a reformed drunkard, preached a form of radical nativist fundamentalism that provided an explanation for the woes confronting the tribes at the beginning of the nineteenth century. If native people would return to their traditional ways and unite, they could achieve personal salvation, and game would return in abundance, as the whites would be beaten back. It was a very appealing doctrine, and Tenskwatawa's teachings spread quickly through the tribes of the northwest.

One of the early converts to the new religion was Tecumseh. The brothers were heirs to the tradition of pan-tribalism that reached back to the middle of the eighteenth century. Tecumseh took over the role of military and political leader, while Tenskwatawa was the latest in a long line of prophets.

Many historians consider Tenskwatawa, better known as The Prophet, as the more important of the two brothers in the history of the pan-tribal movement. As the founder of the new religion, it was he who revived the alliance that had lain dormant for a decade following the natives' defeat at the Battle of Fallen Timbers in 1793 and the subsequent Treaty of Greenville two years later. But Tecumseh was by far the greater leader of the two and the one who united the tribes in war. Moreover, it was the legend of his earthquake prophecy that would have devastating consequences for at least one tribe.

In the summer of 1806, Tecumseh and his brother had established a new village in response to Tenskwatawa's growing reputation and influence. The site they chose—near Greenville in western Ohio, on the U.S. side of the boundary delineated by the 1795 Treaty of Greenville—became the headquarters of The Prophet's new religion. The location had been revealed to Tenskwatawa by the Master of Life in a vision.

Here, The Prophet became one of the most important Native American leaders of the region, as members of all the northern tribes flocked to hear him and receive his teachings.

There was a steady influx of new arrivals to the Greenville settlement. By 1807, the village had almost sixty lodges and a 34-foot-wide by 150-foot-long council house that was built by men and women working together. Throughout the northwest and beyond, Native Americans were taking up The Prophet's teachings.

At that point, neither of the brothers had wanted a war with the United States. The numbers of pilgrims arriving at Greenville, however, alarmed the white settlers, and tensions began to rise. In fact, the overwhelming majority of those who came to Greenville to hear The Prophet were not hostile, but in the spring of 1807, several settlers were murdered by an unknown band of Indians, causing a general panic among the whites of the region. Without any evidence, William Wells, the Indian agent at Fort Wayne, blamed the killings on Indians en route to or from the Greenville settlement, and he had the audacity to invoke the authority of President Jefferson in demanding that Tecumseh and The Prophet remove themselves and their village from the Greenville location. "Brothers," wrote Wells in a letter to Greenville, "it is now more than twelve Moons since you settled on the Lands of the United States at that place during which time you have Kept the minds of your Brothers the white people in a continual State of uneasiness. . . .

"Brothers this makes it proper that you should reside no longer at that place or on the Lands of the United States, and makes it my duty to request and urge you in the name of the Great Chief of the United States to move from that place and off of the Land of the United States immediately."

Initially, Tecumseh and Tenskwatawa had no intentions of acceding to Wells's impudent demand—after all, this was the place that the Master of Life had designated to The Prophet as the location for his religious center. But an unexpected event soon forced them to abandon the settlement in an effort to avoid a war with the United States.

*   *   *

ON JUNE 22, 1807, forty miles off the coast of Virginia, an officer from the British warship *Leopard* boarded the American frigate *Chesapeake* and demanded to search the ship for deserters from the Royal Navy. When the captain of the American ship refused, the British officer returned to the *Leopard,* which then opened fire on the *Chesapeake,* killing three Americans. The American captain surrendered, and the British boarded the *Chesapeake* and took four prisoners.

U.S. relations with the British had already been strained over the Crown's blockade of American trade with Europe, a consequence of Britain's war with Napoleon. After the *Chesapeake* affair, war with the British seemed inevitable, and Native Americans were caught in the middle.

U.S. officials, remembering that the tribes of the northwest had, for the most part, fought with the British during the Revolutionary War, were convinced that the British in Canada were cultivating the tribes' friendship in order to ensure their alliance in the coming war. The British had certainly curried favor with the Indians, and for American officials like William Henry Harrison, British provocation of the Indians was a convenient explanation for Indian hostility. "I really fear that this said Prophet is an engine set to work by the British for some bad purpose," Harrison wrote to Secretary of War Henry Dearborn in July 1807. The following month he expressed the unfounded opinion that the Shawnees were "entirely devoted" to the British. In August he also wrote to the Shawnee chiefs to admonish them for listening to The Prophet. "My children it must be stopped," said Harrison with his characteristic hard-nosed, nonnegotiable tactlessness. "I will suffer it no longer. You have called in a number of men to listen to a fool who speaks not the words of the Great Spirit, but those of the Devil and of the British agents."

Thomas McKee, the British Indian agent at Fort Malden, had a more realistic view of the situation. "The discontent of the Indians arises principally from the unfair purchases of their lands," he wrote shortly before the *Chesapeake* incident, "but the Americans ascribe their dissatisfaction to the machinations of our government."

Finally, wishing to escape the escalating tension, Tecumseh and

The Prophet decided to heed William Wells's warning and move their village. In early 1808, they relocated about 125 miles west to where the Tippecanoe River joined the Wabash in Indiana Territory. There, they established a new settlement that the whites called Prophetstown.

The move accomplished a number of things. First, it put the brothers further away from the reach and influence of the U.S. government. In addition, the new location had more game than the Greenville area. Also, by moving west, they were closer to the tribes in Illinois and Michigan, which had been notably open to The Prophet's teachings. Finally, it sent a message to the government that indicated their determination to defend their remaining lands.

INCREASINGLY, white Americans were also looking west. The Lewis and Clark expedition (Spring 1804–Fall 1806) had established beyond any doubt the vastness of the continent, and settlers were forsaking the eastern states for the promise of the frontier. They poured into southern Indiana, and it was only a matter of time before they would begin moving onto tribal territory.

The protection of their remaining land was increasingly the most important issue facing the tribes. Accordingly, the focus of the pan-tribal movement began to shift from the religious and spiritual to the political and military, and Tecumseh began to surpass The Prophet as its paramount leader.

In the summer of 1809, Tecumseh traveled through the northwest on a recruiting trip. In keeping with his advocating a return to traditional ways, he dressed in a style that had become obsolete half a century earlier—unadorned buckskin shirt, breechcloth and fringed leggings, moccasins decorated with porcupine quills rather than European trade beads. In his nose he wore three small silver crosses. His head was shaved except for a scalp lock that fell loosely down his back. Wherever he went, he made an impression and attracted a following.

But when Tecumseh returned to Prophetstown in the fall, there was the ominous news of the Treaty of Fort Wayne, with its cession of three million acres. Harrison had assured the signers, "This is the first request [*sic*] your new Father (President Madison) has ever made you [and] it will be the last, he wants no more of your land agree to the proposition which I now make & . . . he will never make another proposition to you to sell your lands." This promise would be broken within eighteen months.

The signing of the Fort Wayne treaty was a watershed moment in the growth of the pan-tribal movement, as alarmed tribesmen all over the northwest suddenly realized that The Prophet's teachings in itself were not enough to protect them from the government's insatiable thirst for their lands. Many now began to view Tecumseh's military leadership as a more powerful path. In the spring of 1810, a thousand warriors flocked to Prophetstown, which had grown to sixty lodges, a large guest house, a council house, a medicine lodge, and a hundred acres of cultivated fields. The Shawnee, Potawatomi, Sac, Fox, Ottawa, Delaware, Kickapoo, Winnebago, and Wyandot tribes were all represented. Even many Miamis, to that point one of the tribes considered most friendly to the government, were now in Tecumseh's camp and could be counted among the confederation forces at Prophetstown.

Governor Harrison had taken the great influx as an ominous sign, an indication that the Indians were preparing for war. He had written to The Prophet, whom he still regarded as the leader of the pan-tribal movement, instructing him to disband his settlement on the Wabash and summoning him to Vincennes for a council. He said that although he considered Tenskwatawa to be an enemy of the U.S., there was "yet but very little harm done but what may easily be repaired. The chain of friendship which unites the whites with the Indians may be received and be as strong as ever—a great deal of that work depends on you— the destiny of those who are under your direction depends upon the choice which you will make of the two roads which are before you. One is large, open and pleasant, and leads to peace security and happiness— the other on the contrary is narrow and crooked and leads to misery, to ruin. . . . What reason have you to complain of the 17 fires [i.e., the United States], have they taken anything from you, have they ever violated the Treaties made with the red men, you say they purchased land from those who had no right to sell. Show the truth of this and the lands will be instantly restored."

Tecumseh, not Tenskwatawa, sent a reply to the governor. He said that while he had no desire for war, it was difficult for him to be peaceful toward those who had stolen his people's land. "The Great Spirit said he gave this great island to his red children," said the Shawnee. "He placed the whites on the other side of the big water, they were not contented with their own, but came to take ours from us. They have driven us from the sea to the lakes, we can go no farther. They have taken upon themselves to say this tract belongs to the Miamis, this to the Delawares & so on. but the Great Spirit intended it to be the common property of all the Tribes, nor can it be sold without the consent of all. Our father tells us that we have no business on the Wabash, the land belongs to other Tribes, but the great spirit order'd us to come here and we shall stay."

AND SO the Vincennes council had been set. Not long before meeting Tecumseh for the first time, Harrison had learned from his informants who the true leader of the pan-tribal movement was. "This brother," he wrote to the secretary of war, "is really the efficient man—the Moses of the family . . . He is . . . described by all as a bold active, sensible man, daring in the extreme and capable of any undertaking."

Chapter Five

—

THE IMPENDING
DESTRUCTION

Following the Vincennes council, Tecumseh began to prepare for the inevitable. He undertook a westward recruiting trip to Canada, where he met with British officials at Fort Malden, below Detroit, to try and enlist their aid in the impending war with the United States. He told them that he did not expect their active participation in a war, but he did hope they would contribute ammunition and supplies. His appeal met with a mixed response. Sir James Craig, the governor general of Canada, made no commitment but promised to send Tecumseh's request to the king. Matthew Elliott, on the other hand, the British Indian agent at Fort Malden, who was married to a Shawnee woman, was more amenable. His wife persuaded Elliott to furnish Tecumseh with clothing and ammunition, as well as promise to send along another shipment of supplies to Prophetstown.

After his meeting with the British, Tecumseh returned home, relieved that his trip had yielded at least some minimal support. Elliott made good on his pledge of provisions, and the winter passed peacefully. But even Governor Harrison, who in December wrote that "there is not at present any probability of an Indian war," knew that trouble was just under the surface: "I believe the Prophet's principle, that their lands should be considered common property, is either openly avowed or secretly favored by all the Tribes, west of the Wabash. A . . . resolution to prevent the sale of any more lands to the United States, was entered into by the chiefs."

The following spring, new hostilities broke out. Potawatomi warriors raided settlements in southern Illinois. The Wea tribe in Indiana, which to that point had been friendly to the government, threatened surveyors sent by Harrison to measure the territory of the Fort Wayne treaty; the surveyors vacated the area in such haste that they left their instruments behind. In May, the Wyandot accommodationist chief Tarhe told William Clark (whom Jefferson had appointed Indian agent for St. Louis in 1807) that "the time is drawing near when the murder is to begin, and all the Indians that will not Join, are to die with the whites." Concerned over this new militancy, Harrison wrote to Washington asking for reinforcements and for permission to attack Prophetstown if he deemed it necessary.

He also sent Tecumseh a belligerent letter, reprimanding the Shawnee chief for inciting a war, and claiming he had been told that Tecumseh was plotting his assassination. He warned, "Do you really think that the handful of men that you have about you are able to contend with the Seventeen Fires, or even that the whole of the tribes united could contend against the Kentucky Fire alone? . . . Brothers, it is not our wish to hurt you. If we did we certainly have the power to do it." Finally, he offered Tecumseh and The Prophet the opportunity to travel to Washington to speak with President Madison.

Tecumseh briefly considered Harrison's proposition. Tecumseh was planning a major recruiting campaign to the south, so he had little inclination to travel to Washington. Such a trip could take six or eight weeks, during which time he would be missing the opportunity to enlist the southern tribes in his confederacy. Besides, what reason was there to believe that speaking to the president would make any difference? Instead, Tecumseh decided that before departing he would again travel to Vincennes to meet once more with Harrison, in hopes of placating the governor—at least until the southern tour was completed.

Before leaving Prophetstown, he carefully instructed Tenskwatawa to avoid any military confrontation with Harrison until he returned from the south. He stressed the importance of having the support of the southern tribes before engaging in hostilities. The Prophet agreed— there would be no fighting in Tecumseh's absence.

When Harrison learned that Tecumseh was coming to Vincennes, he cautioned him to bring only a small group with him. Tecumseh ignored the governor's instructions and was accompanied by an even larger escort than he'd had the year before; close to three hundred warriors arrived at Vincennes on July 27, 1811, and set up camp nearby. In town, Harrison had assembled eighty regulars and eight hundred militia, and the night before the council was to begin, the governor whipped the militiamen up to the point where, by John Badollet's account, it was only "with difficulty, that they could be refrained from running to Tecumseh's camp" to massacre the Indians.

The meeting lasted only a couple of days. Tecumseh had learned from the first council that Harrison was not an honest man, and it had therefore been a mistake to be forthcoming with him. Now, Tecumseh disguised his long-range intentions. He admitted that he had assembled a confederation of northern tribesmen who were united and under his direction, but he insisted that there was no reason for Harrison to be concerned over this. In creating this alliance, he had merely followed the example set for him by the United States—a union composed of all the different "fires." And since Native Americans did not complain about the confederation of white people, why should white Americans begrudge the native tribes the same type of affiliation? Indeed, as soon as the council ended, he planned to make a visit to the southern tribes to recruit them into the union. Tecumseh insisted, however, that he did not intend for his confederacy to enter into a war with the United States.

Harrison was not fooled. He demanded to know if Tecumseh intended to prevent white settlers from occupying the Fort Wayne treaty lands, and the chief replied that he hoped everything would remain as it was until he returned, and that if the whites agreed not to occupy those lands before spring, he would then travel to Washington to see President Madison. In response, Harrison disdainfully told Tecumseh that the president "would put his warriors in petticoats sooner than he would give up a country which he had fairly acquired from the rightful owners."

Observing Tecumseh for a second time, Badollet recorded his strong impressions: "The more I think of that man and the measures he pursues, the more I am convinced that his superior mind (I mean Tecumseh) has seen the impending destruction of the indians in their present mode of life," and "to prevent their ultimate annihilation . . . teaches them how to draw their subsistence from their own resources."

Even Harrison gave grudging respect to Tecumseh. It was after this meeting that he wrote of the Shawnee leader as "one of those uncommon geniuses" noting, "No difficulties deter him. His activity and industry supply the want of letters. for Four years he has been in constant motion. You see him today on the Wabash and in a short time you hear of him on the shores of Lake Erie or Michigan, or on the banks of the Mississippi and wherever he goes he makes an impression favorable to his purposes."

As intended, following the meeting with Harrison, Tecumseh set out on his southern journey. He hoped the peace would keep until his return.

IN FACT, Harrison was also dissembling in his talks with Tecumseh. Before the Shawnee even arrived at Vincennes for their second meeting, Harrison had received his response from Washington. On July 17, two months after the governor had written for permission to attack Prophetstown, Secretary of War William Eustis wrote, "If the prophet should commence, or seriously threaten, hostilities he ought to be attacked; provided the force under your command is sufficient to ensure success."

Three days later, Eustis softened this order, saying he had "been particularly instructed by the President, to communicate to your excellency his earnest desire that peace may, if possible, be preserved with the Indians. . . . [H]ostilities (of any kind or to any degree not indispensable required) should be avoided." Noting that reinforcements had been dispatched to Kentucky, Eustis cautioned Harrison that although the troops were at his disposal, "the President indulges the hope and expectation that your exertions and measures with the Indians, will be such as may render their march to the Indiana territory unnecessary."

But the president was one thousand miles away, and Harrison had ideas of his own. With Tecumseh gone from Prophetstown, the governor saw his opportunity to render the pan-tribal movement a paralyzing blow. Just after Tecumseh's departure, he wrote to Eustis, "There can be no doubt but his object is to excite the Southern Indians against us. . . . I do not think there is any danger of any hostility until he returns. And his absence affords a most favorable opportunity for breaking up his Confederacy. . . . I hope . . . before his return that that part of the fabrick, which he considered complete will be demolished and even its foundations rooted up."

Harrison went to work drumming up support for his upcoming mission. He dispatched couriers with secret correspondence to key individuals. Captain Daniel Bissell was told to prepare the Kentucky troops for an "expedition about the 20th. of Sept." A number of individuals with military experience received letters offering them the chance to join the expedition. His missives to Governors Ninian Edwards of Illinois and Benjamin Howard of Upper Louisiana enlisted their backing and forewarned them of the need to alert their militias.

Edwards was only too happy to throw his support behind Harrison—the previous month he had already written the secretary of war to say, "I consider peace totally out of the question; we need not expect it till the Prophet's party is dispersed . . . and there seems to be no reasonable ground to hope for a change for the better, whilst he is permitted to increase his strength with impunity."

On August 13, Harrison informed Eustis of his communications with the other governors: "the President may rest assured that our united councils and exertions will be directed to preserve peace with the Indians. I believe, however, that we all agree in opinion as to the necessity of breaking up the Prophet's establishment upon the Wabash. . . .

"But let me assure you Sir, that I feel most forcibly the responsibility imposed upon me, by the president's directions 'to preserve peace if possible.' And that recourse to actual hostilities shall be had only when every other means shall have been tried in vain to effect the disbanding of the Prophet's force."

Harrison was blowing smoke. He clearly had every intention of invading Prophetstown and was simply indulging in the cynical albeit time-honored political tradition of talking peace while preparing for war. Harrison had become obsessed with the need to destroy the settlement. There was little doubt that the only way to disperse the inhabitants of Prophetstown would be by force, and John Badollet correctly analyzed the situation when he wrote that "extirpation or forcible removal appears to be the ardent wish" of Harrison.

As a warning, Harrison sent a menacing message to the residents of Prophetstown, ordering them to forsake The Prophet and his settlement, in return for which they would not be attacked. He also wrote to the neighboring Miami, Eel River, and Wea tribes, warning them to remain neutral: *"My Children.* My eyes are open and I am now looking toward the Wabash. I see a dark cloud hanging over it. Those who have raised it intended it for my own destruction; but I will turn it upon their own heads. . . .

"My Children. be wise and listen to my voice. I fear that you have got on a road that will lead you to destruction. It is not too late to turn back. Have pity on your women and children. It is time that my friends should be known. I shall draw a line. Those that keep me by the hand must keep on one side of it and those that adhere to the Prophet on the other."

The Wea chief Laprusieur sent back a reply stating that he was a friend of both the Americans and The Prophet. He also let Harrison know that his threats were not effective. *"Father* Your speech . . . has not scared us, we are not afraid of what you say. . . . We have our eyes on our lands on the Wabash with a strong determination to defend our rights, let them be invaded from what quarter they may; that when our best interest is invaded, we will defend them to a man."

Harrison was furious and sent a letter to John Johnston, the Indian agent at Fort Wayne, instructing him to tell the tribes in that area that "the war that may be waged against us by any of the Tribes shall be the last they shall ever make, as it is the positive determination of our Government . . . that the War once begun it will be pursued to the utter exterpation of those who shall commence it or until they are delivered to such a distance as to preclude all probability of their ever again annoying us."

At the end of September 1811, Harrison began the northward march from Vincennes to Prophetstown with a force of more than a thousand men. About a third were regulars, over four hundred were Indiana militia, approximately 120 were mounted Kentucky volunteers, and eighty were Indiana riflemen. They made two-thirds of the 180 miles in less than a fortnight, then stopped for two weeks to throw up a fort near present-day Terre Haute.

On October 10, while Fort Harrison was being completed, a sentry was shot in the legs by a party of Shawnees from Prophetstown. The incident was exactly the provocation Harrison had been looking for. If he had had any lingering hesitation about attacking the settlement, he now threw all reluctance aside. "I had always supposed that the Prophet was a rash and presumptuous man," he wrote to Eustis on October 13, "but he has exceeded by [*sic*] expectations. He has not contented himself with throwing the gauntlet but has absolutely commenced the war."

Recalling Eustis's admonition that he could attack Prophetstown "provided the force under your command is sufficient to ensure success," Harrison requested reinforcements: "A few companies more would make success unequivocal."

A party of friendly Delawares was accompanying Harrison's expedition, serving as messengers and interpreters. In a last-ditch attempt to give the appearance of trying to avoid hostilities, Harrison sent the Delawares to Prophetstown to persuade Tenskwatawa to "lay aside his hostile designs." The messengers set out three conditions whereby Prophetstown could avoid being attacked—conditions Harrison knew very well Tenskwatawa would reject: first, evict all the Potawatomis, Kickapoos, and Winnebagos from Prophetstown; second, turn over all

Indians who had committed depredations against the U.S. and its citizens; third, return all horses stolen from white settlers. The Delawares returned to Fort Harrison to report that they had been poorly received and that the inhabitants of Prophetstown had heaped "the most contemptuous remarks upon them" and upon the whites who had sent them.

On October 29, the requested reinforcements having arrived, Harrison's troops resumed their march. On November 5, they were a dozen miles from Prophetstown, and the following afternoon they advanced to within one mile of the settlement.

As Harrison's army began its march from Vincennes, Tenskwatawa was caught in a dilemma. Tecumseh had very specifically ordered The Prophet to avoid any conflict until his return from the south, when, with the southern tribes presumably enlisted in the confederation, it would clearly be a far more propitious time to strike. But now Harrison was advancing on Prophetstown with a large force. And when the Long Knives, as the natives called U.S. soldiers, built a new garrison on Fort Wayne treaty lands, Tenskwatawa took it as a sign that Harrison was determined to bring about a confrontation.

Very well, then, Tenskwatawa would give the governor what he wanted. A victory over the Long Knives would surely regain for him some share of the leadership of the pan-tribal movement that had shifted to Tecumseh in the past couple of years. To simply retreat in the face of U.S. threats, on the other hand, would diminish his stature. Overestimating his own prowess, The Prophet decided to ignore his brother's instructions and engage Harrison's troops.

As the Long Knives moved north, Tenskwatawa rebuffed every one of Harrison's overtures to "negotiate." When the army marched to within a mile of Prophetstown, however, the Shawnee seer was suddenly unsure of himself—he was, after all, not a war chief but a religious leader, with no experience leading warriors in battle. Now, with the enemy at the gates, he sent out a small group of warriors to speak with Harrison in an attempt to stall for time. The messengers asked the governor to postpone a discussion until the following day, and Harrison, perhaps thinking of Eustis's instructions to fight only as a last resort, agreed to their request. Both sides also agreed to observe a truce until after the following day's conference.

After the short meeting, the U.S. troops set up camp on a ridge about a mile northwest of Prophetstown. Expecting that the negotiations would do nothing to break the stalemate, Harrison made plans to spring a surprise attack and catch the Indians as they were returning to their homes after the council the next day.

Tenskwatawa, however, under pressure from the hotheads in his camp, was a jump ahead. Disregarding the agreed-upon truce, he decided to attack before dawn. A battle plan was drawn: under cover of darkness, the warriors would surround the enemy encampment, and a select party of one hundred warriors would slip silently between the sentries to infiltrate the camp. They would then find Harrison's tent and kill him, which would cause disorder among the U.S. troops. Tenskwatawa assured them that while the darkness would blind the Long Knives, it would not affect the tribesmen themselves and that they would be able to see clearly. He also promised to send rain to dampen the Long Knives' gunpowder and to make the warriors invulnerable to the Long Knives' bullets. Tenskwatawa assured a victory and whipped his warriors into a froth.

After 4:00 a.m. on November 7, having surrounding the bivouacked troops, the warriors' confidence rose even higher when a cold rain began to fall, just as The Prophet had predicted. Moreover, the Long Knives had built bonfires, illuminating their encampment and making it visible from the outside but impairing their own capacity to see beyond the site. The Prophet's medicine appeared to be very strong.

At about 4:30 a.m., however, as they were sneaking through the Long Knives' picket line, one of the warriors was spotted by a sentry, who fired his rifle to alert the troops and then quickly retreated toward safety. Alarmed at the shot, other sentries also abandoned their posts and ran for the camp. Harrison had suspected the possibility of a surprise attack and had ordered his men to sleep "on their arms," as one officer later wrote; when the sentry's shot rang out, the troops awakened, reached for their weapons, and "formed in half a minute." At the same time, those warriors who had successfully infiltrated the picket line jumped up and let out a prearranged war cry, which signaled the rest of their fellows that the advance party had been discovered and to begin their assault on the camp.

Fighting broke out everywhere, as the two armies fell upon each other. From outside the camp, warriors with blackened faces poured volleys of bullets into the illuminated camp while some of the soldiers fired blindly into the darkness and others hastily strove to extinguish the bonfires that made them easy targets.

Harrison, who was awake and pulling on his boots when the first shot rang out, immediately left his tent and began to ride toward the northwest corner of the camp, where the U.S. line was in danger of buckling under the weight of the Indian offensive. With him, on a white horse, was a Colonel Abraham Owen. Two warriors who had crept into the camp undiscovered were close by Harrison's tent, and as he and Colonel Owen galloped by, they mistook the colonel for the governor and shot him dead. Harrison rode on unharmed.

The fighting continued for more than two hours. Bloodcurdling war whoops mixed with the agonized cries of the wounded and the fearful bellowing of stampeding cattle. Finally, with daybreak approaching and their ammunition dwindling, the tribesmen retreated to Prophetstown. Reports of the number of warriors at the battle vary, but the highest estimates run no more than six to seven hundred. Under cover of darkness, they had been able to fight the Long Knives at an advantage, but daylight would quickly reveal their inferior numbers and give the Long Knives the upper hand, especially with the tribesmen's ammunition running out.

Harrison's army suffered over 60 dead and 120 wounded. Casualties on the other side are harder to assess, but a good estimate is about 50 killed and perhaps 75 wounded.

Tenskwatawa had spent the battle on a nearby hill, chanting and praying for success. As the battle ended, he returned to Prophetstown, where he was accosted by furious warriors who threatened to kill him for misleading them. He begged them to regroup, offering to make new medicine that would assure them a victory, but the angry tribesmen left the settlement in disgust.

Expecting the Indians to renew their assault, Harrison's army spent the rest of the day and part of the next building fortifications and taking care of their wounded. When there was no further attack from the Indians, the troops marched on Prophetstown late on November 8. Finding it abandoned, they confiscated cooking implements and other useful items, then set fire to more than five thousand bushels of corn and beans, and also torched the lodges.

Immediately after the engagement, Harrison began trumpeting the Battle of Tippecanoe as an unqualified victory for the United States. He declared triumphantly that "the Indians have never sustained so severe a defeat, since their acquaintance with the white people," and vowed that it had put an end to the Indian problem in the northwest. "I think upon the whole, that there will be no further hostilities," he boasted in a letter to Eustis a short time after the battle.

His self-aggrandizing reports were reflected in newspaper items throughout the country, such as the letter from "a gentleman in Vincennes to his friend" in Lexington, published in the *Lexington American Statesman*. "The Governor on this occasion has proved himself to be a General," stated the writer. "The disposition of his forces, his great caution against surprise, and his perfect self command and coolness during the whole engagement, mark him for a commander."

In fact, the Battle of Tippecanoe was hardly the decisive military triumph that Harrison portrayed. The U.S. troops did little more than hold their position against a significantly smaller force while suffering a greater number of casualties. Nor was the battle the end of the pan-tribal movement, as would quite soon become apparent. Nonetheless, it was enough for Harrison's political ambitions, as three decades later "Tippecanoe and Tyler too" would make his presidential campaign slogan the first in American history that bragged of a Pyrrhic victory.

The confederation did, without doubt, suffer a significant blow. The winter's store of staples was gone, and the village lay in ashes. Of no less significance was the blow to Tenskwatawa's credibility. Never again would he command the respect and devotion of vast numbers of tribesmen. From this point forth, the main mantle of leadership of the pan-tribal movement shifted to The Prophet's brother.

TECUMSEH, who knew nothing of what had transpired at Prophetstown, was having problems of his own. His visit to the Chickasaws, in what is now northern Mississippi, yielded no success, and traveling further south to the Choctaws, he was met with a similar lack of enthusiasm. The government's civilization program, which converted hunters into farmers, had been more successful among the southern tribes than it had been in the north. Equally important, the southern tribes had experienced a considerable amount of intermarriage with whites, and many of the chiefs were of mixed blood. Consequently, Tecumseh was preaching a return to traditional Native American culture to people who had already begun to make the transition to white ways, and who in many cases were part white themselves. The chiefs who were in power enjoyed the backing of the U.S. government, and they were not about to advocate a program that challenged their own authority.

The Creeks of Alabama, on the other hand, despite their history of intermarriage, could be expected to be more receptive. These, after all, were the people of Alexander McGillivray, who a quarter-century earlier had led the militant pan-tribal resistance to the U.S. land grab in the south. In addition, Tecumseh had a familial connection with the Creeks of Tuckhabatchee, where the annual council of the Creek Confederacy was being held. Perhaps most important, the Creeks were extremely disgruntled about a series of roads that the federal government was building on their lands, roads that would greatly increase the amount of traffic passing through their territory. Now, shortly after Tecumseh's arrival, Indian agent Benjamin Hawkins was presenting them with the fait accompli of another road. After three days of protest from the Creeks, Hawkins put an end to the discussion by informing them that he had "not come there to ask their permission to open a road, but merely to inform them that it was now cutting."

As Tecumseh had expected, many Creeks received his message with enthusiasm. But Big Warrior, the head civil chief of Tuckhabatchee, was still a holdout. In the Creek chief's lodge, Tecumseh gave his talk and presented gifts, but when Big Warrior still refused to make a commitment, Tecumseh's legendary earthquake prediction was born. If he could unite the tribes, and if the British went to war alongside them, Tecumseh had a chance at defeating the Long Knives. And when the earth began to tremble on December 16, it appeared to many that the Shawnee had commanded nature itself as his third ally.

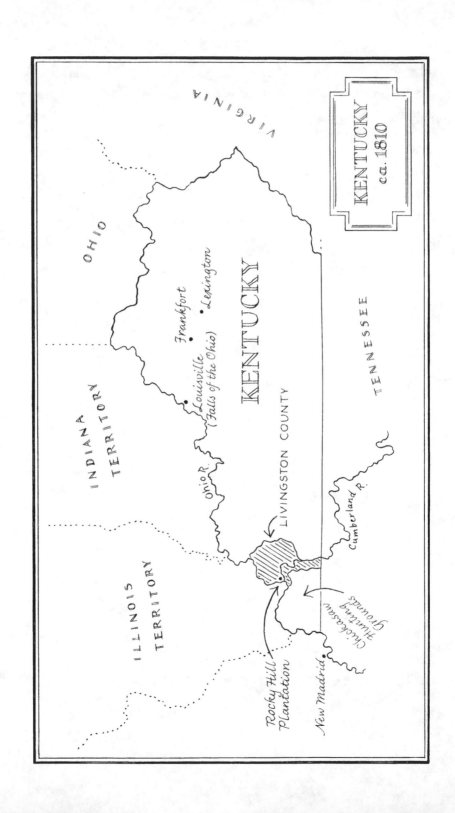

KENTUCKY
ca. 1810

VIRGINIA

OHIO

INDIANA TERRITORY

ILLINOIS TERRITORY

KENTUCKY

Frankfort
• Lexington
Louisville
(Falls of the Ohio)

Ohio R.

LIVINGSTON COUNTY

TENNESSEE

Cumberland R.

Chickasaw
Hunting
grounds

Rocky Hill
Plantation

New Madrid

Chapter Six

THE BLOODY GROUND

A T T H E E N D of the eighteenth and beginning of the nineteenth centuries, the politics of the frontier was influenced more by Indian relations and relations with Spain, France, and Britain than it was by slavery. But slavery was a ticking time bomb that would soon dominate the politics of both westward expansion and north-south relations, and in these years, the coming explosion was already discernible. At the 1792 convention where the new state of Kentucky's constitution was written, the most contentious issue had been whether to include in state law the right to hold slaves. The question was a critical one, for it would set a precedent for westward expansion.

Of the many thousands of settlers who emigrated to Kentucky, a large number were from Virginia. The migration had been going on since the end of the Revolution, when the commonwealth of Virginia, unable to pay many of her soldiers, gave them grants of land in Kentucky County, which had been annexed in 1776. Many of these former soldiers moved west; others, unwilling to uproot their lives, sold their grants. By the end of the 1790s, twenty thousand people a year were emigrating to Kentucky from the eastern states, and during the course of that last decade of the eighteenth century, the immigrant population jumped from 7,000 to over 220,000.

As part of Virginia, slavery had been legal in Kentucky County; in the first federal census of 1790, Kentucky's slave population numbered 12,430. So when the opportunity for statehood arose, the large number of former Virginians living in Kentucky—backed by powerful Virginians such as Thomas Jefferson and James Monroe, who held vast parcels of land in Kentucky—were determined to ensure that the new state was a slave state.

Nevertheless, at the 1792 constitutional convention, a group of clergymen had argued fervently against the practice. Taking their example from the Northwest Ordinance of 1787, which had forbidden slavery north of the Ohio River (although it also provided for the return of escaped slaves to their owners), the ministers managed to gather sixteen votes on their side. After a heated debate, however, they were outvoted by the twenty-six plantation owners at the convention, and Kentucky entered the union as a slave state.

Tennessee also became a slave state four years later, and in 1798, another vigorous debate had been held in Congress over the admission of the Mississippi Territory as a slaveholding territory. As in the cases of Kentucky and Tennessee, the wealthy planters of Mississippi prevailed.

Nevertheless, slavery's opponents were gaining strength and clearing the northern states of the barbaric practice. One by one, following the example of Vermont, which outlawed slavery in 1777, the northern states gradually passed legislation prohibiting the possession of human chattel. By the time of the Louisiana Purchase in 1803, Connecticut, Massachusetts, New Hamphire, New York, Ohio, Pennsylvania, and Rhode Island had all banned slavery.

The Louisiana Purchase once again thrust the issue of slavery before the nation. Under French law, slavery had existed in Louisiana but was on the decline at the time of the purchase. Article III of the purchase treaty stated that the inhabitants of Louisiana would become Americans, with "the enjoyment of all the rights, advantages and immunities of citizens of the United States; and . . . they shall be maintained and protected in the free enjoyment of their liberty, property and the religion which they profess." Proponents of slavery interpreted the provision to justify the possession and sale of human chattel.

An equally determined group was opposed to the notion. In 1805–06, a faction of congressmen led by James Hillhouse of Connecticut was successful in at least temporarily preventing further importation of slaves into the newly acquired territory, but it was a short-lived victory. By the time Louisiana was admitted to statehood in 1812, interstate commerce in slaves was flourishing, and for slave owners, the frontier beckoned.

AMONG the tens of thousands who relocated to Kentucky with their slaves were the Lewises of Albemarle County, Virginia. The once proud Lewises had been reduced to poverty, and they were hoping for a fresh start on the frontier. But in moving from Virginia to Kentucky, the Lewis family merely went from bad to worse as their luck continued to decline in their new surroundings. The shocks that would ultimately cause the Lewis dynasty to crumble—just as they would bring down so many physical structures—were the New Madrid earthquakes.

ON THE morning of November 20, 1807, three families named Lewis had set out from central Virginia, bound for the Kentucky frontier. With all their meager earthly goods—including furniture, clothing, household items, and farm implements—piled high onto wagons and their slaves walking alongside, they began the 160-mile carriage trip to Pittsburgh, where they would board a flatboat for the dangerous river voyage to Livingston County in westernmost Kentucky. Like so many others, they sought a new life in the west.

The move was hard on Lucy Jefferson Lewis, the oldest woman in the group. Now in her mid-fifties, she remembered the good days, when her husband was a rich and influential landowner and planter. How quickly and inexorably their fortunes had ebbed. As the carriage pulled away from the plantation that had been home, she had her last chance to look at not too distant Monticello, the home of her brother, currently in his second term as president of the United States. She would never see him again.

Descendants of General Robert Lewis, a Welsh lawyer who emigrated to Virginia in 1645, the Lewises were one of the colony's most influential dynastic families, with sundry branches and many distinguished members. (Meriwether Lewis, William Clark's partner on their already famous expedition across the continent, was a cousin.) As part of Virginia's ruling class, the Lewises owned extensive tracts of land, had numerous slaves, occupied positions of authority in local government, and fought in the Revolution.

When Charles Lewis, Jr., the great-great-grandson of General Robert Lewis, died in 1782 at the age of sixty-one he owned 4,500 acres and fifty-seven slaves. One of his sons, Charles L. Lewis, married Thomas Jefferson's sister Lucy, attained the rank of colonel in the Virginia militia, and served, albeit with no particular distinction, in the War of Independence. After the war, Colonel Lewis's personal fortunes flourished. By 1791, he had inherited the title to three thousand acres and owned forty slaves; he also had a tavern license, was involved in real estate promotion, and ran a stage line with twenty horses and four wagons. Colonel Lewis and his wife had nine children and lived in a large home within sight of Monticello. Lewis was so prosperous that, in 1792, Jefferson wrote, "C. L. Lewis my brother in law . . . is becoming one of our wealthiest people."

Ten years later, Colonel Lewis was indigent, dependent on his children for support. Beginning with the colonel's decline, the fall of the Lewis family would be swift and relentless. The story of how Colonel Lewis, in the space of a decade, went from being one of Albemarle County's wealthiest people to a state of utter destitution is at least partly the story of how Virginia's ruling class recklessly destroyed the colony's fertile soil.

Virginia was an agricultural-based class society, with the wealthy plantation owners at the top of the social order. In general (there were exceptions, naturally), these men were an easygoing, good-natured, indolent lot. Their plantations were run by overseers, as most of the planters considered it beneath their dignity to involve themselves in such menial affairs. The Anglican minister Reverend Andrew Burnaby, who toured the region before the Revolution, observed that Virginia's upper-class men were "extremely fond of society and given to convivial pleasures," and that they were not inclined to "show any spirit of enterprise, or expose themselves willingly to fatigue." Their generosity and ostentation led to "a disregard of economy," which caused many Virginians to "outrun their incomes."

Thomas Jefferson had similar opinions about his fellow Virginians. In an assessment of their makeup, Jefferson wrote, "I have studied their character with attention. I have thought them . . . aristocratical, pompous, clannish, indolent, hospitable, and . . . disinterested. . . . I have always thought them so careless of their interests, so thoughtless in their expences and in all their transactions of business that I had placed it among the vices of their character."

By their lack of initiative and foresight, these sociable, insular, indolent, pleasure-seeking, profligate men managed to wreak devastation on Virginia's environment during the colonial and post-revolutionary periods.

For the entire seventeenth and nearly all of the eighteenth centuries, tobacco was king in Virginia, almost to the exclusion of all other crops. The cultivation of tobacco grew out of the early settlers' need for an exchange crop and blossomed into a monocultural farming system that, in a relatively short time, stripped Virginia's forests, utterly depleted the colony's rich soil, and brought on social ills as well. Jefferson, himself a onetime tobacco farmer, summed up the situation when he wrote, "It is a culture productive of infinite wretchedness. Those employed in it are in a continued state of exertion beyond the powers of nature to support. Little food of any kind is raised by them; so that the men and animals on those farms are badly fed, and the earth is rapidly impoverished." Elsewhere he wrote, "The unprofitable condition of Virginia estates in general leaves it now next to impossible for the holder of one to avoid ruin. And this condition will continue until some change takes place in the mode of working them."

COLONEL Charles L. Lewis was a perfect example of a man brought to ruin at least in part by the squandering of land. By the time he had inherited his property from his father, the soil had been fairly well exhausted. On top of that, a series of droughts alternating with ravaging rains, along with pest infestations and poor yields, combined to make the years between 1792 and 1800 a bleak period for Albemarle County farmers.

There are also indications that Colonel Lewis was somewhat unstable. His business affairs are filled with dishonest and shady dealings. Two later accounts describe him as "taciturn, moody, abstracted, and queer," and "to say the least, a very strange man."

In fact, the Jefferson, Randolph, and Lewis families were rife with many generations of first-cousin intermarriage—Colonel Lewis and his wife, Lucy Jefferson (whose mother was a Randolph), were themselves first cousins. The three families were riddled with many of the genetic infirmities that accompany such consanguinity, frequently showing up as physical, mental, and/or psychological disabilities. Writing about the Lewises, Jefferson referred to the "hypochondriac affections" that seemed to be "a constitutional disposition in all the nearer branches of the family."

In fact, the Lewis, Randolph, and Jefferson families all exhibited physical, mental, and/or psychological problems. Thomas Jefferson had three siblings who were, as one of his biographers has written, either "simple-minded" or markedly "deficient" in intellect. Three of his five children died in infancy, and one of his grandsons was epileptic. Jefferson himself suffered from severe, prolonged headaches.

The Randolph family in particular was riddled with mental and physical instability, including retardation, insanity, epilepsy, alcohol abuse, morphine addiction, and criminal behavior. According to Rev. Hamilton Wilcox Pierson, who knew them, "The Randolphs were all strange people."

In addition to the farming problems and Colonel Lewis's personal predilections, a combination of poor business decisions, the economic depressions of the times, and just plain bad luck led the colonel to ruin. In 1794, he was forced to give up his tavern license as well as sell the stage line and seven of his horses. Two years later, the number of slaves he owned had been reduced from over forty to seventeen, and five more horses were sold. By 1803, he had lost the rest of his slaves and horses. Of his original 3,000 acres, only 750 remained; the rest he had given to his three oldest sons, Randolph, Lilburne, and Charles (who would die in August 1806 while serving in the army) as their inheritance. But the depleted soil on those remaining 750 acres could not be farmed, which left Colonel Lewis with no source of income. By September 1803, all of his remaining acreage was sold—the proceeds were not even enough to cover his debts.

Fortunately for the colonel and his wife, several of their grown children, including Randolph and Lilburne, were able to care for them, and from 1803 on, the Lewis children looked after their parents. But the two brothers' fortunes also went into decline. The land they had received from their father was exhausted, and in 1806, they decided to emigrate to Kentucky, where virgin land could be had for a small fraction of Virginia prices.

Lilburne and Randolph sold their property and made a trip to western Kentucky to look for acreage. With the rapid settlement of Kentucky well under way, their plan was not merely to buy land to live on, but to acquire other property for speculation. Using the proceeds from the sale of their Virginia property, they were able to purchase several large tracts in Livingston County. Randolph paid over $9,000 for close to 4,000 acres, and Lilburne spent more than $8,000 on 1,500 acres.

In November 1807, the land-poor families of Randolph and Lilburne Lewis, together with their parents, left Virginia for the Kentucky frontier. The parents and their three younger children were now totally dependent on Randolph and Lilburne. The party that said farewell to Albemarle County that day consisted of Randolph, his wife, Mary (a second cousin), their seven children and seven slaves; Lilburne, his wife, Elizabeth (Mary's sister), their four children and fourteen slaves; and Colonel Charles L., his wife, Lucy, their three unmarried daughters, and four slaves. As they got under way, they had bright hopes for the future.

The Lewises were hardly the first Virginians to think of relocating to Kentucky. From their home county of Albemarle alone, three hundred other families had made the arduous move. Friends and relatives of the Lewis family—many of whom had left Virginia during the decade-long series of natural disasters in the 1790s—could be found throughout the state.

WESTERN Kentucky, the Lewises' destination, was not exactly the paradise they envisioned. In the eighteenth century, a Native American had ominously referred to the lands below the Kentucky River as "the bloody Ground." The violent and corrupt nature of western Kentucky society in the early nineteenth century provided a context in which the Lewis brothers' ghastly murder of the slave George was not entirely an aberration.

Logan County, two counties east of Livingston County where the Lewises would settle, was nicknamed "Rogues' Harbor" and was estimated to have the greatest concentration of criminals on the frontier. "Here many refugees, from almost all parts of the Union, fled to escape justice or punishment," wrote one frontiersman, "for although there was law, yet it could not be executed, and it was a desperate state of society. Murderers, horse thieves, highway robbers, and counterfeiters fled here until they combined and actually formed a majority . . . and they really put all law at defiance, and carried on such desperate violence and outrage."

Livingston County was not far behind when it came to violence. Public brawling among lower-class whites—often precipitated by bouts of drinking—was a commonplace spectator sport. It was not at all unusual for one of the combatants in these spectacles to bite off an ear, lip, or nose of his opponent. The county court records reveal two such incidents in September 1810 alone. In the first, a James Stevenson "did unlawfully make an assault on William Love . . . and without being compelled thereto in self defense, did bite off the ear of him the said William Love." In the second case, a Robert Woods, "being a wicked and evil disposed person . . . did make an assault on the body of one Jeremiah Moore . . . and unlawfully bite off the lip of said Jeremiah Moore."

Vincent Nolte, a frontier merchant, described one appalling custom in his memoirs. "A frightfully cruel practice prevailed at that time among the greater part of the rude inhabitants of the western states," wrote Nolte. "It consisted in allowing the finger-nails to grow so long, that, by cutting them, you could give them the form of a small sickle, and this strange weapon was used, in the broils that constantly occurred, to cut out the eyes of the hostile party. This barbarous action was called *gouging*. In this excursion through Kentucky I saw several persons who lacked an eye, and others, both of whose eyes were disfigured."

Gouging—which was punishable by imprisonment for two to ten years and a fine of up to $1,000, two thirds of which went to the victim—was vigorously prosecuted, and eventually began to disappear. Unfortunately, it was replaced by an equally, if not more, barbaric practice. Andrew Melish, who traveled extensively throughout the United States from 1806 to 1811, noted that while gouging was "not now so common as formerly" in Kentucky, many of the "quarrelsome miscreants" had instead "adopted the practice of *stabbing*."

When white Americans tired of fighting amongst themselves, they had African-Americans and Native Americans to abuse, and it was not only the lower classes who were given to this type of violence. In 1804, the Livingston County coroner's jury found that Thomas Hawkins and his wife had murdered one of their female slaves, who suffered "an exceeding bad wound behind the right ear, supposed to be struck with a club or some other unlawful weapon. The appearance of the wound had affected the side of the head unto the left nostril and Blood appeared to issue therefrom, together with sundry smaller wounds appeared to be from severe whipping."

But slaves were not only in danger of being beaten by their masters. The type of treatment to which they might be subjected can be inferred from an incident that occurred in August 1809, when Richard Ferguson, a Livingston County justice of the peace, and his friend James McCawley, a tavern owner—about whom we will soon hear more—arrested a slave named Bob and beat him within an inch of his life.

Bob's crime was being out on his own, in violation of the Kentucky statute that stated, "No slave shall go from the tenements of his master or other person with whom he lives, without a pass, or some letter or token, whereby it may appear that he is proceeding by authority, from his master, employer or overseer; if he does, it shall be lawful for any person to apprehend and carry him before a justice of the peace, to be by his order punished with stripes, or not, in his discretion." If the justice's discretion were so inclined, the offender could "receive, on his or her back at the public whipping post, any number of lashes not exceeding thirty nine."

Since Bob's offense was a misdemeanor and not a felony, Ferguson, as a justice of the peace, had the power to mete out the punishment without summoning a jury. He and McCawley zealously seized the opportunity to uphold the law and dragged the unfortunate man to the whipping post in the Livingston County public square. There, in their eagerness to carry out justice, they "with hands, fists, feet, sticks, and clubs . . . an assault did make on . . . negroe man Bob. They did then and there, beat, wound, and ill treat and with a rope they then and there hung said negroe man Bob up by the neck till he was nearly dead, and other outragious violences did to said negroe man Bob."

Bob's owner, ferryman Isaac Bullard, sued Ferguson and McCawley, charging that as a result of the beating he "wholly lost the services and labor of said negroe man for the span of two months." Bullard asked $500 in damages. The jury agreed that the punishment Ferguson and McCawley administered had been extreme, but awarded Bullard a mere $7.60, the average two-month rental fee for an adult male slave.

Native Americans were similarly at risk. Kentucky settlers had waged a long, intermittent war against the Shawnee and other tribes, with depredations and atrocities carried out by both whites and natives, and most Kentuckians accordingly had little use for any Indian.

In 1803, three Chickasaws were among a group of men drinking at James Ivy's tavern in the small town of Eddyville. One Chickasaw named Jimmy had been plied with liquor by the crowd until he slumped to the floor, dead drunk. One of the whites dragged Jimmy over to a corner, where he would be out of the way of the trouble that was about to start. The other two Chickasaws also sensed danger and left the tavern. A couple of white men, Matthias Cook and Isaac Ferguson, followed them out and began battering them with heavy wooden clubs. Cook and Ferguson would likely have killed the two Chickasaws had they not been restrained by some of the other men present.

In the meantime, inside the tavern, a man named Reuben Cook had dragged Jimmy out of his corner, thrown him down in front of the fireplace, and proceeded to kick burning embers onto the semiconscious man's skin. Badly burned, Jimmy managed to crawl outside, where Ferguson and the two Cooks attacked him again, kicking him and pounding him with their clubs. Then they dragged him away. A white man who tried to intercede on Jimmy's behalf was threatened with a beating and backed off.

When Jimmy was found, he was lying face down in the mud, barely alive. His skull was bashed in on one side and his face was mutilated. He was taken to James Ivy's house, where he died two days later. In a subsequent trial, the murderers were acquitted by a jury.

WESTERN Kentucky was also a politically corrupt society, governed as it was by a closed circle of powerful individuals who promoted and protected their own interests. The Kentucky frontier was an oligarchy, where position, influence, and justice were customarily bought and sold by the ruling class, and abuse of power was a fact of life. Only the governor, lieutenant governor, and members of the Kentucky state legislature were elected. Local officials were all appointed, in some instances by the governor, in some by other local officials. The county court—the most powerful and important governmental structure in Kentucky— was responsible for the control of virtually all public affairs and business dealings in the county. There was not even a notion of separation of powers, as the county court's responsibilities were not merely judicial but executive and legislative as well.

Justices of the peace—who, sitting together, formed the county court—were appointed for life. Upon resigning, they chose two candidates as potential successors, one of whom was appointed to the open post by the governor. The county court in turn chose all county officials.

The offices of sheriff, deputy sheriff, clerk, and constable were custom-arily sold or rented out, despite the illegality of the practice. The sheriff was the most powerful person in the county, and it was entirely common for the office of sheriff to be sold at public auction, which caused one detractor of the system to charge that the position was "hawked about the streets, and sold like a horse in the public market, so that he who had the most money might get the office." In the six-year period between 1807 and 1813, Livingston County had eight different sheriffs, despite the fact that the office of sheriff carried a two-year term.

James McCawley and Richard Ferguson, the two men who brutal-ized the slave Bob, were both public officials in Livingston County. McCawley was a trustee of Smithland town, the neighborhood where the Lewis family settled. He later became a town magistrate. Over the course of time, McCawley was in court four times for assault, as well as for perjury and contempt of court. Ferguson, as already noted, was a justice of the peace. In 1801, Ferguson was indicted for "committing a riot . . . by abusing and tarring the clothes and cutting the same and confining James Axley . . . and other enormities then and there." Despite this charge and a number of other court appearances, Ferguson went on to rise to the position of Smithland's representative on the county court.

About two months before they nearly killed Bob, these two pillars of society, acting together with two other brutes, pummeled one William Barker to the point that he was not expected to live. Later that same day, they ganged up with nine others to give a man named Sam McAmy a similar thrashing.

Such were the quality of men who occupied positions of leadership in Livingston County, and it provides a telling glimpse into Lilburne Lewis's character to learn that both McCawley and Ferguson became close friends of his.

The Lewis family arrived in the Smithland area in 1808. A few years later, a traveler wrote of Smithland, "A more miserable looking place exists nowhere. It contains a few wretched buildings . . . Here the slaves are more numerous than the whites, and many of the former appear far better in point of morals and intelligence."

*   *   *

THE LEWISES' Kentucky properties lay at the confluence of the Ohio and Cumberland rivers, approximately seventy-five miles northeast of New Madrid. Livingston County was the southwesternmost county in Kentucky; the only part of the state that lay west of Livingston County was the Chickasaw hunting lands. Lilburne's property was on a high bluff looking out over the Ohio, and in keeping with Virginia tradition, he gave his estate a name: Rocky Hill.

The first year in Kentucky passed relatively uneventfully as the three families were occupied with clearing land and building houses. In 1809, however, a succession of events sent Lilburne Lewis's life careening out of control. The troubles began in April, when Elizabeth, his wife of twelve years to whom he was deeply devoted, died at age twenty-seven. Lilburne was now left with five children to look after, the youngest of whom was only two.

Soon after Elizabeth's death, the financial pressure began to mount. In May, Lilburne was sued for $500 for collection of an old debt incurred on his first trip to Kentucky in 1806.

During the summer, Lilburne's household was beset by a series of illnesses and other health concerns, including malaria, digestive problems, insomnia, and body lice. During August and September, the head of the family, three of his children, and six of his slaves repeatedly needed treatment. Lilburne ran up a bill of $65 with Dr. Arthur Campbell of Smithland. Not surprisingly, the doctor soon began demanding payment.

By the end of the year, Lilburne realized he was not capable of caring for five children, and in December, he took his two oldest daughters, aged nine and eleven, to Mercer County, some 175 miles east of Smithland, to be boarded and schooled. The cost—$100 a year—added to Lilburne's growing financial woes.

It was a bad time to be owing money in Kentucky. The entire country was in an economic depression, and as the Kentucky House of Representatives wrote in a letter to Governor Charles Scott on December 20, 1809, "our commerce is embarrassed, and the scarcity of specie has become proverbial."

Lilburne's annual earnings were only about $250, which he received for renting out seven of his slaves. Neither he nor Randolph were able to sell any of the investment properties they had bought, and by the beginning of 1810, Lilburne was desperate for income. In addition to the financial problems, there were two more deaths in the family. In October 1809, a shocking piece of news arrived from Tennessee. Lilburne's second cousin Meriwether Lewis—Colonel Lewis's grandfather and Meriwether's grandfather were brothers—had committed suicide. At the time, Meriwether Lewis was governor of Upper Louisiana, having been appointed to the position by Thomas Jefferson in 1807. (It was in his obituary of Meriwether that Jefferson wrote of the "hypochondriac affections" to which he was disposed and which afflicted "all the nearer branches of the family of his name.")

In late May of the following year, Lilburne and Randolph's mother, Lucy Jefferson Lewis, died of a lingering illness at the age of fifty-seven. In the space of thirteen months, Lilburne had lost his wife and his mother.

Nonetheless, together with Randolph, Lilburne gradually began to get involved in community life. He served on a circuit court grand jury and joined the Kentucky militia, where he would eventually rise to the rank of captain. He also found temporary employment.

Eighteen-ten was a census year, and Lilburne applied to the federal marshal of Kentucky, Colonel Joseph Crockett, for the position of Livingston County census taker. The colonel, also a former resident of Albemarle County, had been appointed to his post by Lilburne's uncle Thomas Jefferson, so it was hardly surprising that Crockett gave Lilburne the job. The county census taker was paid two and a half cents for every person recorded. In 1810, Livingston County had 3,674 residents—2,932 whites, 718 slaves, and 24 free blacks—and Lilburne earned $91.85 for his work.

If he had any income other than his census pay and the rental fees for some of his slaves, there is no record of it. For the year of 1810, Lilburne's total earnings appear to be less than $350.

In November of that year, it seemed that Lilburne's fortunes might be changing for the better when he married Letitia Rutter. Letitia was a catch. The Rutters were one of the most powerful families in Livingston County and deservedly known as upstanding citizens. Moreover, Letitia was extremely attractive. One of the only two surviving accounts of her describes as "a very beautiful young lady—one of the belles of Livingston County." The other calls her "accomplished and . . . a bright eyed, pulsing, Kentucky beauty."

Unfortunately, Letitia was not only beautiful but also a "cold, proud and scornful young wife." The new marriage was not a happy one, and it quickly became yet another in Lilburne's accumulating series of misfortunes.

In late February 1811, Lilburne's brother Randolph, who had been ill since January, died of unknown causes. He was thirty-eight and left eight children, the oldest of whom was nineteen. Lilburne was now the head of the clan. His income was a mere dribble. His new marriage was heading for the rocks. He was woefully ill-equipped to handle the familial responsibility that had fallen upon his narrow shoulders. There seemed to be no way out of his morass.

In March, the lawsuit over the 1806 debt was finally brought to judgment, and Lilburne somehow scraped together the $500 to pay off the bill. Meanwhile, Dr. Campbell kept pressing his suit for the money Lilburne owed him for medical services.

At the time of his death, Randolph Lewis had been serving as a Livingston County justice of the peace, and after he died, the county court nominated Lilburne to fill his brother's position. The county court, composed of the justices of the peace, submitted the customary two candidates to the governor, with Lilburne's name in the first position. Ordinarily, it was a rubber-stamp formality for the first nominee to be approved, but for some reason, Governor Scott passed over Lilburne and appointed the second candidate, Amos Persons.

In June, Lilburne's daughters, now eleven and thirteen, arrived from Mercer County, sent home because their tuition had not been paid. By summer, Letitia Lewis was pregnant, and Lilburne's "cold, proud and scornful young wife" became increasingly temperamental. Tensions in the Rocky Hill household were running extremely high. Lilburne began drinking heavily and spending evenings by himself, brooding over his life gone sour.

In October, the arrival of Isham Lewis, Lilburne's shiftless younger brother, brought matters to the boiling point.

LILBURNE was ten years older than Isham. As the youngest of the four Lewis brothers, Isham was the only one who inherited no land from his father. In April 1809, Isham had written to his uncle Thomas, whose second term as president had just ended, asking for Jefferson's help in finding some gainful employment. In a bitter and self-pitying letter, Isham confessed that he had no way of earning a living and claimed that his desperate situation was "brought on not from my own imprudences but those of an unfortunate father whose promises of wealth and neglect to bring me up in any useful pursuit has brought on me the want of the former and occasions me to deplore his inattention to the latter."

Jefferson wrote back, graciously offering to teach his nephew the rudiments of surveying and to furnish him with recommendations that would help him get a position. "The public lands in the Orleans and Mississippi territories are now under a course of survey, and offer, I think the best chance of employment. I am acquainted with the surveyor general, Mr. Pease, and could give you a letter which might probably induce him to employ you as a surveyor, if there be any room: and this would give chances of doing something for yourself."

Isham spent three weeks with his uncle at Monticello learning to survey. Then he set out for Mississippi in late May, armed with letters to Seth Pease and Gideon Fitch, who also worked at the U.S. Surveyor General's office in Mississippi. In recommending Isham, the former president wrote of the "shipwreck of the fortunes of his family" and asked his acquaintances to "befriend him in getting into emploiment."

On his way to Mississippi, Isham stopped at Rocky Hill to visit his relatives. It was the summer of 1809, when there was so much illness in Lilburne's household, and Isham contracted malaria. After several months of recuperation in Kentucky, he set out and reached Mississippi later in the spring.

There is no record of Isham's ever having worked as a surveyor in Mississippi. There is evidence, however, that he had financial difficulties, for in April 1810, he borrowed $235. A year and a half later, he was sued for repayment of the loan and skipped out on the court hearing. A fugitive from Mississippi justice, Isham returned to Kentucky in October 1811.

By the time Isham arrived at Rocky Hill, Lilburne Lewis was manifesting signs of psychological instability. Lilburne was the intersection, as it were, of three deeply flawed families. His grandmother was Mary Randolph Jefferson and his mother Lucy Jefferson Lewis. The genetic load of recurring first-cousin intermarriage had created a structural weakness that was hidden by a thin covering, and on the night of December 15, 1811, the veneer of sanity was stripped away, as Lilburne's slave George was beheaded, dismembered, and thrown into the fire.

The slave system was built on brutality, and in western Kentucky, brutality was a daily fact of life. Yet some acts, even those committed by a slave owner against his slave, strained the limits of civilized behavior. Even in his madness, Lilburne must have understood that his deed, if discovered, would be punishable. He obviously understood that he needed to permanently dispose of the body. But little did he suspect that on the eve of December 15, 1811, nothing was permanent.

Chapter Seven

—

THE MONSTER OF
THE WATERS

S LAVERY AND INDIAN relations were two key elements of the
early frontier, but in time, both would be overshadowed by the
relentless advance of technology. The Indians of the Ohio and Mississippi valleys would be defeated by sheer numbers, military organization,
and superior weapons. Slavery would cling stubbornly to the land south
of 36'30" (as established by the Missouri Compromise of 1820) until the
Civil War finally put an end to the pernicious institution. But technology would only gain momentum, moving ever faster and thereby promoting the third key element of the early frontier—settlement.
Emerging technology would bring ever-increasing numbers to the
west, helping them establish small villages that would grow into larger
towns that would in turn evolve into great cities. When the first of the
New Madrid earthquakes struck, not far from its epicenter there was a
notable symbol of emerging technology and the westward push—the
steamboat *New Orleans.*

By the beginning of the second decade of the nineteenth century,
the stream of immigrants to the west had grown to a raging torrent.
The Louisiana Purchase of 1803 opened up vast new possibilities for
white pioneers, and the Lewis and Clark expedition confirmed the

seemingly inexhaustible territory that was now part of the United States.

More than ever, the Ohio and Mississippi rivers were the lifeblood of the west, as transportation and commerce on the waterways increased to accommodate the new population. Both immigration and the flow of produce from and goods to the frontier greatly intensified the amount of river traffic. But shipping was still a crude business, and upriver travel remained a grueling and time-consuming undertaking.

The *New Orleans* was a pioneer in her own right, the first of a long and proud line on the western waters, as steamboats would revolutionize river travel in the west, and with it, the shipping industry and westward expansion would change overnight.

As SHE left the dock in Pittsburgh, the cheers of the crowd onshore were drowned out by the roar of the steam engine and the sonorous blasts of the boat's booming whistle. For dramatic effect, the huge craft first started upstream, then made a wide, sweeping downstream turn into the Monongahela current. Nicholas and Lydia Roosevelt stood proudly on the deck of their new steamboat and waved to the enthusiastic throng on the bank. It was a magnificent send-off and a glorious moment for the Roosevelts.

When the couple steamed off in October 1811, they were leaving from essentially the same point and embarking on essentially the same voyage as George Morgan in 1789 and the Lewis family in 1807; they were, in fact, following the same route taken by tens of thousands of other emigrants to the west since the end of the American Revolution. But there was one essential difference—the *New Orleans* was the first boat on the Ohio River to be moving under her own power.

The course was well known by now, and before starting out, every potential river traveler with any sense stopped in at Zadok Cramer's shop on Pittsburgh's Market Street and invested one dollar in a copy of Cramer's book, *The Navigator*, which contained "directions for navigating the Monongahela, Allegheny, Ohio and Mississippi rivers."

In writing of the impending voyage of the *New Orleans* in his 1811 edition, Cramer fully understood the significance of the moment: if successful, he pointed out, the steamboat "must open to view flattering prospects to an immense country, an interior of not less than two thousand miles of as fine a soil and climate, as the world can produce." Cramer went on to wax eloquent on the "immensity of country we have yet to settle, the vast riches of the bowels of the earth, the unexampled advantages of our water courses, which wind without interruption for thousands of miles, the numerous sources of trade and wealth opening to the enterprising and industrious citizens. . . . Thus, the rise and progress of the trade and the trader on the western waters; thus, the progress of our country from infancy to manhood; and thus, the flattering prospects of its future greatness through the channels of the Ohio and Mississippi rivers." If the *New Orleans* proved triumphant, Cramer concluded, the United States would "ere long have steam boats of all sizes and fashions, running up and down our numerous rivers with . . . ease and facility."

The new era that Zadok Cramer correctly foresaw would be ushered in by Nicholas Roosevelt's vision and persistence and Lydia Roosevelt's loving support and faith in that vision.

NICHOLAS ROOSEVELT was born into one of New York City's most prominent Dutch-American families in 1767. The Roosevelts, as numerous and influential in New York as the Lewises were in Virginia, were artisans and merchants. Nicholas's father, Jacobus, was a goldsmith and shopkeeper in Greenwich Village who, though past fifty at the outbreak of the American Revolution, nevertheless signed up to fight for the colonists' cause. When New York City soon afterwards became a burned-out battleground, Jacobus moved his family upstate to the farm of his friend Joseph Oosterhaudt, near Esopus (later Kingston), where Mrs. Roosevelt and the children remained for the duration of the war.

The young Nicholas was curious and creative, and with a lot of free time on his hands, he experimented with various mechanical devices. During the summer of 1781, he began work on an idea he had been mulling over for some time. Several years earlier, while out fishing on

Minetta Brook north of Greenwich Village, he had come upon a mill house, and as he watched the huge wheel that ran the mill, he suddenly saw the house transformed into a boat. A germ of an idea formed in his fertile young mind, and now he set out to determine whether a boat could actually be propelled by such a method.

He spent long hours painstakingly crafting a wooden model that had two vertical wheels, one on either side of the body, just as the mill wheel had been mounted alongside the mill house. Each wheel had four paddles made, as Roosevelt would write many years later, "of pieces of shingle attached to the periphery of the wheels whereby to take a purchase on the water." He used whalebone and hickory springs to propel the boat along "by the agency of a tight cord passed between the wheels and being re-acted on by the springs."

After days of work, the little boat was ready for launching. The boy could barely contain his excitement as he ran down to the creek near Oosterhaudt's farm to test his new invention. Reaching the stream, he walked along the bank to a fishing hole he knew well, where the water would be deep and calm enough to give his device a trial run. At the pool, he wound up one wheel and then, pressing it firmly against his body with his arm in order to preserve the tension, spun the other to tautness. He knelt and placed the little boat in the water, then took a deep breath and released the wheels. With a surge, the boat skated out onto the stream, continuing to forge along until the tension in the springs wound out.

Nicholas Roosevelt stood up, grinning from ear to ear. At the tender age of thirteen, he had invented the method of propulsion that would later be proven the most efficient way of moving steamboats.

WHEN THE Roosevelt family returned to New York three years later, Nicholas chose not to follow his father in the hardware business and instead went about becoming a mechanic, which at that time required a knowledge of various skills, including those of the metallurgist, engineer, and machinist. The Industrial Revolution was taking hold in the country, and the prospects looked bright for a man with Roosevelt's talents. By the end of the decade, he was deservedly regarded as one of New York's foremost mechanics.

In 1793, Roosevelt was approached by General Philip Schuyler, who wanted to reopen his once productive New Jersey copper mine, which had become flooded after several years of neglect. Schuyler offered the twenty-five-year-old prodigy a partnership if he could drain the mine and get it running again. Roosevelt, who had been studying the steam engines imported from the Boulton and Watt company of Birmingham, England, jumped at the offer, and he proceeded to set up the first machine shop and foundry in the United States that was capable of producing engines. The Soho Works built the steam engines that pumped the water out of the mine shaft, but the quality of copper recovered from 360 feet below the earth's surface was a disappointment and not of a high-enough quality to warrant keeping the mine open. That was no great loss, however, because the engine factory quickly became a profitable enterprise. By age thirty, Nicholas Roosevelt was acknowledged to be the premier engine maker in the United States.

He hired James Smallman, formerly of Boulton and Watt, and together they designed and obtained a patent in April 1798 for "a double steam Engine, which improvement has not been known or used before." In their application, Roosevelt and Smallman described their innovation as, "Two air pumps . . . so constructed as to make the vacuum perfect both ways, which gives our Engines . . . five and five-sevenths Horses power more than the highly famed engines which are built by Messrs. Watt and Boulton." The projected uses for this machine included "raising water from mines, for vessels particularly of small burthen, for rolling Grist and saw mills, and indeed for every purpose to which power is required."

FOUR MONTHS before the engine patent was granted, New York state chancellor Robert Livingston had written to Roosevelt, proposing that they collaborate on a steamboat. Livingston would put up the money and design the propulsion system, and Roosevelt would build the engine. A third partner, Livingston's brother-in-law John Stevens, would be responsible for the design of the boat itself.

The idea of a boat powered by steam was not new. Ever since the invention of the first practical steam engine by Edward Somerset, Marquis of Worcester, in the mid-seventeenth century, creative minds had been searching for a way to use the power generated by steam to move a vessel. Thomas Newcomen's 1705 engine—the first capable of harnessing steam power for mechanical motion—resulted in several unsuccessful attempts to build a steamboat. In 1773, the Count d'Auxiron constructed a boat with side paddle wheels, but the weight of the huge engine, which sat on a heavy brick foundation, sank the boat. Another experiment by the Marquis of Jouffroy d'Abbans on the River Saône ten years later also used paddle wheels for propulsion and was relatively successful until, after fifteen minutes, the vibrations of the engine caused the 130-foot boat to come apart at the seams.

The race to build a steamboat crossed the Atlantic, and during the 1780s two Americans became bitter adversaries in their attempts to come up with a workable boat. John Fitch, a brilliant but unschooled and ill-mannered genius, and James Rumsey, a polished member of the upper class, engaged in an acrimonious struggle—Fitch had the better ideas while Rumsey had the support of powerful friends, but unlike Fitch, Rumsey never succeeded in building a viable boat.

Fitch's first designs employed a series of oars on either side, creating the effect of a huge water bug. These early boats had very limited success, but in the summer of 1790, using a steamboat with paddle wheels, Fitch actually hauled passengers up and down the Delaware River at the astonishing rate of eight miles per hour. But the boat was too new and strange, and it failed to attract the numbers of passengers that would have made its operation profitable, so the investors behind Fitch's invention withdrew their support. Moreover, Fitch's ill-tempered personality and disheveled appearance earned him the enmity of such influential men as Benjamin Franklin and George Washington, and the subsequent damage to his reputation kept him from gaining the recognition for his landmark achievement.

*   *   *

A DEPENDABLE steamboat still did not exist when Robert Livingston asked Nicholas Roosevelt in late 1797 to build the engine for his proposed boat. Livingston was among the most powerful men in the country. He had served on the Declaration of Independence framing committee, written most of the constitution of New York state, and as the state's chancellor, administered the oath of office to George Washington at the latter's presidential inauguration. (A few years later, as ambassador to France, Livingston would negotiate the Louisiana Purchase.)

Livingston also imagined himself an inventor and believed he had a realistic design for a steamboat. "Mr. Stevens mentioned to me your desire to apply the steam machine to a boat," wrote Livingston to Roosevelt. "Every attempt of this kind having failed, I have constructed a boat on perfectly new principles. . . . I was about writing to England for a steam machine, but hearing of your wish, I was willing to treat with you on terms which I believe you will find advantageous."

The "perfectly new principles" of Livingston's design involved two horizontal wheels submerged on vertical shafts that would force a stream of water between them and thus propel the boat forward. Given his mechanical knowledge, Roosevelt doubted that Livingston's propulsion system could provide enough power. The mechanic suspected, without having to take the time and pains of building such a contraption, that it would not be an efficient machine.

But he needed the work, and besides, when in time it became apparent, as it most certainly would, that Livingston's scheme was harebrained, he, Roosevelt, would be waiting in the wings with the idea he had so successfully tested on Jacob Oosterhaudt's farm almost fifteen years earlier. So Roosevelt said yes, he would build the engine for Livingston's boat.

There were problems as the boat took shape, however, as conflicts arose between Roosevelt and Livingston. The chancellor was constantly meddling, demanding alterations and modifications in the design. On September 6, 1798, Roosevelt wrote the chancellor to "recommend that we throw two wheels of wood over the sides fastened to the axes of the flys with 8 arms or paddles . . . and that we navigate the vessel with these."

When the chancellor did not respond, Roosevelt wrote, "I hope to hear your opinion of throwing wheels over the sides," to which Livingston replied, "I say nothing on the subject of wheels over the sides as I am perfectly convinced from a variety of experiments of the superiority of those we have adopted."

As Roosevelt had all along known it would, the boat made a poor showing in a trial run in October, whereupon John Stevens came up with an alternative design that employed stern wheel paddles mounted on the back of the boat, an adaptation of one of John Fitch's ideas. Roosevelt suggested that the chancellor's propulsion method "be contrasted with paddles upon Mr. Stevens' plan, or wheels over the sides, so as to fairly ascertain the difference of the application of the power." Livingston answered that "as for vertical wheels they are out of the question."

Roosevelt was a sensitive man, and he began to weary of Livingston's dismissive disdain. True, the chancellor was putting up the money, but the mechanical expertise was Roosevelt's—he was a partner and he should be treated as an equal. It was clear to Roosevelt that Livingston's propulsion system was worthless and Stevens's method almost as far-fetched. Moreover, unlike these two wealthy amateurs, Roosevelt had a system that he knew worked.

When Stevens's design was tried out, it was initially more successful than Livingston's—until the stern paddles shook the boat so violently that, like Jouffroy d'Abbans's earlier attempt, the craft came apart. And so two years of work produced no immediate results. Livingston and Roosevelt's first venture into steamboats came to an end, and the two dissolved their association.

Six years later, while in Paris, Livingston would meet Robert Fulton, who was conducting steamboat experiments on the Seine, and suggest to him that "wheels over the side" might be a good idea. The suggestion would lead the two men to build the first truly viable steamboat, the *Clermont*, named for Livingston's estate on the Hudson River.

Four years after that, they and Roosevelt would become partners in building the first steamboat in the west.

AFTER parting company with Livingston, Roosevelt become involved in other projects, one of which was to have disastrous long-term effects on his financial condition. Federalist president John Adams, a staunch advocate of maintaining a large navy, had ordered the construction of six seventy-four-gun frigates, and Roosevelt was awarded the contract for the sheet copper that would line the bottoms of the ships. He borrowed large sums from the Navy Department to build a rolling mill, hire workers, and buy the vast amount of copper needed for such an undertaking.

While he was working on the copper project, Roosevelt was approached by the architect Benjamin Henry Latrobe, an English immigrant who was well on his way to becoming one of the most important architects in America. Latrobe was a renaissance man with wide-ranging talents and interests; he was a musician and artist, an inquisitive scientist, and knew eight languages. He had emigrated to the United States in 1796, in grief following the death of his wife in childbirth, leaving two young children behind in England.

Latrobe had been commissioned by the city of Philadelphia to build an underground water delivery system and needed two enormous steam-driven pumps of the kind that only Roosevelt was capable of building. Both men were creative minds and incurable optimists, and when Latrobe walked into Roosevelt's factory in October 1799, the two instantly recognized each other as kindred souls. The thirty-four-year-old architect and the thirty-one-year-old mechanic talked long into the night, touching on a wide range of subjects. A measure of Latrobe's sweet nature and innate belief in the goodness of his fellow man—some might call it naïveté—was demonstrated by his endorsing, on the occasion of their very first meeting, Roosevelt's promissory notes to the navy. Roosevelt, in turn, already deeply in debt, showed his faith in Latrobe by mortgaging his engine works in order to finance the building of the engines for the water system.

Latrobe and Roosevelt quickly fell into a fast friendship. But there were also significant differences in the personalities of the two men, differences that would begin to surface over time.

In March 1801, Roosevelt was left on the brink of ruin when the newly inaugurated Republican president Jefferson, who was opposed to building up the navy, canceled the order for the six "74s," as the frigates were called. Soon thereafter, Roosevelt, "a broken man," as one of his relatives later characterized him, was imprisoned briefly for the debts incurred in the copper-rolling venture. As the signer of Roosevelt's notes, Latrobe's financial situation was also imperiled. The Philadelphia water system caused the two of them further financial problems, as there were a number of difficulties with its functioning, and the final cost—$350,000—was almost triple the original estimate. Overrunning the costs in this way was to become a hallmark of Roosevelt's business dealings; he was unquestionably a great mechanic and innovator as well as a good-hearted person, but he was a terrible businessman who had no qualms about playing fast and loose with his investors' money. Latrobe, on the other hand, was a man who wore responsibility like a well-tailored cloak, and Roosevelt's dealings were becoming a source of anguish for him.

DESPITE the financial problems hanging over their heads, there was a saving grace for both men. In May 1800, Latrobe had remarried, and it was a very happy union. His new wife, Mary, insisted that he send to England for his two children. The nine-year-old Lydia and eight-year-old Henry arrived in the fall of the year, and soon afterwards, Roosevelt traveled to the Latrobes' home in Wilmington, Delaware, to meet the children.

He quickly became a regular visitor to the Latrobe household, and over the next few years spent a fair amount of time with the family—particularly with Lydia. She was a lively child, and Roosevelt was positively captivated with her. He loved listening to her high-spirited, whimsical chatter, and he could not take his eyes off her expressive, animated face. By the time she was thirteen, Roosevelt was hopelessly in love with this magical creature who was described by her father as "a fine sensible young woman" who, though prone to "uneveness of temper," was nonetheless "abounding also in excellent qualities of solid value." She was educated, artistic, responsible, and "an excellent house-keeper & nurse both for the children & the sick."

To the parents, the time Roosevelt spent with their daughter was nothing more than a demonstration of the affection of an older relative for a younger one—he was simply "Uncle Nick." But in December 1804, Latrobe returned from a three-week business trip to find a letter from Roosevelt to Mary that threw Lydia's parents into a state of turmoil.

Latrobe read the letter with disbelief. Here was his best friend, a thirty-seven-year-old bachelor—not four years younger than himself—professing love for his thirteen-year-old daughter, asking for permission to become engaged to her, and declaring that Lydia was of like mind about him! Certainly, Lydia was an unusually mature young woman. And without question, he was "a man of exceptionally good moral char-acter." But even by the standards of the day, it was an extraordinary dec-laration. After a few days, Latrobe wrote Roosevelt that he would meet him in Philadelphia, to "talk over all our matters including that on which you have written to Mrs. Latrobe." On that subject, wrote Latrobe, "we had better *talk* than *write*. Perhaps it will be still better to *laugh*—*13 Years and 6 months.*" In closing, Latrobe assured him that "if there is anything certain under heaven, it is that You hold the first place in our esteem, good opinion, & friendship."

The parents' incredulity over this news was more than understand-able. The difference in their ages was only one factor—there was also the question of Roosevelt's financial instability, not to mention the lia-bility he posed to Latrobe as the signer of his notes. Over the next few weeks and months, however, it became apparent that the attraction between Roosevelt and Lydia was mutual. They were deeply in love. Against their better judgment, the Latrobes gave the betrothal their blessing after Lydia's fourteenth birthday in March—but only on the condition that there be a one-year moratorium during which time the lovers would refrain from being in each other's company or even com-municating by letter. If they still felt the same after the hiatus, they would be free to marry. For his part, Latrobe informed his brother that he hoped something would happen in that time "to break off the connexion."

In fact, something did happen, but not for any lack of communication between the lovebirds. Going against the terms of the year-long probation, Roosevelt and Lydia carried on a clandestine weekly correspondence; once, he even stole down to Wilmington to see her when her parents were gone to Washington. But toward the end of 1805, some unknown disagreement arose between them, and whatever the issue was, it was serious enough to cause Lydia to "break off the connexion." She refused to answer Roosevelt's letters and called off the wedding, which had been scheduled for March 23, 1806, her fifteenth birthday.

Roosevelt was devastated by Lydia's rejection. Latrobe, for his part, was furious over the deceit that had been carried on behind his back. For a time, relations between him and Roosevelt grew strained, even unfriendly. But the friendship repaired itself over time, and by the beginning of 1807, the men once again enjoyed each other's company as before.

That year, Latrobe moved his family to Washington, where he had been commissioned to redesign the presidential home. In the capital city, the Latrobes entertained the greats and near-greats of the day, and Lydia, who had by now blossomed into a striking young woman, received a number of marriage proposals, all of which she declined. In fact, she was still carrying a torch for Roosevelt. When her father spoke approvingly of one particular suitor, a certain captain in the navy, Lydia told her mother that "he was not to be compared with Mr. Roosevelt."

That Roosevelt was also still smitten with Lydia became apparent when he visited the Latrobes in September 1808. Mary Latrobe was confined to bed, recovering from a miscarriage she had suffered several days earlier. When Latrobe was called out on business, Roosevelt and Lydia were left alone for a short time. The spark that had lain dormant for three years burst into flames. Roosevelt proposed. Lydia accepted.

This time, the parents were in agreement that the marriage was the right thing. Besides the obvious deep devotion and passion that existed between their daughter and Roosevelt, they had been persuaded by the example of their friends James and Dolley Madison. Soon to be president, the wizened Madison was seventeen years older than his vivacious wife, and they were clearly well suited. It was settled, then, and on November 15, 1808, Lydia became Mrs. Roosevelt.

After a tearful farewell, the newlyweds boarded a carriage for New York, where they were to live with Roosevelt's longtime friend and business associate, Jacob Mark, and his wife. Once again, Nicholas Roosevelt's future looked bright.

But nothing panned out for several months, and by February 1809, Roosevelt was still without any income. Latrobe, still liable for the notes he had signed for Roosevelt ten years earlier and now carrying the additional burden of concern for his distant daughter's well-being, wrote to his friend Robert Fulton, asking him and Chancellor Livingston to take Roosevelt on as a third partner in their steamboat endeavor.

Two and a half years earlier, Fulton and Livingston's *Clermont*—using Roosevelt's wheels-over-the-side design—had made the first truly successful steamboat voyage, chugging steadfastly up the Hudson River from Greenwich Village to Albany, cutting the normal four-to-nine-day sailing time down to thirty-two hours. Apparently neither man had had any qualms about using Roosevelt's idea without consulting or compensating him. "Fulton I respect and love and believe him honest, tho' devoted to his own interest," Latrobe confided in a letter to Lydia. "Of the Chancellor I have no good opinion."

Aware that if Roosevelt patented his invention it would adversely affect their business, Fulton agreed to take him on as a partner, but not in the Hudson River venture. Given Roosevelt's eccentric personality and the potential for harm in the patent matter, Fulton and Livingston agreed it would be better to have him out of the way. So, with Fulton and Livingston supplying the capital, the Mississippi Steamboat Navigation Company was formed with Roosevelt as a partner, and he was dispatched to Pittsburgh to investigate the possibility of running a steamboat down the Ohio and Mississippi to New Orleans. Thus it was that in the spring of 1809, Nicholas and Lydia Roosevelt left New York for the city named for William Pitt.

George Morgan, a patriot of the American Revolution and the founder of New Madrid, was a merchant, Indian agent, farmer, and land speculator. Morgan envisioned New Madrid as a great utopian metropolis in Spanish Louisiana. *(Used by permission, State Historical Society of Missouri, Columbia, and Washington County, Pa., Historical Society)*

James Wilkinson was Morgan's nemesis. Wilkinson, one of the boldest scoundrels in early U.S. history, was on the payroll of Spain at the same time he was commanding general of the western army of the United States. He was twice court-martialed and acquitted in the course of his checkered career. This portrait was painted by Miss Levy after Gilbert Stuart. *(Courtesy of the Louisiana State Museum)*

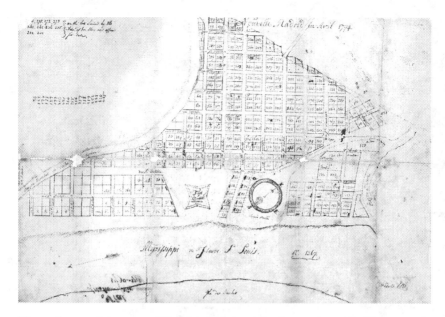

The earliest surviving map of New Madrid, dated April 1794, shows Fort Celeste and the grid of streets, but none of the environmental amenities that George Morgan had planned. *(Missouri Historical Society, St. Louis)*

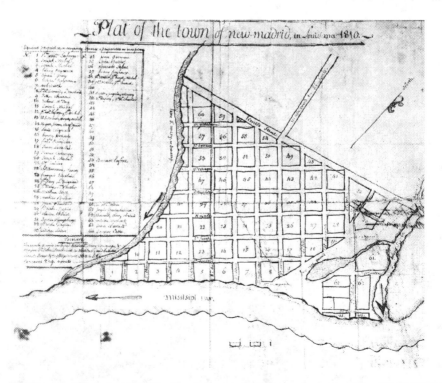

By 1810, the Mississippi River had carried away the fort and two rows of New Madrid's streets. A little more than a year later, the town was all but destroyed in the New Madrid earthquakes. *(Missouri Historical Society, St. Louis)*

(LEFT) Tecumseh, the great Shawnee leader, organized a pan-tribal military confederation to resist U.S. expansion in the Old Northwest Territory and southeastern United States. Legend has it that he prophesied the first of the New Madrid earthquakes, a prophecy that had an effect on the War of 1812. There is no authenticated portrait of Tecumseh; this version of a drawing by French trader Pierre Le Dru is believed to be the most accurate likeness that exists. *(Cincinnati Museum Center–Cincinnati Historical Society Library)*

(RIGHT) Tecumseh's brother Tenskwatawa, also known as The Prophet, was a reformed alcoholic whose life-transforming vision led him to form a new religion, with pan-tribalism and a return to traditional ways as the two basic tenets. This portrait is by J. O. Lewis, ca. 1823–24. *(Indiana Historical Society)*

William Henry Harrison, governor of the Indiana Territory and later president of the United States, was Tecumseh's main adversary. Ruthless in his acquisition of tribal lands for the United States, Harrison was determined to stamp out Indian resistance in the Old Northwest. This portrait, ca. 1800, is attributed to Rembrandt Peale. In the original, Harrison wore civilian clothes; the major-general's uniform was overpainted during the War of 1812. *(Indiana Historical Society)*

A river scene, from *The Keelboat Age on Western Waters* by Leland D. Baldwin, shows a flatboat and two keelboats, the main types of river transportation before steamboats. *(© 1941 by University of Pittsburgh Press, © 1969 by Leland D. Baldwin. Reprinted by permission of the University of Pittsburgh Press)*

Jolly Flatboatmen in Port, an 1857 painting by George Caleb Bingham, depicts a romanticized version of rivermen at their recreation. In reality, they were a hard-drinking, profane, rough-and-tumble lot. *(The Saint Louis Art Museum, Museum Purchase)*

Nicholas Roosevelt, the great-granduncle of Theodore, was a mechanic, metallurgist, machinist, civil engineer, and the foremost engine maker in the United States at the beginning of the nineteenth century. In his boat, the *New Orleans*, he made the first steamboat voyage on the Ohio and Missis-sippi rivers, thereby proving that they were navigable by steamboat and leading to a revo-lution in transportation and commerce that helped open the west.

Lydia Roosevelt, though twenty-four years younger than her husband, was his constant companion and greatest supporter. Intrepid and fiercely independent, Lydia took her two-year-old daughter on the inaugural steamboat voyage on the western rivers, beginning the trip when she was eight months pregnant and giving birth to her second child while en route.

The *New Orleans*, here pictured in a replica version built for the 1911 centennial celebration, was the first steamboat to attempt and conquer the Ohio and Mississippi rivers. On its maiden voyage, the boat was caught in and survived the first New Madrid earthquake. *(The Historic New Orleans Collection, accession no. 1974.25.33.84, detail)*

In August 1810, Tecumseh and Harrison, both attended by entourages, met face-to-face at a conference in Vincennes. The meeting came within a hair's breadth of erupting into violence when Tecumseh called Harrison a liar. In W. Ridgeway's painting of the climactic moment, Tecumseh's outfit and those of his fellow tribesmen are not authentic. *(Indiana Historical Society)*

The Battle of Tippecanoe, in November 1811, pitted Harrison's troops against the residents of Prophetstown, the community founded by Tecumseh and The Prophet that served as the headquarters of the pan-tribal movement. Although Harrison's troops did not win a clear victory, the inhabitants of Prophetstown abandoned the settlement after the fight, allowing the American soldiers to burn the village to the ground and destroy the winter's store of food. *(Indiana Historical Society)*

In May 1813, U.S. troops under Harrison's command met a combined army of British and Native Americans at the Battle of Fort Meigs in Ohio. The pan-tribal forces captured five hundred U.S. soldiers, and a brutal massacre ensued. Alerted to what was taking place, Tecumseh rushed from the battlefield to intervene and stop the slaughter of prisoners. The Battle of Fort Meigs was the pan-tribal confederacy's last victory in the War of 1812. *(Indiana Historical Society)*

(LEFT) *The Great Earthquake at New Madrid* shows the devastation on land during one of the three major earthquakes in the New Madrid sequence. Of the more than two thousand earthquakes that hit the Mississippi River Valley between December 1811 and April 1812, three would have measured near or over 8.0 on the later-devised magnitude scales. The New Madrid quakes were felt as far away as Mexico, Canada, Boston, New Orleans, and the Rocky Mountains. *(From Devens,* Our First Century*)*

(BELOW) *Scene of the Great Earthquake in the West* depicts the turbulence on the Mississippi River. Huge sections of riverbank caved in, the level of the river rose by as much as thirty feet, and uplifted land twice caused the mighty river to flow backwards. *(From Howe,* Historical Collections of the Great West*)*

MURDER! HORRID MURDER!

An 1812 newspaper headline trumpets the story of the brutal murder of a slave by Lilburne and Isham Lewis—nephews of Thomas Jefferson—and the Lewis brothers' subsequent botched suicide pact. The murder was brought to light by the New Madrid earthquakes. *(Courtesy of University of Kentucky, Lexington)*

Death of Tecumseh, a Currier & Ives lithograph from 1846, shows the Shawnee leader being slain by Colonel Richard Mentor Johnson at the Battle of the Thames in October 1813. In fact, there is no decisive evidence to show who killed Tecumseh. *(Library of Congress, Prints & Photographs Division, LC-USZC4–1581)*

Andrew Jackson with the Tennessee forces on the Hickory Grounds [Ala.] A.D. 1814. Jackson took the lead in defeating the Creeks in the Creek War of 1813–14 and went on to achieve his legendary victory over the British at the Battle of New Orleans, the last battle of the War of 1812, on January 8, 1815. *(Library of Congress, Prints & Photographs Division, LC-USZC4–4084)*

*   *   *

AT THE END of the first decade of the nineteenth century, Pittsburgh was a bustling, industrial, rough-hewn, rapidly growing inland seaport. Between 1800 and 1810, the population of the city doubled to 4,740 (and would double again in the next five years).

As the Roosevelts approached Pittsburgh in their springless carriage—there was not a set of springs made that could hold up against the shocks of the overland journey—they could see why the city was well on its way to earning the moniker of the Birmingham of America. As Zadok Cramer wrote of the place he lived, it was "enveloped in thick clouds of smoke, which even affect respiration; the appearance of the houses is dark and gloomy, from the general use of coal, particularly in the numerous manufacturies, which send into the air immense columns of smoke." The pollution was so bad that the smoke, noted Cramer, "descends in fine dust which blackens every object; even snow can scarcely be called white in Pittsburgh."

One of Pittsburgh's main industries was boatbuilding. Between 1800 and 1810, sailing ships built in the city's shipyards traveled down the Ohio and Mississippi and continued on to such far-flung places as Liverpool, Lisbon, St. Thomas in the Virgin Islands, and sundry other world ports. But the manufacture of oceangoing vessels had begun to drop off by the time of the Roosevelts' arrival in Pittsburgh because these craft had deep hulls, which made it rather impractical to negotiate the relatively shallow rivers with their hidden sandbars and other lurking dangers.

The construction of riverboats now constituted the mainstay of the boatbuilding industry. Built for transporting people and products up and down the Ohio and Mississippi, there were two basic kinds of boats that made these trips.

The great majority of river craft were the flatboats—as many as two thousand or more flatboats could be found on the two rivers at any given time. Also called broadhorns or arks, they were sometimes further designated as Kentucky or New Orleans boats depending on their projected destinations. These behemoths were essentially enormous, enclosed floating boxes with flat bottoms and bows angled to ease their passage through the water (although arks sometimes had a pointed bow). Flatboats were between twenty and one hundred feet long and from twelve to twenty feet wide. They were steered by a long oar that functioned as a rudder and two more long oars on the sides (hence the name broadhorns). These primitive craft generally cost about a dollar a foot for a twelve-foot-wide boat, with the price increasing according to the width. Many had brick fireplaces and chimneys. Flatboats were strictly one-way vessels; upon arriving at their destination, they were dismantled and sold for lumber or burned for firewood.

The other class of riverboats were the keelboats, the largest of which were sometimes called barges. These boats, with their keels and pointed bows and sterns, were the thoroughbreds of the river—sleek, hydrodynamic craft that were capable of upriver as well as downriver travel. Keelboats were between forty and eighty feet in length and seven to ten feet in width, although the largest of the barges could sometimes come in sizes up to 120 feet long and twenty feet wide. On downriver trips, the crew sat in seats in the bow and rowed. These boats had a cabin in the center, around which there was a footway where the crew walked as they set poles on upriver passages. Besides poling, the other main way of getting a keelboat upstream was for the crew to walk on the riverbank and haul it by ropes, an operation so exhausting that the men were entitled to a break every hour. Keelboats were often also fitted with a mast and sail, which, when the wind was right, could be a great asset in moving the boat against the current. These classy boats cost between $2.50 and $5 a foot, depending on width. In 1811, there were approximately four hundred keelboats running up and down the Ohio River.

Before Nicholas Roosevelt's steamboat transformed western trade and transportation, 90 percent of river traffic was downriver. The time and effort it took to get a keelboat from New Orleans to Pittsburgh made it an inefficient means of transport: the average voyage from Pittsburgh to New Orleans took four to six weeks, while the return trip required a minimum of four months. At best, a keelboat owner could make two round-trips a year if all conditions were favorable.

Roosevelt's determination would change all that in the most dramatic fashion, but before he and his bride could make the trip down the western rivers by steamboat, they had to first determine whether such travel was even a feasible option.

THERE WERE well-founded doubts about whether steamboats could handle the treacherous western rivers. To ascertain the practicality of steamboat travel on these rivers, the initial part of the Roosevelts' mission was to undertake an exploratory voyage from Pittsburgh to New Orleans.

Together, Nicholas and Lydia looked at all the standard options in the way of boats, and found none of them satisfactory. Instead, they determined to have a flatboat built to their own specifications, a big boat, with all the "necessary comforts." Lydia, employing the skills she had inherited from her architect father, designed the interior. The boat, as she later related, had a "comfortable bed room, dining room, pantry, and a room in front for the crew, with a fire-place were the cooking was done." The boat had a crew of five—"a pilot, three hands and a man-cook"—and Lydia had a maid. In order that the passengers and crew might enjoy the river on balmy summer evenings, "The top of the boat was flat, with seats and an awning."

The Roosevelts' marriage was, to put it mildly, unusual for the times. They were close companions and partners, equals in all matters. They made decisions together and consulted each other when in doubt. It is difficult to say enough about Lydia Roosevelt's iconoclasm. Here was an eighteen-year-old woman who had been raised in privilege and comfort, about to embark on a trip that challenged the hardiest of souls—not out of necessity, but because she had no intention of letting her husband face the unknown alone, besides which, she would not dream of missing such a magnificent adventure. And to top it all off, she was pregnant. By the time the flatboat reached Louisville, where they spent three weeks, Lydia had already begun to show, and when they arrived in New Orleans at the beginning of December, half a year after departing, she was seven months along.

Although the flatboat voyage had a serious purpose—Roosevelt was constantly putting out in the large rowboat with two or three of the crewmen, taking soundings, gauging the current, noting the topography and hazards of the river—it was also a working vacation, a belated wedding present. The newlyweds took their time, enjoying what was surely the most convention-shattering honeymoon cruise of its day. They made their leisurely way down the river, stopping and introducing themselves to the residents of the small settlements that dotted the shores, Roosevelt assuring everybody that they would be back soon enough, but in a very different kind of vessel.

Near Yellow Bank, about 150 miles from the mouth of the Ohio, Roosevelt made a valuable discovery—coal. He bought and opened several mines in anticipation of using their coal to fuel a steamboat that was still little more than a figment of his imagination.

The days and nights rolled by. The Roosevelt boat floated by day and tied up to the shore at night. On the hottest summer nights, the newlyweds bedded down right on the deck, with the crew moving about. September was beautiful on the Mississippi, with its cooler temperatures and shorter days. In the evenings, Nicholas and Lydia sat on the roof of their floating home and listened to the sounds of the river and woods before retiring to their comfortable bedroom.

One night, they were awakened by two Indians, who had somehow managed to board the boat and find the Roosevelts' cabin. "Whiskey!" demanded one of them. Seeing that they were not hostile, Roosevelt got out of bed and tried, without success, to persuade them to leave the boat. Finally, realizing that there would be no getting rid of them without acceding to their demand, Roosevelt managed to locate a bottle and bade them continue on their way.

A few weeks later, one of the crew took sick with a fever, and it quickly spread to everyone else on board except Lydia. For the next three weeks, wrote her father, she "cooked & baked for the whole crew . . . nursed all the sick, scoured & washed what was absolutely necessary."

When the crew finally recovered, the group got under way again. As the boat reached Natchez, Lydia's maid and husband were still both under the weather, but the five crewmen were ready for some action, so they tied up for the night and went ashore to paint the town. Soon after they left, there was a sudden drop in the level of the river, causing the boat to hit the mast of a sunken vessel. It sprang a leak, taking on so much water that "they would have gone to the bottom" were it not for the seven-months-pregnant Lydia, who "baled from *Nine* in the evening till *One* in the morning when the crew returned."

With the flatboat out of commission, the comfort level of the trip changed drastically, as the party continued downriver in the large rowboat. The pilot, an experienced river man, assured them they would have no trouble finding lodgings for the week or so it would take to reach New Orleans. But the first night out, they discovered that most river dwellers had apparently had one too many unpleasant experiences with overnight guests, and they were "refused all applications," as Lydia wrote. So passengers and crew were forced to spend the night on the rowboat, which they dragged partly onto the shore. The nights had grown cold by now, and the Roosevelts made their bed on a large traveling trunk positioned between the stern and the first seat, over which they spread a buffalo robe for warmth.

An hour after dark, they were suddenly awakened by the sound of scratching on the side of the rowboat. Waking from a fitful sleep, Roosevelt glanced over the side and saw a good-size alligator, who had taken the boat for a log, and was trying to climb aboard. Grabbing the pilot's cane, he whacked the edge of the boat and the reptile splashed back into the river. The next four nights were passed in this fashion— restless sleep broken by fending off the gators.

The fifth night they got lucky and were taken in by an elderly French couple, who let them spread their buffalo robes on the floor before a roaring fire. They were safe here, but during the night they were woken up more than once by the old man and woman, who were devout Catholics and had come into the room to kneel before the crucifix.

The next night, a "pouring rain came up," and the crew rowed hard for Baton Rouge, finally making the town at nine o'clock. By Lydia's account, Baton Rouge "was a miserable place at that time, with one wretched public house; yet we felt thankful that we had found a shelter from the storm. But when I was shewn into our sleeping room, I wished myself on board the boat. It was a forlorn little place opening out of the bar room, which was filled with tipsy men looking like cutthroats. The room had one window opening into a stable yard, but which had neither shutters nor fastenings. Its furniture was a single chair and a dirty bed. We threw our cloaks on the bed and laid down to rest, but not to sleep, for the fighting and the noise in the bar room prevented that." At the crack of dawn, the party was up and out and back on the rowboat, "feeling thankful we had not been murdered in the night."

The following three nights they slept on sand beaches, "fancying every moment, that something terrible might happen before morning." They finally reached New Orleans around December 1. The trip had been a graphic demonstration of the need for better transportation.

The Roosevelts booked passage on the first boat they could find. Their relief at being on the way back to New York, however, was tempered when the captain came down with yellow fever and it spread to the crew and passengers. At least one passenger, a nephew of James Wilkinson, died on board. After a month, the Roosevelts were able to disembark at Old Point Comfort, Virginia, in Chesapeake Bay. From there they continued on to New York by stagecoach, arriving in mid-January 1810, nine months after they had left—and just in time for Lydia to deliver a daughter.

If Lydia had had any quit in her, she would have shown it right then and there. But after a short respite of a few months, during which time Roosevelt presented a thorough, detailed report to Fulton and Livingston, the intrepid couple, with the infant Rosetta in tow, set out once again for Pittsburgh. Roosevelt's partners had been sufficiently persuaded by his report that they entrusted him with overseeing the construction of a steamboat to conquer the western rivers.

THE BOAT was designed in New York by Fulton. Its dimensions were to be 116 feet long and twenty feet wide. As usual, however, Roosevelt had grander ideas than other people. He showed the plans to Lydia, who agreed that bigger was better, and together they redesigned the craft. When Andrew Melish saw the *New Orleans* just after its launch, he called it "the largest vessel I had ever seen which bore the name of a boat," and recorded the dimensions as "length 148 feet 6 inches; breadth 32 feet 6 inches; depth 12 feet." The Mississippi had never heard of such a large, stable vessel.

The steamboat was, as the *Pittsburgh Gazette* observed, "built with the best materials and in the most substantial manner." The lumber— white pine—came from the forests east of the city, which entailed the hiring of large crews to fell the trees, cart the logs to the Monongahela, and float them down to the Pipetown shipyard on rafts. A new saw pit was built to accommodate the enormous amount of timber that had to be processed into planks. Accomplished machinists were imported from New York and New Jersey, as were the copper boiler plates for the engine. The expenses mounted, and as the project went along, Roosevelt soon found himself in the familiar predicament of having spent his associates' money rather too lavishly. Fulton and Livingston wrote repeatedly to Roosevelt, cautioning him about the escalating costs, but to no avail. When, after more than a year, the *New Orleans* was finally finished in the summer of 1811 at a cost of $38,000, Livingston wrote such a blistering letter that Roosevelt never forgave him.

It was several months after the boat's completion before the trip to New Orleans could be undertaken because the Ohio River was simply too low, but finally, on October 15, the 371-ton steamboat was launched on the Monongahela. She puffed up and down the river, leading the *Gazette* to conclude that the boat "fully answers the most sanguine expectations."

A new era of American life, and of the life of the Mississippi, was at hand. As with the spread of telegraph machines a few decades later, which would give a large number of adventurous boys like Thomas Edison a new option for leaving home, steamboats and the river now beckoned to America's restless youth. On the heels of the *New Orleans* there would soon follow the *Vesuvius,* the *Aetna,* the *Comet,* the *Despatch,* the *Enterprise,* and the *Washington.* In the second decade of the nineteenth century, and for decades after, young opportunists like Samuel Clemens (the future Mark Twain), would answer the siren call of the steamboat's whistle.

*   *   *

ON SUNDAY, October 20, the *New Orleans* embarked for points west and south. In addition to the Roosevelt family, "a captain, an engineer named [Nicholas] Baker, Andrew Jack, the pilot, six hands, two female servants, a man waiter, a cook, and an immense Newfoundland dog, named Tiger," were also aboard as the steamboat eased out into the river, first starting upstream and then turning down.

Lydia had caused a minor scandal among Pittsburgh's upper crust by departing on the voyage while eight months pregnant with her second child. Tongues wagged in disapproval over her condition as well as over her taking the two-year-old Rosetta along on such a highly uncertain enterprise. She might be heedless of the danger to herself, but what about the little one, not to mention the unborn? Lydia laughed off such criticism. She had been in on the planning of this boat, and she had frequented the Pipetown shipyard to check up on the interior details as the vessel took shape. She had suffered through one inclement night when the Monongahela flooded and lifted the half-built boat off its dry dock; the swollen river would have prematurely launched the boat had Roosevelt and his workers not dashed down to the shipyard and somehow managed to throw cables onto the deck to secure it. Lydia certainly was not about to miss the reward. She, every bit as much as her husband, took great pride in the *New Orleans*.

The final product was a handsome beast, "built after the fashion of a ship," according to one account, with portholes in the sides and an eight-foot-long, sky-blue bowsprit with a carved figurehead. There was a great smokestack in the middle and two masts fore and aft. The wooden "wheels over the side," fitted with iron paddles, could be raised or lowered in the water to compensate for the weight on board. The two cabins, which were in the hold, were "elegant, and accommodations for passengers not surpassed." The forward cabin was for gentlemen, the aft for ladies. Between the cabins, with their finely appointed wooden walls, and steerage, up to eighty passengers could be lodged on the *New Orleans*.

Unfortunately, there were no paying passengers despite the *Pittsburgh*

Gazette's glowing description of the boat's accommodations. Perhaps it was skepticism about the boat's ability to make the trip or fear of an engine explosion and subsequent fire (a not uncommon hazard with steam engines), but whatever the reasons, not a soul besides the Roosevelts, their dog, and their crew were aboard the *New Orleans* when she left Pittsburgh.

As she moved downstream, Engineer Baker and his crew in the sweltering boiler room kept the fire well stoked. The steam from the boiler entered the thirty-four-inch cylinder, with its hand-filed walls, and was compressed and exhausted by a huge piston; at top speed, the engine was capable of 18 rpm. If there had been any qualms about the boat's performance, "The regular working of the engine, the ample supply of steam, the uniformity of the speed, inspired at last a confidence that quieted the nervous apprehensions of the travellers." Pilot Andrew Jack was more than pleased at the boat's handling, steering as she did with ease—not to mention his satisfaction at moving along the water at the unheard of rate of twelve miles per hour.

The first night out was clear, with a near-full moon, so Pilot Jack kept the boat running. Lydia had established a bedroom for herself and her husband in the ladies' cabin, with its four berths, but she and Nicholas were far too excited to sleep, and they spent most of the night on deck. In the morning, Roosevelt assembled the passengers and crew on deck to acknowledge the cheers of the crowd as the boat chugged by a small village.

The steamboat went through six cords of wood in twenty-four hours of running. To save time, Roosevelt preferred to buy wood from settlers along the river rather than have the crew cut it, but that was costly—$2.50 per cord. Stopping in Wheeling to replenish the wood supply, Roosevelt offset the price tag of the fuel with his 25-cent guided tour of the *New Orleans*.

On the morning of Sunday the 27th, after one week on the river, with Lydia feeling her delivery impending, the *New Orleans* cruised past Cincinnati "in fine stile," as the *Liberty Hall* noted. "Her appearance was very elegant and her sailing beyond anything we have ever witnessed," reported another Cincinnati newspaper.

*   *   *

LATER that day, the steamboat turned a Kentucky farmer named Weldon into a would-be latter-day Paul Revere.

Ever since the *Chesapeake* incident in 1807, relations between the United States and Britain had been strained. When American public opinion clamored for war after the *Chesapeake* episode, British authorities in Canada revived their support of the native tribes of the Old Northwest in order to ensure their alliance in the event of war. Naturally, this enraged white America even further, particularly when Indian attacks on settlers escalated.

At the same time, the British continued to seize U.S. ships and impress American sailors. Jefferson and Congress had instituted an embargo on trade, but it had failed to force Britain to end the impressments. British ships lingered off the U.S. coast, waiting to intercept American vessels. In May 1811, the U.S. frigate *President,* sent out to cruise the coast and protect American craft, fired on the British ship *Little Belt,* killing nine sailors and wounding twenty-three others. Tensions between the two nations grew. War now seemed inevitable.

Weldon's farm was on the Kentucky side of the river, opposite the small settlement of North Bend, which was a few miles above the mouth of the Miami River. Along with everyone else in the Ohio Valley, Weldon had heard the talk of an impending war with Britain, and when the *New Orleans* came puffing along, he assumed the worst. Weldon and his two sons went racing over to his downstream neighbors, the Bush family, crying, "The British are coming down the river!" The Bushes went running to the riverbank in time to see the steamboat, as Philip Bush later wrote, "making her dignified appearance and slowly marching down the stream, seeming with her lever beams to be warning everything to clear the track—

"My father who was about 44 years old, had never heard of such a thing, but stood looking on, smiling as much at his own ignorance as at the monster of the waters.

"We of course let her pass and in wonder & silence returned. The only suggestion that I recollect of being my own That it must be some kind of a sawmill intended for the West."

The following midnight, "the monster of the waters" arrived in Louisville and created havoc among the town's 1,500 citizens. Two days later, the Roosevelts became parents for a second time, as Henry Latrobe Roosevelt came bawling into the world in the Roosevelts' cabin on the *New Orleans*.

Several days after the birth, the elite of Louisville held a dinner in honor of Nicholas Roosevelt. He tried to use the occasion to recruit investors for the Ohio Steamboat Navigation Company, a second firm formed by himself, Fulton, and Livingston for the purpose of developing steamboat traffic on the Ohio. But the prospective investors were reluctant. For one thing, there was considerable skepticism about the steamboat's ability to negotiate the treacherous Falls of the Ohio, just a few miles south of Louisville. Moreover, many were unconvinced of the boat's capacity to move upstream against the powerful current of the big river. This is not the Hudson, they reminded him.

The following week, Roosevelt held a dinner of his own on the *New Orleans,* to which he invited those who had feted him earlier. In the middle of the sumptuous meal, the boat began to rumble and lurch, and soon it became clear that it was moving. A panic swept through the dining room. The elegantly dressed guests, assuming that the boat had slipped its moorings and was headed downstream toward the Falls, pushed their chairs back from the table, and rushed out onto the deck, fully prepared to jump for their lives.

When they got outside, however, they saw that the *New Orleans* was not headed toward the Falls at all; rather, the boat was moving steadily upstream at about four miles per hour. Roosevelt watched with bemused satisfaction as it slowly dawned on his guests what was happening. First there was relieved laughter, then a hearty cheer and sustained applause. It was a masterful stroke of public relations, but it failed to loosen any pockets—when Roosevelt asked his amazed company who among them would be the first to subscribe to the Ohio Steamboat Navigation Company, the guests congratulated him on his ploy, but still held out. How the boat fared on the Falls still remained to be seen.

*   *   *

THE FALLS of the Ohio, at a large bend in the river, was the single most perilous obstacle between Pittsburgh and the Mississippi. As many as a dozen boats a year were lost in trying to navigate the Falls, and countless others were delayed due to low water, all of which resulted in considerable financial losses. It was not uncommon for boats to unload their cargo in Louisville and have it transported by land to Shippingport, just below the Falls—that way, if the boat perished on the rocks, at least the goods would be saved; if the boat made it successfully through, the cargo would be reloaded downriver. The rapids, eddies, islands, and rocks encountered in the two-and-a-half-mile passage were capable of demolishing the most stalwart boat. On one disastrous day four years before the voyage of the *New Orleans,* two seafaring sailing ships, the *Tuscarora* and the *Rufus King,* both smaller than the *New Orleans,* had dramatically wrecked there. At about that same time, another oceangoing ship, the *Penrose,* waited an entire year until the water rose to where the Falls was safe to navigate.

When the water was high, the Falls was easily negotiated, the only noticeable effect being an acceleration of speed as a boat entered the area of the rapids. But when the river was low, the exposed rock shelf, formed by 400-million-year-old fossil beds that stretch across the mile-wide river, presented a grave danger.

Now, as Roosevelt awaited the autumn swell in the river before proceeding, he hatched the scheme of excursion trips upriver. "Frequent experiments of her performance," reported the *Liberty Hall,* "have been made against the current since her arrival; in the presence of a number of respectable gentlemen, who have ascertained with certainty she runs thirteen miles in two hours and a half."

Hearing of these outings and of the delay in her itinerary, the people of Cincinnati—having been passed by once—were soon clamoring for the chance to ride the steamboat. Roosevelt seized the opportunity: what better way to prove the steamboat's capability against the current than to make the 180-mile upriver trip? In late November, then, with the river still showing no sign of a major rise, Roosevelt returned to Cincinnati, where, over the course of a week, the *New Orleans* was, according to the *Liberty Hall*, "an object of much curiosity." The one-dollar jaunts added up. "Several short trips have been performed up and down the river from this place, and numbers have gratified themselves by taking passage in these short voyages."

When the boat returned to Louisville at the end of the month, there was another week's wait, but finally, on December 8, the river rose to where there was a five-inch clearance below the steamboat's hull. It was hardly an optimal situation, but Roosevelt could wait no longer.

Predictably, Lydia insisted on being aboard for the trip down the Falls. Her friends, even her husband, implored her to take the children in a carriage and meet the steamboat in Shippingport. But Lydia was nothing if not headstrong; she relented for the children but not for herself. The children were sent on to Shippingport with the two maids.

Today, a canal on the Kentucky side of the river allows for smooth passage, but in 1811, there was no such channel. Instead, there were three possible routes, two of which—Kentucky Chute, between the Kentucky bank and Rock Island, and Middle Chute, between Rock and Goose islands—were too narrow for the *New Orleans*. Indian Chute, the widest and northernmost passage between Goose Island and the Indiana shore, was the only choice. With this channel, however, in addition to the low water level, care had to be taken to avoid the rough, sharp limestone that lined one side of the bed.

The essence of successfully negotiating the Falls was velocity. The rapids coursed at fourteen miles per hour, and the boat had to exceed that speed; otherwise it was at the whim of the current. To build up a head of speed, the *New Orleans* started upstream, turned after half a mile, and then steamed down toward the Falls.

Roosevelt was up in the bow with Andrew Jack and the falls pilot who had been hired on for the trip. Lydia stood in the stern with Tiger, her Newfoundland. In the boiler room, Baker the engineer fed extra wood onto the fire, building the blaze up to get the maximum amount of steam from the boiler. The safety valve screamed in protest as the engine reached its maximum 18 rpm. Approaching the Falls, they could see a thick mist, like a cloud of smoke, rising toward the sky. When they entered the rushing rapids, no conversation could be heard above the roar of the churning river, so the two pilots communicated with the man at the helm by hand signals, urgently gesturing where he should steer. The steamboat worked its way across an eddy and entered Indian Chute. Waves crashed against the foam-covered rocks, and the din was now deafening. In the stern, Lydia hugged the rail as Tiger crouched apprehensively near her. The violence of the rushing water threw a heavy spray up onto the deck, drenching the passengers and crew.

Suddenly, there was a slight jarring of the boat. Roosevelt's heart stopped for a moment. They had hit limestone. He had no time to dwell on the possible consequences, however, for seconds later they were propelled into the biggest drop in the Falls, and the boat plunged forward and downward as Roosevelt's stomach jumped into his throat.

Then, without warning, it was calm. It took a moment to sink in, before a shout went up. They had made it, with no more than a five-inch margin for error. Roosevelt went running down to the stern, where he and Lydia embraced. Now, if only the damage from that scrape was not debilitating.

They put up at Shippingport, to the welcome of cheering crowds. When the damage to the hull was assessed, there was, incredibly, nothing but a small scrape.

AFTER THE successful descent, the *New Orleans* spent several days in Shippingport. There the boat was thoroughly inspected from top to bottom while she was loaded with supplies and wood before resuming her voyage.

The cost of wood had added a considerable expense to the voyage—an expense Fulton and Livingston were sure to find objectionable. Now—Roosevelt silently congratulated himself—they were only two days from Yellow Bank and the coal mines he had the foresight to buy two years earlier. A full load of coal would save both time and money on the four-hundred-mile haul from New Madrid to Natchez, between which there were no sizable settlements at which to buy wood.

They left Shippingport on the morning of Friday the 13th. When they arrived at Yellow Bank two days later, they were stunned to find an immense pile of coal stacked up on the shore. Roosevelt cursed the poachers who had made off with some of his fuel, but then realized it was a small price to pay for having it already quarried. The crew went ashore and began to load the precious fuel onto the boat.

As they were working, local squatters came creeping out of the woods. Approaching warily, the vagabonds asked fearfully if the boatmen had heard any untoward noises coming from the river or the forest that day. Had the crew hands not felt the earth tremble, as they, the squatters, had?

The crew denied having felt or heard anything unusual and continued their work. But when they stopped and thought about it, they agreed that the weather was strange. It was unusually warm for December. The air was hazy, and the sun was red.

The crew loaded as much coal as the boat would hold. By the time they were done, it was too late in the day to resume their voyage, so Roosevelt and Andrew Jack resolved to get an early start the next morning. Passengers and crew turned in early that night.

Part Three

UPHEAVAL

Chapter Eight

———

ALL NATURE WAS
IN A STATE
OF DISSOLUTION

A BILLION YEARS AGO, the present continent of North America was part of a much larger body of land that geologists call Rodinia. The history of the earth's continental crust reveals a cyclical process: over the course of millions of years, continents drift together to form one (or more) huge landmass, and subsequently these supercontinents develop rifts and split up into smaller components, which later come together again and then once again break apart.

Sometime between 700 and 550 million years ago, the supercontinent Rodinia began to separate into smaller pieces. Huge blocks of land tore away from the main body and drifted off to form new continents; one of them, which geologists have named Laurentia, was the predecessor of North America. In the continent's original form, what is now the Gulf of Mexico extended up to the southeast corner of present-day Oklahoma; the continental shoreline ran from there to Austin, Texas, in a southwest direction, and to Pensacola, Florida, in a southeast direction.

About 540 million years ago, after the breakup of Rodinia, continuing smaller rifts sent fractures into Laurentia, including one that ran north from the Gulf coast up into what is now the bootheel region of Missouri, as yet another part of the Laurentian continent threatened to break off and float away. As the continental crust ripped apart, molten rock or magma from deep below the crust came flowing up to the surface.

But for unknown reasons, the rifting stopped, and the process of separation was never completed. As the molten rock cooled, the rifted area sank below sea level, in much the same manner as a cake will fall when removed from an oven under certain conditions. The separations in the crust now formed the boundaries of a rift valley in the bedrock, extending over an area more than 350 miles long and more than fifty miles wide, throughout what would later become the lower Mississippi Valley.

About 250 million years ago, the continents once again came back together, creating the supercontinent of Pangaea. Fifty million years later, as Pangaea broke up, the continent of North America was formed.

About 60 million years ago, when the great inland sea that had covered a large part of North America began to drain, the Mississippi River took shape, taking the path of least resistance by following the rift valley that had been created after the breakup of Rodinia. Over the deep fractures and faults of the old rift valley the earth's surface sagged further, eventually reaching a depth of three miles. As the Mississippi River swept along, it deposited a massive volume of sediment eroded from higher parts of the continent, filling the rift valley with silt and creating the land that now forms the eastern part of Texas, southernmost Arkansas, all of Louisiana, southern Mississippi, and the southwest corner of Alabama. And though the rift valley, which is now called the Reelfoot Rift, gradually became buried miles below the river, it nevertheless persisted as a zone of weakness in the form of a scar in the continental crust.

The rift valley was under constant stress from the westward spread of the North American tectonic plate away from the Mid-Atlantic Ridge on the ocean floor, where new crust is continually being created. Slowly, these forces build, until something yields. At intervals in the course of the past sixty thousand millennia, the faults in the bedrock under the rift valley have failed, releasing an enormous amount of energy and triggering an earthquake or a series of earthquakes.

At the beginning of the nineteenth century, the stresses had been building for about 350 years. Just after 2:00 a.m. on December 16, 1811, the New Madrid fault system had once again borne all the stress it could absorb. There could be only one outcome.

IT BEGAN without any warning. December started out rainy, but the days leading up to the first earthquake were unusually warm, "a balmy Indian summer," as New Madrid resident James Ritchie testified. "The weather was warm and smoky, and had been for some days, not a breath of air stirring, so thick and smoky that the Kentucky shore, one mile distant, could not be seen at all."

The thickness and haziness of the air did not deter the French residents of New Madrid from holding their customary Sunday night dance on December 15. It was holiday season, after all, and the mood was festive.

By 2:00 a.m., the townspeople were safely asleep in their beds. At a quarter past the hour, there was a sudden loud rumbling, likened in many eyewitness accounts to distant thunder, or the rolling of wagons across pavement, or a deafening crash resembling "the discharge of heavy artillery." All at once, the earth began moving, and throughout New Madrid, sleepers were jolted from their slumber and sent flying from their beds, while articles of furniture were propelled across rooms. The wooden houses shook and jumped, as men, women, and children went shrieking into the streets in their nightclothes. Many of the terror-stricken inhabitants, having no idea what was happening, ran aimlessly about in confusion. Quickly, there ensued a "complete saturation of the atmosphere, with sulphurious vapor, causing total darkness," as Eliza Bryan wrote in her oft-cited account.

As people stood choking and gasping from the fumes that seared their lungs, a young mother suddenly realized that in the confusion of grabbing the children and rushing from their home, she and her husband had left their infant behind. The woman urgently implored her husband to go back for the baby, and the father "determined to rescue it, or die in the effort." But before he could start back toward the house, a second shock, even more powerful than the first, sent people reeling. "We were all thrown on the ground," the father related. "It was so dark that we could see only when the pale, sickly flashes of lightning illuminated the scene. One of the flashes followed, or rather accompanied, the second shock, and by the aid of it I saw the people all prostrated on the ground."

Pandemonium now reigned supreme. The air was rent by a cacophonous din, as countless numbers of ducks, geese, swans, and other river birds that had been sleeping peacefully flew aimlessly about, screeching with terror. Huge trees swayed and bowed like saplings; many snapped like twigs and went crashing to the ground. Cattle stampeded through the streets, bellowing in fear, while horses and other livestock, seeking protection, stuck closely by the human beings. Smaller birds landed on the heads and shoulders of some people, as if to comfort themselves by contact with another creature, however alien.

With the ground heaving and pitching about him, the man whose infant had been left behind desperately made his way back toward the house. He was flung to the ground a dozen times as he bravely negotiated the few yards to the entrance. Finally, reaching the steps, he pulled himself up and crawled into the building, "where the cries of the affrighted child could be heard." He seized the baby and cautiously crept back outside to rejoin his wife.

Altogether, the racket, the darkness, the convulsions of the ground, and the overall chaos—not to mention the strong smell of sulfur, which is traditionally associated with the devil—convinced many that the Day of Judgment was at hand. Catholics and Protestants alike dropped to their knees in fervent communal prayer and "solemn supplication;—for in that fearful hour, human aid was unavailing," as one eyewitness put it. Afraid to return to their houses, the residents of New Madrid passed the rest of the cold night huddled together in the streets.

Lesser shocks continued throughout the night—one firsthand account mentions eight more shakes before daybreak. When day finally arrived, dawn brought little comfort to the afflicted, according to the man who had rescued his baby, since "no sun shone on us to gladden our hearts. A dense vapor arose from the seams of the earth, and hid it from view."

By 6:30, there was enough light to survey the extent of the wreckage. Many chimneys were toppled, and several houses suffered structural damage. Hardly a building escaped completely unscathed. Fences were down everywhere.

At about 7:15 a.m., the earth unleashed another awful tremor, the most severe one yet. It lasted several minutes, beginning with a shaking like its predecessors, but then turning into a terrifying series of hard vertical jolts, which caused a renewed and intensified panic in humans and animals alike. River traveler William Leigh Pierce wrote that "confusion, terror and uproar presided," as "those in the town were . . . running for the country, whilst those in the country fled with like purpose towards the town."

Every person in New Madrid would forever remember those terrible events. "[T]he earth seemed convulsed . . . ," one man wrote to his friend in Lexington, Kentucky. "The loud hoarse roaring which attended the earthquake, together with the cries, screams, and yells of the people seem still ringing in my ears."

NEW MADRID was hit hard, but it was not the scene of the worst destruction that day. Thirty miles downriver, the small settlement of Little Prairie—at the site of present-day Caruthersville, Missouri—with its twenty houses and between six and eight miles of cultivated land, was damaged badly by the first shock, which brought down many chimneys and some buildings. But it was the large aftershock after dawn, with its vertical bouncing, that completely devastated Little Prairie, destroying virtually every structure and producing alarming deformation to the surrounding land.

Godfrey Lesieur, who was eight years old at the time, saw the ground "rolling in waves of a few feet in height, with a visible depression between. By and by those swells burst, throwing up large volumes of water, sand and a species of charcoal."

The exploding earth left fissures, ten feet wide and deep, and up to four and five miles long. In a number of cases, large trees that straddled the ground where a fissure opened were split several yards up the trunk. Little Prairie resident James Fletcher watched as a granary and a smokehouse sank into a fissure and disappeared, after which the gap in the ground closed up, permanently burying the buildings.

Everywhere, the earth was opening and various substances were thrown high up into the air. In some places, sand and other materials were forced up through large circular holes. Water came rising to the surface and was sometimes sent spouting up in geyser-like streams. Fletcher noted that "The earth was, in the course of 15 minutes after the shock in the morning nearly *entirely* inundated with water."

With the water level climbing about him, Little Prairie resident Michael Braunm observed the bed of the river suddenly rise up "like a great loaf of bread to the height of many feet, the uprising being accompanied by a terrible rumbling noise." At its height, the "loaf" burst, as "great quantities of sand, water and a black sulphurous vapor" were sent shooting upward.

The terrified citizens of Little Prairie instinctively retreated from the river. Braunm put his wife on a horse and carefully led the mount around many fissures, seeking safety.

As the water rose all about the area that had been Little Prairie, one woman led her children out of the house and sat them on a tree trunk that lay on the ground. Returning to her house for a supply of provisions, she roused her husband from his state of stunned inertia and emphatically instructed him to take a canoe paddle and follow her. When they reached the log, she commanded him to row them to safety while she tightly clutched the children to her.

After wandering about in panic for several hours, some two hundred citizens of Little Prairie gathered at the house of Captain Francis Lecuer, a community leader. While there, they somehow heard that the hills west of the town had not been damaged, so they quickly set off in that direction.

Meanwhile, Captain George Ruddell, another leader of the Little Prairie settlement, was standing in his yard near the river when the daylight aftershock hit. He looked on with unbelieving eyes as the bank caved in about thirty yards back from the water. As far up- and down-river as he could see, acres upon acres of land went plunging into the current. One of his cows came rushing toward him in terror; the ground in her path suddenly opened up, and unable to check her momentum, the poor beast went plummeting into the chasm. Ruddell turned back in time to see his flour mill destroyed and one corner of his house sinking down. Across the bayou, he observed what had been a swamp suddenly lift up and become dry land, while the side he stood on was rapidly falling and filling with water.

The rest of Ruddell's family had fled from the house and were running toward the woods when all at once the earth's surface cracked, opening up a gaping gulf before them. Ruddell urgently stumbled to join them and had just caught up when another shock came on. The water was now up to their waists. With Ruddell in the lead, they began wading toward the ridge west of Little Prairie.

As they slogged through the flood, Ruddell suddenly fell headlong into a fissure that was hidden by the muddy water. The others rushed to his aid and helped him crawl out. Several more times in the family's eight-mile trek to dry ground, Ruddell fell into concealed crevices. All the while, earsplitting explosions echoed around them, and the earth burst everywhere, throwing up mud, sand, water, and coal nearly a hundred feet toward the sky.

Through sheer determination, the Ruddells finally reached higher ground, where they joined James Fletcher, Michael Braunm and his wife, the couple who used the log to rescue their children, and virtually the entire rest of the population of Little Prairie. The refugees set up camp on the ridge.

A man aboard a boat that came along the shore of Little Prairie later in the day wrote that "the inhabitants had fled from their houses in great terror. A negro man, who told us that he was the only person then in the place, informed us that the swamp at the back of the prairie was completely inundated." On every hand was "a melancholy spectacle of desolation." The village of Little Prairie was a ruin. Between the quake and the flood, not one of the community's houses was left standing.

Throughout the Little Prairie area, the deformation to the land was stunning. One of the most dramatic events occurred about ten miles from Little Prairie—an incident that, as Lesieur wrote, "those who did not see would pronounce fabulous." It happened on the farm of a family named Culberson on the bank of a small river called the Pemiscot. At this particular place, the river made a sharp turn, and the Culbersons' house stood on the point inside the bend; a well and a smokehouse were located on the acre between the house and the river. After the big after-shock on the morning of December 16, Mrs. Culberson went out to get water and meat for breakfast, but to her astonishment, there was no well or smokehouse to be seen. She looked around and spotted them on the other side of the river. A large enough fissure had opened that the river broke through the point, severing the land with the well and smoke-house and carrying them over to the other bank.

EARTHQUAKES, along with volcanoes, hurricanes, and tornadoes, are among the most powerful natural forces on the planet, capable of caus-ing widespread, catastrophic destruction. Only in the most severe cases, however, such as the New Madrid shocks, do their full range of effects come to bear.

There are essentially four types of earthquakes: tectonic, volcanic, and collapse quakes, which are natural phenomena, and explosion earthquakes, which are human-induced, triggered by the detonation of chemicals or nuclear devices. Volcanic earthquakes occur in conjunction with volcanic activity, and collapse earthquakes are small quakes caused by the collapse of a mine or underground cavern.

Tectonic earthquakes are by far the most common. Of these, the great majority of earthquakes occur along the boundaries of the earth's tectonic plates as they push together, pull apart, or slide alongside one another.

Occurring as they did in the middle of the continent, the New Madrid earthquakes are highly unusual—only about 10 to 20 percent of earthquakes are intraplate quakes. Whereas the frequency of earth-quakes is relatively high along plate boundaries, in their interiors, the rate of stress buildup is much slower. The west coast of the United

States, for example, is located at the boundary of the North American and Pacific plates, and so California sees more than its share of tremors. Unlike the frequent activity in these more active seismic zones, movement in the middle of the plates is sporadic. Active periods are separated by long dormant stretches. Recent seismologic studies indicate that intraplate zones in Canada, Oklahoma, India, and Australia appear to be quiet for tens or even hundreds of thousands of years between episodes of activity. The New Madrid fault system, while still relatively quiescent compared to places like California and Alaska, has been somewhat more active, at least in the past eleven hundred years. Paleoseismologic studies conducted by geologists Martitia Tuttle and Eugene Schweig indicate that major earthquakes along the New Madrid fault system appear to have occurred in about A.D. 900 and again about 1450.

Although intraplate quakes represent a small percentage of earthquakes worldwide, two other major quakes in U.S. history have been of this type. One occurred before the New Madrid series and one after.

On November 18, 1755, the northeast part of the country was struck by a powerful temblor known as the Cape Ann earthquake. It was felt over a wide area ranging from Lake George, New York, to Halifax, Nova Scotia, to Chesapeake Bay, Maryland. A ship about two hundred miles east of Boston felt the quake so intensely that sailors on board believed they had run aground. Boston suffered extensive damage. "The Convulsions were so extreme" wrote the *Boston Weekly News-Letter*, "as to wreck the Houses in this Town to such a Degree that the Tops of many Chimnies, and some of them quite down to the Roofs, were thrown down, and several of the Roofs upon which they fell were beat in . . . and great Quantities of Bricks, Tiles and Rubbish fell into many of the Streets, Lanes and Alleys." A hundred chimneys were reported leveled and more than 1,200 others partially destroyed. Stone fences collapsed throughout the countryside, especially on a line between Boston and Montreal. In the area surrounding Boston, soil liquefaction produced many fissures, some of which emitted fine sand and water. Estimated to have had a magnitude of 6.0 to 6.5, the Cape Ann earthquake still stands as the most powerful shock ever to hit the northeastern United States.

Another devastating intraplate earthquake ruined Charleston, South Carolina, on August 31, 1886. "The temblor came lightly," wrote eyewitness Paul Pinckney, "with a gentle vibration of the houses as when a cat trots across the floor; but a very few seconds of this and it began to come in sharp jolts and shocks which grew momentarily more violent until buildings were shaken as toys. Frantic with terror, the people rushed from the houses, and in so doing many lost their lives from falling chimneys or walls." The death toll for the Charleston quake has been placed at between sixty to a hundred people. Approximately 90 percent of the buildings of the city of 49,000 inhabitants were damaged to the extent that they were no longer fit for habitation. By far the largest earthquake to strike the southeastern U.S., the Charleston quake was felt as far away as Boston, Milwaukee, Chicago, Cuba, and Bermuda. Fissuring was extensive over an eight-hundred-square-mile area, and sand blows threw up large quantities of water and sand. The magnitude of the Charleston earthquake is estimated to have been greater than 7.0.

WHEN a fault ruptures below the earth's surface, it causes a release of energy in the form of seismic waves. P or primary waves, which proceed away from the source of the quake with the same mechanics as sound waves, have the greatest velocity and are therefore the first to reach the surface. Like sound waves, P waves alternately compress and extend, behaving in much the same way a Slinky toy does when motion is transmitted along its length. S or shear waves, more powerful and slower moving, follow on the heels of the P waves. The motion of S waves can be likened to a sidewinder rattlesnake, which propels itself forward by a transverse motion—an S wave's ground motion is in a plane perpendicular to the direction in which the wave is moving.

When P waves reach the surface, they can release energy in an explosive form, sounding like "the discharge of heavy artillery." Some of the S wave energy can also be converted to the rumbling noises described as distant thunder or the rolling of wagons across pavement. Both types of ominous sounds were experienced during the December

16 quakes, sometimes almost simultaneously, as reported by a man on a boat on the Mississippi that was tied up near New Madrid: "The sound was in the ground, sometimes muffled and groaning; sometimes it cracked and crashed, not like thunder, but as though a great sheet of ice had broken."

In addition to the P and S waves, earthquakes create surface waves. Slower moving than the P and S waves, some—called Rayleigh waves—cause oceanlike ground undulations that resemble water waves. As they move underfoot, objects on the surface move up and down, much as a cork floating on a pond bobs up and down in an elliptical motion as a boat's wake passes by. Other surface waves, called Love waves, cause the ground to shake sideways. It was surface waves that knocked the residents of New Madrid to the ground.

P and S waves radiate out from the point of initial rupture—the hypocenter or focus—within the earth. The most shattering quakes—and the most common—are those with a shallow focus, i.e., close to the surface. Quakes with an initial rupture of less than forty miles deep are considered shallow-focus. The New Madrid earthquakes, needless to say, were of this type.

The point on the earth's surface directly above the quake's focus is called the epicenter, which is something of a misnomer. Living on the surface, we naturally assume ground zero to be a surface location, but the action starts far below; the epicenter gives us a reference point on the surface. Little Prairie was harder hit by the 7:15 a.m. aftershock than New Madrid because it was thirty miles closer to the epicenter, which was most likely located near the present-day town of Blytheville, Arkansas, less than twenty-five miles south of Little Prairie.

CHARLESTON, on the Atlantic coast of South Carolina, shares a similarity to the New Madrid Seismic Zone in that they both have large amounts of unconsolidated sediment at the surface, a circumstance that creates the potential for an earthquake to be especially devastating. In the case of New Madrid, a vast volume of alluvial deposit brought down by the Mississippi River is topped by a fine silt known as loess, which was deposited during the last glacial period that ended twenty thousand years ago. As a result, the Mississippi floodplain contains one of the largest blankets of unconsolidated sediment in the United States. When seismic waves are generated in rock, they travel very quickly, but when they hit this unconsolidated sediment, which is many tens of feet deep, the velocity of the waves decreases, and they become more amplified, in the same way that ocean waves, which travel quite rapidly in the open ocean, slow down from friction as they approach the beach, causing their amplitude to increase and thereby form breakers. When seismic waves hit unconsolidated sediment, the energy gets trapped between the rock below and the air above, and it bounces around, with most of the motion becoming horizontal, resulting in much greater shaking at the surface, which in turn causes greater damage to structures and soil. The New Madrid earthquakes thus combined the worst of circumstances: shallow focus, intraplate shocks, in an area with an enormous amount of unconsolidated sediment.

Along with the shaking and sound came another terrible phenomenon known as soil liquefaction. Liquefaction, one of the most destructive effects of an earthquake, occurs when the intense shaking of the ground dislodges water from the soil, causing it to behave like a dense fluid rather than a moist solid mass—in a graphic description, one writer observed that the ground "quivered like the flesh of a beef just killed." Liquefaction can result in landslides—California earthquakes frequently cause mudslides—lateral movement, and eruptions of liquid and solid matter. At Little Prairie, the quakes caused all of these phenomena.

The huge concentration of unconsolidated sediment on the west bank of the Mississippi was particularly volatile. The ground on the west bank was and is very moist, situated on the floodplain of the river. At the time of the New Madrid quakes, much of it was swampland. When soil liquefaction occurs, the top layer is essentially floating on the layer of liquefied sand beneath it—Jared Brooks, a Louisville engineer and surveyor who kept careful track of the entire New Madrid sequence with primitive instruments, was quite accurate when he wrote, "It seemed as if the surface of the earth was afloat." If there is any degree of slope to the land, everything starts flowing downhill. On a steep slope, landslides are likely to occur, as in the caving in of the riverbanks. On a slight slope, fissures open, most of which, but not all, soon close up again.

The shaking also causes water pressure to build up between the particles of sand. Finally, the pressure breaks through the silt, throwing up sand and anything else that may lie buried. One of the most exciting items to be ejected in the New Madrid earthquakes was the fossilized skull of an extinct species of buffalo.

Lesieur and others reported that material was expressed through fissures, while some witnesses stated it was sand blows that brought matter up to the surface. Sand blows, a type of eruption that was common in the Little Prairie area, burst out through a circular opening. In addition to measuring a number of these sand blows—one was sixteen and a half feet deep and sixty-three feet in diameter at the mouth—William Leigh Pierce also weighed some of the extruded pieces of coal, many of which were between fifteen and twenty pounds. To this day, the Little Prairie area is pockmarked by the evidence of sand blows from the New Madrid earthquakes.

ONE OF the most common phenomena associated with earthquakes is the toppling of chimneys. Of the thousands of chimneys that came down in the December 16 quake, one—seventy-five miles northeast of New Madrid—was of particular significance.

In the main house at the Rocky Hill plantation, Lilburne Lewis's wife, Letitia, was within earshot of the weeping and wailing issuing from the kitchen cabin on the night of December 15. Letitia and Lilburne had been married little over a year, and she almost certainly regretted the union, especially now that she was eight months pregnant. As Lilburne had deteriorated since their marriage, her disdain for him had grown. Now, with anguished cries issuing from the kitchen cabin, it seemed that her drunken husband and his good-for-nothing brother Isham were descending to a new level of depravity.

Soon after the brothers left the kitchen cabin and the burning remains of George behind, the first quake struck, sending the inhabitants of Rocky Hill out of their living quarters and into the night. The traumatized slaves, still reeling from the murder, added fear to their grief. For them, it was a night of compounded horror.

Toward morning, the sky lightened to reveal that the quake had brought down the kitchen cabin's chimney. When the stack collapsed, it had smothered the fire in the fireplace. The incriminating evidence had not been destroyed. Later in the day, when the ground stopped moving for a time, Lilburne and Isham gathered the terrified slaves and had them reconstruct the chimney, but with one added ingredient. While most survivors of the first quake were worrying about their families, livestock, and food supply, the Lewis brothers were focused on masonry. Having failed to incinerate George's remains, they now incorporated them into the stonework.

About 125 miles northeast of Rocky Hill, the steamboat *New Orleans* was resting quietly on the evening of December 15. Apart from not having been able to recruit any investors for the Ohio Steamboat Navigation Company, the voyage of the *New Orleans* was going as well as Nicholas Roosevelt could have hoped. The boat had performed admirably at the Falls, and she was on a reasonably timely schedule. And now Roosevelt was the proud father of a son.

Like everybody else within a three-hundred-mile radius of New Madrid, those aboard the steamboat were awakened by the 2:15 a.m. shock. With the shakes continuing throughout the night, they passed the rest of the anxious time without sleep. Yet they may have been the most fortunate of everyone in the area—because of the size and stability of their boat, the water was safer than land.

As soon as it was light enough to travel, the *New Orleans* was able to get under way. Moving downstream, the vibrations and noise of the engine kept the people on board from feeling the impact of the ongoing shocks, including the powerful aftershock that morning. But the Roosevelts' Newfoundland dog, Tiger, felt the tremors and alternated between whining and growling as he prowled around the deck, and laying his head softly in Lydia Roosevelt's lap, which indicated to the humans that "it was a sure sign of a commotion of more than usual violence."

Insulated from the quake's effect by this awesome new vehicle of a dawning age, those aboard the steamboat calmly ate their breakfast, but as the *New Orleans* continued downriver, signs of the quakes became more readily apparent. The passengers saw trees swaying as if in a high gale although, in fact, there was no wind blowing. They watched as an enormous section of riverbank suddenly tore away and dropped into the river. As the boat grew closer to the epicenter, it was lifted by quake-induced waves, and many on board the *New Orleans* were struck with seasickness.

The boat's pilot, Andrew Jack, who was on intimate terms with the river, found the channel altered to the point where he was forced to concede he was lost. New hazards lay everywhere, and heretofore reliably deep water was now filled with uprooted trees. Without the familiar channel, Jack chose to stay in the middle of the river and hope for the best. It slowed him down, but it was a much safer way to proceed.

As the big boat passed the small settlements along the lower Ohio, the evidence mounted. Henderson, Highland Creek, Shawnee Town, and Cash Creek all showed earthquake damage. All along the route, banks were caved in and trees were down, and the shapes of familiar islands were changed.

The following night, the *New Orleans* put up about six miles above the junction of the Ohio and Mississippi, and not more than twenty-five miles from the Rocky Hill plantation. Not long after the crew and passengers had retired, there were urgent cries for help from the forward cabin. Assuming an Indian attack, Roosevelt jumped out of bed. He quickly grabbed the ceremonial sword from the outfit he wore for official receptions, and flew out the door of the family's sleeping quarters.

Reaching the forward cabin, Roosevelt found not Indians but flames. Roosevelt's mind jumped to the worst conclusion—an engine explosion, the most dreaded hazard on steamboats. But as he glanced around the room, he saw the real cause. In anticipation of the following day's needs, the crewman who had been assigned to tend the fire had stacked up a pile of green wood near the heating stove to dry it out. Exhausted by the stress of the past two days' events, the man had fallen asleep, and the wood caught fire. The flames quickly jumped to the finely crafted wood of the cabin walls, and suddenly the whole boat was imperiled. Roosevelt regained his wits and took command, urgently barking out orders. With Roosevelt encouraging his men all the while, the blaze was soon extinguished, but not before the exquisite paneling of the forward cabin was all but destroyed.

The following day, when the *New Orleans* reached the confluence of the two rivers, the water level in the big river was unusually high and the current had slackened, an unmistakable indication of flooding. When the big boat arrived at New Madrid that afternoon they found the place in a shambles. The entire town had dropped fifteen feet, down to the level of the Mississippi. A huge chunk of the riverfront, including the city cemetery, was gone, carried away by the river. Many chimneys and fences were down; others fell before their eyes. Houses were damaged. What had been a large plain behind the town was now a lake. The earth's surface was rent by hundred-foot-long chasms. People and animals wandered about in a state of somnambulance.

As the huge boat approached, many of the townspeople fled in terror. The braver among the inhabitants, however, hailed the boat and begged to be taken aboard. Their frantic pleas for help threw Roosevelt into a quandary. There were far more people wanting to board the *New Orleans* than the boat's store of provisions could possibly accommodate. Moreover, these refugees had no place to go, and when they were put ashore at Natchez or New Orleans, they would have no means of support.

The Roosevelts looked at the heartrending scene, and despite their instinct to take the refugees aboard, they knew they had no choice. Sadly, "there was no choice but to turn a deaf ear to the cries of the terrified inhabitants of the doomed town."

As bad as the damage was on land, conditions were worse on the river. The *New Orleans* had been protected by her weight and size. The rest of the boats on the Mississippi were tossed about like toys in a bathtub.

Firmin La Roche, a sailor by trade, was the captain of a small fleet of three boats transporting furs from St. Louis to New Orleans in

December 1811. (After the Battle of Tippecanoe, riverboats increasingly tended to travel in groups as protection against Indian attack.) There were eleven other men on the three boats; on La Roche's vessel were a crewhand named Henry Lamel, a slave named Ben, and Fr. Joseph, a French priest who had been a missionary among the Osage and was now returning to France. The convoy left St. Louis on December 8 but twice in the first week was delayed en route for repairs.

On the evening of December 15, the convoy tied up about eight miles north of New Madrid, at a landing near the home of La Roche's cousin, John Le Clerq. The boatmen ate supper and retired for the night.

At about 2:15 a.m., La Roche was jolted awake by a thunderous crash that turned the boat on its side. Lamel, sleeping in the next bed, was flung on top of La Roche, and the two men landed hard against the side of the boat.

La Roche, Lamel, Ben, and Fr. Joseph scrambled to the deck to see what had happened. The impenetrable darkness was filled only with sounds—an unidentifiable crashing and grinding, and booming explosions and ominous rumblings emanating from the depths of the earth. For almost an hour, they had no reference point until, at around 3:00 a.m., the haze cleared enough for La Roche to see thousands of trees crashing down and huge sections of shoreline tumbling into the river.

With the boat pitching and rolling, Lamel managed to cut the rope that was tied to a log near the bank. The boat had just begun to float away from shore when it was lifted by a monstrous rush of water from downstream. "So great a wave came up the river," wrote La Roche, "that I never have seen one like it at sea."

The four men grabbed on to whatever part of the boat they could and held on for dear life. Trying to row or steer was futile—not capsizing or being thrown overboard was the best they could hope for as they were swept along by the gigantic wave. The river rose to as high as thirty feet above its normal level, and the boat was carried upriver, toward St. Louis, for more than a mile. The mighty Mississippi was running backwards!

The angry river was surging and roiling. John Weisman, a flatboat pilot who was transporting Kentucky whiskey, reported that "if my flatboat load of whiskey had sprung a leak and made the 'Father of Waters' drunk it could not have committed more somersaults. It seemed that old Vesuvius himself was drunk." Vessels were tossed about so violently that experienced boatmen had trouble staying on their feet.

Sandbars and the points of islands dissolved into the furious waters, taking countless numbers of trees down with them, thereby creating new hazards for already beleaguered riverboat pilots. Great quantities of long-submerged trees were also dislodged from the river bottom, freed from the depths "to become merciless enemies of navigation," as one later report so aptly phrased it.

One man whose boat was wrecked on a planter climbed onto its trunk as his vessel went down. Grateful at least for his life having been spared, he soon realized to his dismay that the snag was slipping down into the raging river. Over the course of the next few hours, he desperately clung to the trunk, calling for help as several boats passed by. Finally, a skiff managed to row a short distance upstream of the man and float down alongside the planter. As it passed under him, the exhausted fellow let go of the trunk and tumbled into the boat.

Neither of Firmin La Roche's other two boats was in sight; one vessel and its crew would never be seen again. "Everywhere there was noise like thunder," wrote La Roche, "and the ground was shaking the trees down, and the air was thick with something like smoke. There was much lightning . . . I do not know how long this went on, for we were all in great terror, expecting death." La Roche, Lamel, and Ben knelt and received absolution from Fr. Joseph.

Finally, the great wave began to subside, and the river gradually resumed its normal direction. Near New Madrid, several boats that had been carried up a small stream just above the town were left high and dry, several miles from the river.

As La Roche's boat was carried back downstream, the sky began to lighten. On the Kentucky side of the river the boatmen saw two houses burning. When they reached New Madrid, there were several more buildings in flames, and a crowd of about twenty terror-stricken people crowded together on the high bank, crying out and cringing in fear.

The crewmen tied up to the shore, but before anyone could disembark, a nearby hickory tree suddenly cracked and came crashing down on the boat. A branch whipped into La Roche's left arm, splintering the humerus like a toothpick. Ben was pinned beneath the tree trunk. The others rushed to his aid, but when they managed, with some difficulty, to pull his body out, it was limp. Ben was dead.

The tree had also damaged the boat, which began taking on water. Thinking they would be drowned, the men frantically climbed onto the shore, dragging Ben's lifeless body with them. When the people on land saw a priest among the group, they all knelt, and Fr. Joseph gave them absolution as well.

La Roche's boat did not sink, however, and the townspeople loudly urged the boatmen to return to their craft, believing they would be safer on the water. Having already experienced several terrifying hours on the river, however, the crew were of the exact opposite opinion, and they chose to stay on land. They hurriedly dug a shallow grave and buried Ben.

All the while, the shocks continued, accompanied by constant sounds issuing from the earth. As soon as it was light enough, the crew set about repairing the boat. When it was mended to the extent that they could continue, the people onshore began crowding on board and dumping the cargo of furs into the river in order to lighten the load. (La Roche later estimated his losses at $600.) Finally, when no more souls could safely fit aboard, they pushed off. Unfortunately, the boat leaked badly, and the overloaded vessel was in danger of sinking. Lamel bailed furiously, but finally La Roche insisted that the passengers be deposited back onshore.

As they made their way toward New Orleans, the boatmen saw evidence of earthquake damage for 250 miles south of New Madrid. Concerning the loss of life, Fr. Joseph wrote, "We made no effort to find out how many people had been killed, although it was told us that many were. We saw the dead bodies of several and afterwards drowned persons we saw floating in the river."

EARTHQUAKES in themselves do not usually kill people. People are killed by the secondary phenomena associated with earthquakes, which include tsunamis, landslides, fires, falling structures, soil liquefaction, and land fissures.

Fires are one of the greatest hazards in an earthquake. In modern quakes they can be caused by exposed electrical wires or broken gas lines. For example, in the 1906 San Francisco quake, for which death toll estimates range from seven hundred to three thousand people, the greatest number of casualties was caused by the resulting fire that swept through the city. In the New Madrid quakes, the burning buildings witnessed by La Roche were a result of candles or overturned woodstoves that still held embers of the previous evening's fire.

The wave that carried La Roche and his crew upriver and created the impression that the river had reversed its flow was another deadly secondary effect. It was similar in cause and result to a tsunami. Two factors most likely were responsible. First, a large piece of land somewhere near Little Prairie was thrust up and temporarily dammed the river— quite possibly the "great loaf of bread" recorded by Michael Braunm, who observed that after the "loaf" burst, the river was running retrograde. When the water upstream, pushed along by the current, hit the wall of land, it had no place to go but back in the direction from which it had come, causing a huge wave, just as deformation of the ocean floor during an earthquake at sea displaces vast quantities of water that can result in a tsunami. In addition, enormous sections of riverbank were caving in all around—a Captain John Davis recorded seeing "30 or 40 acres" fall—and when they did, they displaced huge volumes of water, adding to the size of the wave. When the land that had dammed up the river began to erode away, which happened relatively quickly because of its soft character, the current once again flowed naturally.

JOHN BRADBURY, a Scottish naturalist engaged in an extensive collection of North American plant specimens, was on a boat about a hundred miles south of New Madrid when the first quake hit. He had been entrusted by a friend with delivering a cargo of a ton and a half of lead from St. Louis to New Orleans; on board with him were a passenger named John Bridge and a crew of five French Creoles, including

M. Morin, the boatmaster or *patron*. On the night of December 15, the boat was tied up to a sloping bank on a small island near the second Chickasaw Bluff, near present-day Memphis, about five hundred yards above a shallow stretch of river so treacherous that it was known as the Devil's Channel or the Devil's Race Ground. Through this channel, the river rushed so ferociously that the roar of the water could be heard for miles. With the sun already having set, Bradbury determined that the channel was too dangerous to attempt and decided to wait until morning.

When the quake hit, Bradbury and the others were awakened by the noise and "so violent an agitation of the boat that it appeared in danger of upsetting." They rushed onto the deck. The caving banks had caused such a swell in the river that the boat nearly capsized and sank.

Morin, the *patron*, was beside himself with fear. "*O mon Dieu!*" he cried, continuing in French, "We are going to die!" Bradbury tried to calm him, but Morin ran off the boat crying, "Get onto land! Get onto land!" The deckhands followed him onto the island.

Bradbury decided to go ashore as well. As he was preparing to leave the boat, another shock was unleashed. When Bradbury reached the island, he found a frighteningly large fissure. With his candle, he walked the length of the fissure and concluded that it was at least eighty yards long; at either end, the perpendicular banks had crumbled into the Mississippi. With a shudder he realized that had his boat been moored to a perpendicular bank rather than a sloping one, he and his companions would have been goners.

As the sky lightened, the horrors began to emerge. "The river was covered with foam and drift timber, and had risen considerably." As Bradbury and his party waited for enough light to embark, a pair of empty canoes came drifting downstream on the faster-than-normal current. These canoes were of the type towed by boats and used for getting ashore and boarding other vessels, and Bradbury took it as "a melancholy proof" that some of the boats they had passed the previous day had perished along with their crews.

The shocks continued; while on the island, Bradbury counted twenty-seven more by dawn. At daybreak, he gave the order to embark, and everyone returned to the boat. Two of the deckhands were loosening the ropes when yet another powerful shock hit. In terror, the two men ran up onto dry land, but before they could get across the fissure that had opened in the night, a tree came smashing down to block their way. The bank of the island was rapidly disappearing into the river. Bradbury called out to loosen the ropes, and the two hands ran back to the boat.

Now they were once again on the river, but as the boat approached the Devil's Race Ground, Bradbury saw that the channel was choked with trees and driftwood that had floated down during the night. The passage appeared blocked. Equally distressing, Morin and his crew appeared to be in such a state of panic that Bradbury concluded they were incapable of getting the boat safely through the channel.

Bradbury thought it prudent to stop once more to give the men time to get their emotions under control. Spying an island with a gently sloping bank, the boat moored again, and the crew began preparing breakfast. Bradbury and Morin went ashore to get a close look at the channel and determine where the safest passage might be. As they stood and talked, the 7:15 aftershock arrived, nearly knocking them off their feet. Another tremor hit while they ate breakfast, and as they prepared to reboard the boat, there was still another, which nearly pitched John Bridge into the river, as the sand suddenly gave way beneath him.

Before giving the order to push off, Bradbury noticed that the deckhands were still in a state of fearful paralysis, so he proposed to Morin that the *patron* give each of them a glass of whiskey to bolster their courage. After they had drunk up, Bradbury gave them a spirited pep talk, reminding them that their safety and the safety of the boat depended on their efforts.

Finally, the boat untied and was once again on the water. Their confidence buoyed by the whiskey and Bradbury's exhortations, Morin and the hands successfully threaded the boat through the perilous channel, making several instantaneous changes in their course in order to avoid disaster. When they had passed the danger, the men threw down their oars and crossed themselves, then gave a loud cheer and congratulated one another on having come through the Devil's Race Ground in one piece.

Bradbury's summing up of the total effect of the December 16 quakes was that they "produced an idea that all nature was in a state of dissolution."

THE CREWS of countless boats either drowned or abandoned their crafts to take their chances on land. The misfortunes of these men proved a source of salvation for the residents of New Madrid. In the days following December 16, the river deposited manna at their shores, as boat after unmanned boat floated down into the New Madrid harbor, bringing a bounty of meat, flour, cheese, butter, and apples. The town was still a disaster zone, but at least the people had enough to eat.

The shaking went on—as Jared Brooks wrote on December 16, "it is doubtful if the earth is at rest from these troubles 10 minutes during the day and succeeding night"—persisting throughout the course of the following days. Three days later, Stephen F. Austin—later known as "The Father of Texas"—landed at New Madrid and recorded his impressions. "The Philanthropic emotions of the soul are never more powerfully exercised," he wrote, "than when called on [to] witness some great and general calamity . . . throwing a hitherto fertile country into dessolation and plunging such of the unfortunate wretches who survive the ruin, into Misery and dispair."

"These emotions I experianced when on landing at N. Madrid the effects by the Earthquake were so prominently visible as well in the sunken and shattered situation of the Houses, as in the countenance of the few who remained to mourn over the ruins of their prosperity and past happiness."

Several days afterwards, the camp of Little Prairie refugees received word that New Madrid had survived and that food was available there. Led by George Ruddell, the two hundred Little Prairie survivors immediately set out on a three-day march and reached New Madrid on Christmas Eve.

AS THE *New Orleans* chugged its way down the hazard-choked river, keeping to the middle as much as possible, those on board continued to witness the aftermath of the earthquake's wrath. Earlier in the voyage, the steamboat had always made fast to the shore at night, but with so many sections of riverbank caving in without warning, that was no longer possible. Instead, pilot Andrew Jack now anchored to any of the larger islands that dotted the river.

One night soon after passing New Madrid, with the shakes continuing, the steamboat put up on the downstream side of one such island, identified by Zadok Cramer in *The Navigator* as Island 32 (the islands were numbered consecutively, beginning at the mouth of the Ohio), about fifty miles below Little Prairie. In the night, the passengers were awakened by the sounds of scraping and banging against the sides of the boat. Several times, the vessel was shaken by severe blows. Conferring with Jack, Roosevelt concluded that the sounds and jolts, which would continue all through the night, were caused by driftwood that was being swept downriver. They passed the word to the other passengers and then returned to bed.

When the people of the *New Orleans* got out on deck the next morning, they were stunned. They were no longer anchored to the island—it appeared that the steamboat had slipped anchor and floated downriver all night.

But Pilot Jack, with his encyclopedic knowledge of the river, looked around and pointed out to the others the landmarks that showed they were in the same spot at which they had dropped anchor the previous day. The boat had not moved at all—instead, the island had broken up in the night and been carried away by the current! The sounds and jolts they had heard and felt throughout the night were caused by pieces of the disintegrating island floating up against the boat.

Island 32 was not the only one to disintegrate. Island 94, known as Stack Island or Crow's Nest Island, about 450 miles below New Madrid and 175 miles above Natchez, also disappeared.

A tale published in the *St. Louis Globe-Democrat* in 1902 purported to tell the story of "The Last Night of Island Ninety-Four." According to this account, on the evening of December 15, a Captain Sarpy was en route from St. Louis to New Orleans in his keelboat, the *Belle Heloise*, with his wife and daughter and a large sum of money. At nightfall, the keelboat tied up at Island 94. This island had been a long-standing lair for river denizens of every stripe, including Samuel Mason, the notorious river pirate who had been apprehended in Little Prairie a decade earlier, only to escape while being transported on the river. Two years before Sarpy's trip, however, a force of 150 keelboatmen had invaded the island and cleaned out the den of thieves, after which the island became a safe haven, and now, Sarpy thought to use the island's abandoned blockhouse to lodge his family and crew for the night.

As Sarpy and two of his men explored the island, however, they overheard talking in the blockhouse and, peering in the windows, listened as a group of fifteen river pirates discussed plans to fall upon the *Belle Heloise* the following morning. Sarpy and his crewmen hurried back to the boat and quietly pushed off, tying up at a hidden place in the willows on the west bank about a mile below Island 94.

The following morning, after weathering a night of earthquakes, Sarpy looked upstream to see that Island 94 had disintegrated—the entire landmass was gone, and presumably, its criminal inhabitants along with it.

Whether or not the story is true, Island 94 did indeed disappear.

As the *New Orleans* made her way south, the going got easier and the evidence of the earthquakes became less apparent. On December 30, the steamboat reached Natchez, where she received a tumultuous reception; the celebration included the first steamboat wedding in history, as Nicholas Baker, the boat's engineer, married Lydia Roosevelt's maid.

Finally, on January 10, 1812, more than two and a half months after leaving Pittsburgh, the *New Orleans* steamed into the harbor of her eponymous city with Nicholas Roosevelt resplendently decked out in his ceremonial garb. Roosevelt had clearly and emphatically proved to the world that those who had doubted the feasibility of steamboat travel on the Mississippi were wrong. Indeed, the *New Orleans* had not merely succeeded in conquering the Mississippi, she had also survived one of the most hazardous events in the history of the river. Soon, many more behemoth steamships would follow her. The west would never be the same.

THE QUAKES of December 16 were felt hundreds of miles away from the epicenter. Five hundred and fifty miles north-northeast of New Madrid, in Detroit, where, according to the legend, Tecumseh had promised the Creeks he would stamp his foot upon arrival and shake down every house in Tuckhabatchee, the Honorable James Witherell wrote that Native Americans in the area saw the waters of Lake Orchard "boil, bubble, and foam, and roll about as though they had been in a large kettle over a hot fire."

Tecumseh, however, was not among those who witnessed this dramatic phenomenon, for (legend notwithstanding) he was nowhere near Detroit when the first quake hit. In fact, while the Shawnee chief's exact whereabouts during the December 16 quake remain a mystery, it is not unlikely that he was in the vicinity of New Madrid.

Little is known about Tecumseh's movements from the time he left the Creeks in September until November, when he again visited the Chickasaws on his way to crossing the Mississippi River. Tecumseh had a female relative—perhaps a sister, more likely a cousin or niece—who lived in New Madrid, and he may very well have stopped to see her as he made his way west.

His path likely took him through the epicentral area of the December 16 quake, for late in December, Tecumseh paid a visit to the Osage tribe in what is now central Missouri. John Dunn Hunter, a white man who lived for years among the tribe as a captive, wrote that the Osage had been "filled with terror, on account of the repeated occurrences of violent tremors and oscillations of the earth: the trees and wigwams shook exceedingly; the ice which skirted the margin of the Arkansas River was broken in pieces."

As expected, Tecumseh gave a stirring speech to the Osage, addressing them "in long, eloquent, and pathetic strains," according to Hunter, as he delivered "a simple, but vehement narration of the wrongs imposed by the white people on the Indians, and an exhortation for the latter to resist them." Capitalizing on the fear the earthquakes had engendered among the tribe, Tecumseh expanded his usual recruitment talk to incorporate the ongoing quakes, saying, *"Brothers*—The Great Spirit is angry with our enemies; he speaks in thunder, and the earth swallows up villages and drinks up the Mississippi. The great waters will cover their lowlands; their corn cannot grow; and the Great Spirit will sweep those who escape to the hills from the earth with his terrible breath."

The prophecy had been fulfilled, claimed Tecumseh.

THROUGHOUT late December and early January, the ground continued to move as a result of ceaseless slipping and shifting of bedrock. Settlers throughout the Ohio and Mississippi valleys now had two all-consuming and well-founded fears. They lived in constant terror, not only of a new major earthquake, but also of the gathering drums—and whoops—of war.

Eighteen-twelve would prove to be a calamitous year. In Russia, Napoleon would meet with disaster. In North America, the year would be a catastrophe for many white Americans, Native Americans, and British as well.

Chapter Nine

——

A REAL CHAOS

T HERE ARE three main types of faults—strike-slip, reverse or thrust, and normal (see Fig. 1). A strike-slip fault occurs where the two sides of the fault move past each other horizontally. A reverse fault, also called a thrust fault, is where the two sides are forced together and one side rides up over the other. A normal fault occurs when the two sides are pulled apart and one side drops down. In the New Madrid fault system, situated as it is in the middle of the continent, where the tectonic plate is being squeezed, strike-slip and thrust are the two types of faults to be found.

FIG. 1. *The three main types of faults.*

Strike slip fault
(right lateral)

Reverse or thrust fault

Normal fault

The New Madrid fault system is a complex network of faults, but the 1811–12 earthquake sequence is believed to have involved three main ones—two strike-slip faults and one thrust fault (see Fig. 2). The strike-slip faults, which run southwest to northeast, are right-lateral types, meaning that if you are standing on one side of the fault, the other side moves in a left-to-right direction. The thrust fault runs essentially perpendicular to them.

During the first great quake on December 16, 1811, as the western side of the southern strike-slip fault moved in a southwest-to-northeast direction, it created stress on the southwest side of the thrust fault. A second massive shock, dwarfing the aftershocks of late December,

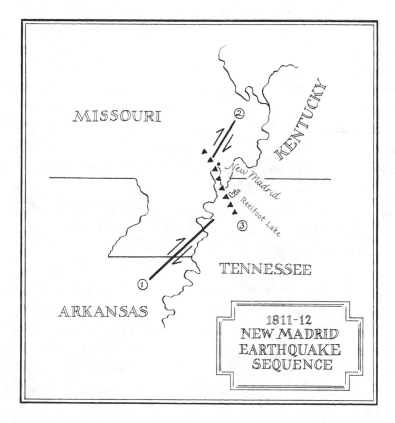

FIG. 2. *The three main faults that were involved in the 1811–12 New Madrid earthquake sequence.*

occurred around 9:00 a.m. on January 23, 1812, as the eastern side of the northern strike-slip fault moved in a northeast-to-southwest direction, stressing the northeast side of the thrust fault. Eliza Bryan wrote that the January 23 quake was "as violent as the severest of the former ones, accompanied by the same phenomena as the former." The combined stresses of these two shocks on the thrust fault would ultimately contribute to a third major quake.

JOHN JAMES AUDUBON, a French immigrant, was twenty-six at the time of the New Madrid earthquakes, years away from the wildlife paintings that would later make him a household name and an American icon. He was living near Louisville and attempting to launch himself as a merchant, and in January he was traveling with a friend named Vincent Nolte, a well-established German entrepreneur who carried on successful business on two continents. A bigger-than-life character, Nolte amassed and lost several fortunes, was involved in any number of adventures and intrigues, and became acquainted with Napoleon, Queen Victoria, Lafayette, and other players on the world stage. Years later, when Audubon was having difficulty publishing his drawings in America, Nolte would arrange for the first edition of Audubon's work in England.

In January, Nolte and Audubon were using one of Nolte's flatboats to move down the Ohio. They disembarked near Cincinnati and proceeded on horseback to Lexington, then the capital of Kentucky, where they went their separate ways.

A few days after leaving Lexington, Nolte was riding by himself through the "vast forest" between Frankfort and Louisville, when his horse suddenly came to a standstill, "as if struck by lightning." Nolte then noticed that the trees began to move strangely, heaving and waving about. Nolte urged his mount on, but with little success. "The animal I bestrode obeyed the spur," he related, "when I attempted to force him onward, with a sort of terror, again stood suddenly still for an instant, and then finally advanced in a tremor. It was some time before he fell into his usual pace."

At the same time, Audubon was on his horse in the Barrens of

Kentucky, near present-day Glasgow, in the south-central part of the state, when he noticed "a sudden and strange darkness rising from the western horizon." Supposing it to be a gathering storm, he decided to make for the house of a nearby friend. After about a mile, he heard what he imagined to be "the distant rumbling of a violent tornado" and spurred his horse to increase his pace. Rather than break into a gallop, however, the animal slowed to a near standstill and began placing "one foot after another on the ground, with as much precaution as if walking on a smooth sheet of ice."

Audubon was about to dismount and lead the horse, when the steed "all of a sudden fell a-groaning piteously, hung his head, spread out his four legs, as if to save himself from falling, and stood stock still, continuing to groan." Thinking the animal about to die, the rider prepared to jump off the horse's back, "but at that instant, all the shrubs and trees began to move from their very roots, the ground rose and fell in successive furrows, like the ruffled waters of a lake."

It now occurred to Audubon that he was in an earthquake. "I had never witnessed anything of the kind before," he wrote, "although, like every other person, I knew of earthquakes by description. But what is the description compared with the reality? Who can tell of the sensations which I experienced when I found myself as it were on my horse, and with him moved to and fro like a child in a cradle, with the most imminent danger around, and expecting the ground every moment to open and present to my eye such an abyss as might engulf myself and all around me?"

As during the December quake, dogs barked and howled, birds screeched and flew aimlessly about, cattle bellowed and stampeded, and wild animals temporarily lost their fear of each other and of humans. The two horses' reactions were typical, and can be likened to the discomfort and agitation of the Roosevelts' dog aboard the *New Orleans*.

In fact, there are many accounts of animals behaving strangely immediately before and during earthquakes. Deodatus de Dolomieu, an eighteenth-century French geologist who studied earthquakes, wrote that "the warning by animals of the approach of earthquakes is a singular phenomenon and ought to surprise us the more because we do not know through what senses they perceive it." There is even a school of thought that believes animals' behavior can be used to predict earthquakes. In China, especially, reports of strange and unusual behavior by animals are used in attempting to foretell impending quakes.

From January 23 "until the 4th of February, the earth was in continual agitation," wrote Eliza Bryan. There were strong shocks on February 4 and 5, and slight tremors on the 6th.

Then, about 3:15 a.m. on February 7, in the worst shock of the entire sequence, the accumulated stresses caused by the strike-slip faults that had ruptured on December 16 and January 23 forced the southwest side of the thrust fault to ride up over the northeast side. The residents of New Madrid were awakened by a series of explosions that finished off what was left of the town. Bryan called it "a concussion . . . so much more violent than those which had preceded it, that it was denominated the hard shock." Roofs caved in, buildings tumbled, and the town was reduced to rubble. Once again, people poured out of their homes and into the streets in panic.

Along with the rest of their neighbors, the Masters family jumped out of bed and rushed to evacuate their trembling house. As they ran to escape, a roof beam collapsed, landing on the family's teenage daughter, Betsey, and breaking her leg below the knee. With difficulty, the family managed to lift the huge timber off the suffering girl's leg. By now, the town was being evacuated, but it was obvious that Betsey could not travel. Callous as it may seem, they moved her to a bed, brought her some cornbread and water, and left her to manage as best she could.

A thousand people of all ages—the combined populations of New Madrid and Little Prairie—abandoned the town. Stopping only long enough to hitch their horse teams and grab some provisions, they fled New Madrid and made their way to the nearest high ground, Tywappety Hill, about thirty miles north of town and seven miles west of the river. There they set up a camp. Somebody suggested that they pray for God's mercy. All knelt together, regardless of denomination, and offered earnest prayers.

One of those on Tywappety Hill was Colonel John Shaw, a merchant who had been boating down the Mississippi to New Orleans on December 16 and was about thirty miles above New Madrid when the first quake struck. By a quirk of fate, he stopped in New Madrid on his way back upriver and was unlucky enough to also get caught in the February 7 shock. With the rest of the inhabitants, Shaw evacuated the town for higher ground.

On Tywappety Hill, he overheard people talking about how Betsey Masters had been left behind. Shaw was incredulous—not only about her being abandoned, but that nobody among those who knew her would go back to check on her. He later related that "though a total stranger, I was the only person who would consent to return and see whether she still survived."

As the ground shifted under his feet, Shaw slowly made his way back to the ghost town and, following the description he had been given, located what was left of the Masters home. He found the girl sitting where she had been left, on the bed, the water and cornbread within her reach.

Shaw splinted the broken leg and made the girl as comfortable as he could, given the circumstances. The wood cookstove was still operable, so he cooked up some food for her and sat with her while she ate. Not wanting to get caught traveling in the dark, Shaw then set out for Tywappety Hill. Betsey Masters eventually recovered, though by what devices it is not known.

Too frightened to return to their homes, the people of New Madrid would continue to live in the camp for over a year. The lightweight shelters, constructed of boards that would prove no danger in the event of further quakes, offered minimal protection from the elements, and the normal routines of daily life became anything but normal.

"New Madrid had been designed as the metropolis of the New World," a commentator wrote shortly after the earthquakes, "but God sees not as man sees—it is deserted by most of its inhabitants." New Madrid founder George Morgan, who died in 1810, was saved the grief of seeing his lofty dream of a great utopian metropolis reduced to a ramshackle tent city.

*   *   *

ON THE Mississippi River, the results were predictably devastating, with effects reminiscent of the December 16 shocks. The river first receded from its shores, leaving many of the boats in the town's harbor on sand. The crews and passengers quickly fled to dry land, as the Mississippi then rose up into a twenty-foot wall of water and overflowed the banks with a fast-moving, retrograde current. The force of the water ripped the abandoned boats from their moorings and carried them up the small creek whose mouth formed New Madrid's harbor. Then, as quickly as it had advanced, the water surged back to the river with such force that entire groves of cottonwoods were torn out of the ground, at the roots. The banks were littered with hundreds of fish that had been unable to swim fast enough to keep up with the water, and the river was now filled with wrecked craft.

Vincent Nolte was tied up in the New Madrid harbor when the quake hit, having reached there on February 6 after meeting his two boats near Shippingport following the January 23 quake and resuming his trip to New Orleans. About twenty other boats that left Shippingport at the same time, traveling in convoy with Nolte's vessels, were also moored in New Madrid that evening.

Nolte was awake working on a cartoon sketch of President Madison when the quake struck. He climbed onto the roof of his boat, where he observed that both his vessels, which were lashed together, were now far from the shore. "The agitated water all around us, full of trees and branches, which the stream . . . was rapidly sweeping away, and a light only here and there visible from the town—in short, a real chaos."

Some of the other boatmen, thinking their chances were better away from the caving banks and falling trees, untied the ropes that held them to the land. Nolte and his crew frantically huddled to decide whether to adopt a similar strategy. Reasoning that night travel was, under the best of circumstances, a dangerous undertaking, and given the numbers of trees that had fallen and were now floating on the current, Nolte decided to wait until daylight to move on.

In the morning, Nolte saw that "the little town of New Madrid, sunken, destroyed, and overflowed to three-fourths of its extent, lay more than five hundred paces from us, with some of its scattered inhabitants here and there visible among the ruins." Nolte's boats were held in place by an island formed by fallen trees. "Of the boats which surrounded us on the evening of February 6th nothing was ever afterwards heard, and we should probably have shared the same fate, had it not been for the plan we adopted of remaining by the shore."

THE BEST account of the February 7 earthquake comes from Matthias Speed, a merchant who was carrying a load of goods to New Orleans. Speed's boat, which was lashed to another craft, was tied to a willow bar on the west bank, across from Island 9, less than ten miles upriver from New Madrid.

About three o'clock, those aboard the two vessels were awakened by the boat's being thrown about and by a sound, according to Speed, "more tremendous and terrific than I can describe or any one can conceive, who was not present or near to such a scene. The constant discharge of heavy artillery cannon might give some idea of the noise for loudness, but this was infinitely more terrible, on account of its appearing to be subterraneous."

Speed and his fellows discovered that the willow bar they had tied to was sinking fast, so they cut loose and made for the middle of the river. The swells were so great that they expected to be taken under at any time and stuffed blankets into the portholes to keep the water from inundating the cabins. Seeing a light onshore, they made an attempt to land, but the landslides and crashing trees made it impossible.

They drifted the rest of the night, and at daybreak found they were at Island 10, only four miles downriver of where they had started. Speed quite correctly deduced that a large block of river bottom must have been thrust up to obstruct the flow of the current. Sticking to the right channel, the two boats bypassed the island and approached New Madrid, where they perceived with horror that they were being swiftly propelled toward a previously unknown waterfall and were so far along into the suck of the falls that they could not stop their momentum. Speed concluded that certain death lay just ahead.

Somehow, by a remarkable stroke of luck, the boats survived the falls and landed at New Madrid. Barely having shaken off their death-defying ride, the boatmen climbed ashore. If they were hoping to find some solace on land, they were sadly disappointed, as they discovered the town to be all but deserted.

Speed stayed around New Madrid until February 12. From some people who had come upriver in a small boat, he learned that seven miles below New Madrid there was another falls that they considered more dangerous than the one he and his boats had come through. This news discouraged Speed from proceeding any further, and he disposed of the merchandise he had on board for a pittance, after which he made his way back north by land, noticing that for ten or twelve miles the earth was cracked in countless spots.

ONE OF THE most dramatic effects of the February 7 quake took place about twenty-five miles southeast of New Madrid in the north-west corner of Tennessee. The region was a swampy forest of cypress, cottonwood, oak, walnut, and other varieties that was frequently flooded by the Mississippi.

An old French trapper named Pierre Nichol was out hunting beaver on the Obion River, when he heard a terrible rumbling noise. Soon the sound had spread, filling the air. Then the ground started its violent shaking, and Nichol had to grab on to a tree to stay on his feet. The forest "swayed and groaned . . . keeping time with the undulating movement of the earth," Nichol said. He looked on in dread as the earth now began to crack, "then to sink, sink, sink, carrying down with it a great park of trees, until the tops of the tallest among them dropped out of sight."

At the same time, a piece of uplifted land dammed Reelfoot Creek. The concurrence of the subsidence and the uplift soon resulted in the formation of a new lake. "In awe and wonderment," testified Nichol, "I stood reeling as one drunk with wine, and witnessed the birth of Reelfoot Lake."

Reelfoot Lake is the largest area of sunklands created by the New Madrid earthquakes—eighteen miles long, five miles wide, and eighteen feet at its deepest point—but there are many others. Some, like the Saint Francis sunklands and Big Lake, both in northeast Arkansas, were caused by warping. Other, less extensive sunken areas, some as small as a football field, caved in because the liquefied sand rising up to the surface removed the underpinnings from below, and as the sand was extruded, the undermined ground sank, leaving previously forested land buried in sand.

In many other places, the opposite occurred as land was thrust up. One of the largest of these sections is called the Lake County Uplift, near Reelfoot Lake, the highest points of which are the Tiptonville Dome and Ridgely Ridge. Throughout northwestern Tennessee, northeastern Arkansas, southeastern Missouri, and southwestern Kentucky, subsidence created new lakes and uplift turned existing lakes into dry ground.

THE MAJOR events of the 1811–12 New Madrid earthquake sequence were felt throughout the United States. In Augusta, Georgia, the editor of the *Herald* wrote of the 2:15 shock of December 16, "So severe a shock of an earthquake we believe was never before experienced here, or as far as we know, in the United States." Augusta is more than four hundred miles southeast of New Madrid.

In Detroit, 550 miles north-northeast, James Witherell wrote of the second December 16 quake, "I felt an unusual sensation; I thought something must be the matter with me. I felt an agitation that I could not account for. But I soon observed that the walls of the house were in motion north and south."

During the January 23 shock in Annapolis, Maryland, 750 miles east-northeast, the 250-foot-high state house vibrated for more than five minutes, and ice skaters on Chesapeake Bay scrambled for shore as the ice began cracking and breaking up. Nearby, in the nation's capital, President Madison mentioned the February 7 quake in a letter to Jefferson, calling it the strongest of the series, noting that it lasted several minutes and was periodically felt for an hour.

The New Madrid quakes caused the earth and buildings to shake in Natchez, Mississippi (375 miles south); the bell in the cupola of the Georgia state house in Milledgeville to peal (425 miles southeast); land to sink in Georgetown, South Carolina; and pavement to crack in Charleston, South Carolina (both about six hundred miles east-southeast). In New York City, nine hundred miles northeast, cups and saucers rattled on breakfast tables, and picture frames jiggled on walls.

Except for the accounts from New Madrid, Little Prairie, and St. Louis, the written record west of the Mississippi is virtually nonexistent. One report stated that the quakes were felt by the Otoes and other Missouri River tribes, and another claimed that "several hunting Indians who were lately on the Missouri have returned, and state that the earthquake was felt very sensibly there, that it shook down trees and many rocks of the mountains, and that every thing bore the appearance of an immediate dissolution of the world!" Because of the sparse number of literate individuals west of the Mississippi, these are the only two reports of the earthquakes' effects in that region, but it is safe to assume that the quakes' westward reach was extensive, possibly as far in that direction as it was to the east.

In all, the felt area of the New Madrid quakes amounted to a million and a half square miles, a staggering range. By comparison, the great 1906 San Francisco earthquake, which caused horrendous damage to a ten-thousand-square-mile area, was barely felt as nearby as Oregon, Nevada, and southern California (see Fig. 3).

The reason for this difference is simple. West of the Rocky Mountains the rocks are younger, warmer, and more fractured, whereas east of the range the rocks are older, colder, and less fragmented. In a western quake, the energy is dissipated more quickly, as it moves along through the cracks and faults in the warmer, weaker rock. In an eastern or midwestern earthquake, however, attenuation is much slower, as the shock is transmitted much more efficiently and can travel hundreds of miles before it dies out. A good analogy would be the difference between striking wood or steel with a hammer—wood absorbs a good deal of the shock and it dissipates, whereas steel is unyielding and the shock is transmitted throughout.

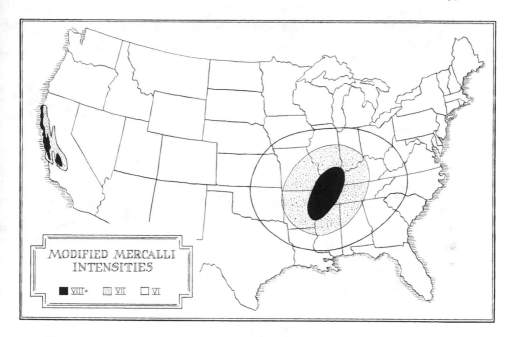

FIG. 3. *The comparative felt areas of the 2:15 a.m., December 16, 1811, New Madrid earthquake and the 1906 San Francisco earthquake (adapted from Johnston, p. 68, original by Andrew Tomko). For an explanation of the Modified Mercalli Intensity Scale, see p. 174ff.*

*   *   *

THERE ARE other questions about the New Madrid earthquakes that, for three reasons, are not so easy to answer: first, there is no instrumental record; second, surface rupture was minimal; finally, much of the firsthand testimony contains conflicting information.

The discrepancies in eyewitness accounts are understandable. As Firmin La Roche wrote about the onset of the quakes, "All of the crew were sleeping and awoke greatly confused and frightened, so that even a few hours after, when we were again safe, nobody could agree in his recollection of that awful night.... When a man expects nothing but instant death it is hard for him to think or notice anything but his danger."

One of the most noticeable inconsistencies concerns the direction of the earth's movement. Many informants describe it as being southwest to northeast, while others say it was east to west, which may have to do with which side of the strike-slip faults the people were on.

Times also vary considerably because timekeeping had not been standardized yet. Each location set its time by the sun, and timepieces were often primitive and unreliable.

BUT CERTAINLY the most significant question that remains unanswered—and a subject of controversy—concerns the size of the principal events in the New Madrid sequence.

There are two ways of describing the size of an earthquake. Intensity measures the strength of the shaking at any given location, whereas magnitude measures the energy released at an earthquake's source.

Before the existence of accurate instruments, an earthquake's size was measured by its intensity. At the beginning of the twentieth century, an Italian seismologist named Giuseppe Mercalli, drawing upon earlier European attempts to quantify the size of earthquakes, developed the Mercalli Intensity Scale. The Mercalli scale assigns values from I to XII, based on the destructiveness to human infrastructure, disturbance of the earth's surface, and degree of animal reaction to the shocks. A modern version, still in use, is called the Modified Mercalli Intensity Scale (see Table 1).

TABLE I.

THE MODIFIED MERCALLI INTENSITY SCALE
WITH MAGNITUDE EQUIVALENTS

Magnitude	Intensity	Description
1.0–2.9	I	I. Not felt except by a very few under especially favorable circumstances.
3.0–3.9	II–III	II. Felt only by a few persons at rest, especially on upper floors of buildings.
		III. Felt quite noticeably by persons indoors, especially on upper floors of buildings. Many people do not recognize it as an earthquake. Standing automobiles may rock slightly. Vibrations similar to the passing of a truck. Duration estimated.

Magnitude	Intensity	Description
4.0–4.9	IV–V	IV. Felt indoors by many, outdoors by few during the day. At night, some awakened. Dishes, windows, doors disturbed; walls make cracking sound. Sensation like heavy truck striking building. Standing automobiles rocked noticeably.
		V. Felt by nearly everyone; many awakened. Some dishes, windows broken. Unstable objects overturned. Disturbances of trees, poles, and other tall objects. Pendulum clocks may stop.
5.0–5.9	VI–VII	VI. Felt by all, many frightened and run outside. Some heavy furniture moved; a few instances of fallen plaster and damaged chimneys. Damage slight.
		VII. Everybody runs outside. Damage negligible in buildings of good design and construction; slight to moderate damage in well-built ordinary structures; considerable damage in poorly built or badly designed structures; some chimneys broken.
6.0–6.9	VIII–IX	VIII. Damage slight in specially designed structures; considerable damage in ordinary substantial buildings with partial collapse; great damage in poorly built structures. Fall of chimneys, factory stacks, columns, monuments, walls. Heavy furniture overturned. Sand and mud ejected in small amounts. Changes in well water. Persons driving cars disturbed.
		IX. Damage considerable in specially designed structures; well-designed frame structures thrown out of plumb. Damage great in substantial buildings, with partial collapse. Buildings shifted off foundations. Ground cracked conspicuously. Underground pipes broken.
7+	X–XII	X. Some well-built wooden structures destroyed; most masonry and frame structures destroyed with foundations. Rails bent. Landslides considerable from riverbanks and steep slopes. Shifted sand and water. Water splashed, slopped over banks.
		XI. Few, if any (masonry) structures remain standing. Bridges destroyed. Rails bent greatly. Broad fissures in ground. Underground pipelines completely out of service. Earth slumps and land slips in soft ground.
		XII. Damage total. Waves seen on ground surface. Lines of sight and level are distorted. Objects thrown into the air.

These intensity ratings help seismologists estimate the magnitude of historic earthquakes that occurred before the existence of accurate seismometers. As related in the eyewitness testimony, the manifestations of the main events in the epicentral area of the New Madrid earthquakes are consistent with Modified Mercalli Intensity values of between IX and XII (See Fig. 4). In trying to assign magnitudes to these earthquakes, however, the lack of any instrumental record is a daunting obstacle.

FIG. 4. *(adapted from Johnston and Schweig, p. 343).*

Seismologists actually employ a number of different magnitude scales, all of which are essentially consistent with the popularly known Richter Scale of local magnitude. In 1935, California seismologist Charles Richter, developing the work done by K. Wadati in Japan, came up with his scale in an attempt to devise a more accurate method of determining the size of earthquakes in southern California.

The Richter Scale is a more objective measure of an earthquake's size than the Mercalli Intensity Scale, but it is by no means a perfect gauge. In fact, it is a secondary measure in that it simply records the displacement of a needle on a seismograph. (The needle is at the end of an arm that pivots at its other end, and a roll of paper moves under the needle, recording every movement of the arm. The larger the earthquake, the greater the movement.) Moreover, the Richter Scale saturates at the high end. At magnitude 8.0 and above, as earthquakes increase in size, the deflection of the needle does not accurately reflect the actual increase in magnitude.

A common misunderstanding about the Richter Scale is the significance of the unit increase. The popular understanding is that an increase of one unit on the scale represents a tenfold increase in size. Actually, the tenfold increase is a measure of ground motion. What is less well known is that the same one-unit increase also represents about a thirty-two-fold increase in the amount of energy released. In other words, a magnitude 7.0 quake creates ground motion ten times greater than a magnitude 6.0 quake, but the 7.0 shock releases thirty-two times more energy than the 6.0.

The Richter Scale worked reasonably well for small and moderate-size earthquakes in southern California, but its limitations led to the devising of new magnitude scales. Small, local seismic events are now usually measured on the body-wave magnitude scale, which measures the strength of the P wave and is accurate up to magnitude 6.5. For larger events, the surface-wave magnitude scale is more reliable. The most accurate scale of all is moment magnitude, which measures the seismic moment, i.e., the energy released in an earthquake by calculating the force and movement of the quake. Particularly at the high end, it is far more accurate than any of the other scales, and today, when magnitude figures are given for contemporary earthquakes, they are on the moment magnitude scale.

THE PRECISE magnitudes of the three main New Madrid earthquakes will probably never be definitively determined. The three major events have been estimated as having had moment magnitudes of between 7.2 and 8.1 for December 16 (2:15 a.m.), between 7.0 and 7.8 for January 23, and between 7.4 and 8.1 for February 7. Whatever the exact magnitudes may have been, one thing is undeniable—the December 16, January 23, and February 7 quakes were huge, and it was only the sparse population of the area and the wooden house construction that kept the death toll from reaching a catastrophic figure.

How many people died in the New Madrid earthquakes is another issue that will never be known for certain. Adding up the victims referred to in the accounts, the number of deaths comes to less than a hundred, although there could have been many more lives lost on the river that were never accounted for.

The New Madrid quakes would have been far more destructive of human life and infrastructure had they taken place close to a center of population. If the epicenter of any of the three major events had, for example, been near St. Louis, with a population of 2,600 at the time, there would almost certainly have been a higher death toll. In March 1812, an earthquake equivalent in size to the largest of the New Madrid quakes hit the highly populated city of Caracas, Venezuela, and more than twenty thousand people were killed.

In Louisville, about 225 miles from New Madrid, Jared Brooks recorded, counted, catalogued, and classified by strength 1,874 shocks between December 22 and March 15, after which he stopped keeping track, although the tremors continued into April. Using six degrees of intensity, he graded eight as "first-rate," which signified "most tremendous, so as to threaten the destruction of the town, and which would soon affect it, should the action continue with the same degree of violence." Ten shocks were "second-rate," i.e., "less violent but severe." Into the third-, fourth-, and fifth-rate classifications fell 35, 65, and 89 shakes, respectively, and there were 1,667 of the final type, which, "although often causing a strange sort of sensation, absence, and sometimes giddiness," the vibrations were generally only perceived by instruments.

AN UNDERSTANDING of plate tectonics did not come until a century and a half after the New Madrid earthquakes. Contemporary and later nineteenth-century theories of causation ranged from the pseudoscientific to the ludicrous.

On the latter side, there was the man who had buried some copper as part of a process for manufacturing counterfeit money and believed that the quakes were a result of the reaction of chemicals on the metal. Another man explained to John Bradbury that the recent comet had two horns, and that the earth had rolled over one and become stuck between the horns—the earthquakes were the earth's attempt to extricate itself; if successful, everything would be fine, but if not, the world would be destroyed. A New Madrid man reported another quaint theory: "One gentleman, from whose learning I expected a more consistent account, says that the convulsions are produced by this *world* and the *moon* coming in contact, and the frequent repetition of the shocks is owing to their rebounding."

On the serious side, nineteenth-century science simply could not explain the New Madrid earthquakes, given the lack of knowledge of plate tectonics. The two main causes ascribed were electricity (or "electrical fluid") and volcanoes. The sometime connection between volcanic activity and earthquakes was known, and it is possible that the recent discovery by Lewis and Clark of volcanoes in the Cascade Range may have played a part in the identification of volcanoes as the cause of the New Madrid quakes.

Louis Bringier, writing a decade after the earthquakes, had a different opinion. "Several authors have asserted that earthquakes proceed from volcanic causes," he wrote, "but although this may be often true, the earthquake alluded to here must have had another cause. . . . It is probable that they are produced, in different instances, by different causes, and electricity is one of them; the shocks of the earthquake of Louisiana, in 1812, produced emotions and sensations much resembling those of a strong galvanic battery."

William Leigh Pierce was convinced that "steam was the more immediate, operative and controlling agent," while Thomas Nutall, an Englishman who traveled through the area less than ten years after the New Madrid events, had "no doubt, but that the decomposition of this vast bed of lignite or wood-coal, situated near the level of the river, and filled with pyrites, has been the active agent in producing the earthquakes."

In a paper presented at the 1883 American Association for the Advancement of Science meeting, James Macfarlane offered that the New Madrid earthquakes were probably not earthquakes at all, but rather "a subsidence due to the solution of underlying strata."

In 1912, Myron Fuller, in his groundbreaking study, *The New Madrid Earthquake,* was the first to identify "faulting in the hard Paleozoic rocks" as "the only probable explanation" of the origin of the 1811–12 New Madrid sequence. Fuller also correctly hypothesized that "it seems clear that the ultimate cause lies in forces operating beneath the embayment deposits."

It was not until the 1960s, with the confirmation of the existence of the tectonic plates that cover the earth's surface, that the stresses on the New Madrid fault system were finally understood. At the Mid-Atlantic Ridge on the floor of the Atlantic Ocean, new continental crust is constantly being created, thereby forcing the North American plate westward at the rate of a few centimeters a year, creating pressure on the failed continental rift valley beneath the Mississippi Embayment. As a region of weakness, the rift valley provides a fertile ground for faulting in the crustal rock, and when the stresses on the faults become too great, one or more ruptures result. The earthquakes of 1811–12 were such a series of ruptures.

NATIVE AMERICANS also had their theories of causation. Throughout the tribes of the affected area, the earthquakes produced fear, awe, and various interpretations.

At the Moravian mission in Goshen, Ohio, a chief told the missionaries that the earthquakes occurred because the Great Spirit was displeased with the whites for taking so much tribal land and for killing so many Native Americans at the Battle of Tippecanoe.

Moravian missionaries in Georgia reported that a tremendous wave of fear and confusion overtook the Cherokee as they tried to find an explanation for the quakes. Some put forth the theory of retribution against the whites, while others felt the tribes themselves were being punished for abandoning the traditional ways. Some claimed that the earth was very old and about to collapse. Others thought a large snake had crawled under their houses and caused them to shake. Still others, including some converts to Christianity who associated the quakes with the Day of Judgment, believed it was the end of the world.

According to John Dunn Hunter, the Osage similarly believed that "the Great Spirit, angry with the human race, was about to destroy the world."

A theory relating directly to Tecumseh's by now legendary prophecy was put forth by one tribesman near New Madrid within days of the December 16 quake. This particular individual declared that "the Shawanoe Prophet has caused the Earthquake, to destroy the whites."

Many of the Creeks, of course, had no trouble interpreting the meaning of the earthquakes. With the fulfillment of Tecumseh's prophecy, they had a clear explanation for the shocks, as well as an unmistakable direction. They began preparing for war.

Tecumseh, meanwhile, continued to canvass the tribes west of the Mississippi as the earth continued to rumble. During this time, he learned of the destruction of Prophetstown, and in late January returned to the burned-out shell on the Tippecanoe to confront the nightmare not only of the destroyed village but also to pick up what pieces of the pan-tribal movement remained and begin rebuilding.

FIVE HUNDRED miles southwest of Prophetstown, the residents of the Rocky Hill plantation were living their own nightmare. Following the murder of George, relations between Lilburne and Letitia Lewis, already cool, became downright icy. Despite the birth of their first child, a son, at the end of January, a ghastly depression descended on Rocky Hill.

After the December quake had extinguished the fire in Lilburne's fireplace, and he had proceeded to wall up George's remains in his rebuilt chimney, there was little reason for him to think he would be brought to account for the murder. But Lilburne's life was cursed.

The big shock of February 7 brought down the restored kitchen cabin chimney, and exposed George's remains yet again. This time, however, before Lilburne could repair the damage, a dog—possibly his own dog, Nero—made off with George's scorched but still fleshy skull. Some weeks later, probably around the middle of March, the dog was lying by the side of the road, busily gnawing away on the charred head, when a neighbor happened along and took the trouble to investigate the strange-looking trophy. The unmistakable scar was still identifiable on George's seared cheek.

Horrified, the neighbor took the grisly evidence straight to the authorities.

Part Four

AFTERSHOCKS

Chapter Ten

———

THE ACCUMULATED LOAD
OF PUBLIC ODIUM

FTERSHOCKS from the February 7 earthquake continued for the rest of the month and on into March. In Louisville, on his primitive instruments, Jared Brooks recorded his second-greatest weekly number of tremors, 221, from March 9 to 15, when the Rocky Hill neighbor likely found George's partly burned, partly eaten cranium.

Owners, overseers, and whites in general were allowed a wide margin of physical abuse of slaves in the antebellum South. Still, it was one thing to beat a slave within an inch of his life, as James McCawley and Richard Ferguson had done to Bob. It was quite another thing again to wantonly murder a man in cold blood, dismember his body, and attempt to dispose of the parts by throwing them in a fire.

In the colonial era, the punishment for killing a slave was simply a fine. By 1812, however, most slave states had laws equating the murder of slaves with the homicide of whites—unless the slave happened to die in the course of "moderate correction" or was slain while resisting the administration of punishment. The murder, in other words, had to be malicious, as opposed to simply careless or in "self-defense."

The enforcement of these laws was another story. There were two main circumstances that diminished the likelihood of any slave owner being indicted and brought to trial for killing a slave. One problem was finding witnesses. Blacks were not permitted to testify against whites, and few whites would take the stand against another white person. But even if there were witnesses who were willing to testify, juries were not likely to convict. In one South Carolina murder trial, just before the jury began deliberations, the jury foreman bluntly stated that he "would not convict the defendant, or any other white person, of murdering a slave." Not surprisingly, the defendant was acquitted. Acquittal was one of the two most common outcomes in these cases; the other was a reduced verdict of manslaughter, which signified that the slave had provoked the owner in some way.

Uncommon though they were, prosecutions of slave owners or overseers for murdering slaves were not unheard of. The more outrageous crimes, like Lilburne Lewis's murder of George, were more likely to be prosecuted than the "ordinary" ones. In general, those slave owners who were prosecuted tended to be excessively violent people, whose aggression manifested itself toward other whites as well as toward their own slaves.

In the decade preceding the killing of George, there had been at least three other slave killings in Livingston County. One involved James Ford, an influential Kirksville man who was a justice of the peace and would later evolve into something of a criminal mastermind. Ford had ordered two of his slaves to tie up a third slave and then ordered one of them to drag the bound man behind a mule through a field of newly cut stumps until the man died. Ford appears never to have been charged. In a second case, a man named Strong clubbed to death a runaway slave near Eddyville in 1804. Strong's crime was recorded in a coroner's jury report in the county records, but an escaped slave was considered fair game, and the case apparently went no further. The third incident occurred the same year and concerned Thomas Hawkins and his wife, who beat and whipped the slave named Rachel so badly that she died. The coroner's jury found that the Hawkins couple had murdered the woman with "malice aforethought" but again, there does not seem to be any indication that they were indicted or prosecuted.

In light of these three cases, the fact that Lilburne's murder of

George was not similarly dismissed is an indication of how offensive the crime must have been to community standards.

OBVIOUSLY, Lilburne never expected to be caught, let alone charged in the killing. After the skull was discovered, however, he had two possible defenses. First, he could claim he had been merely administering a beating—"moderate correction"—to George when he inadvertently killed him, as an accidental slaying carried no penalty in Kentucky. But if that was his intention, it did not look good for him that the incident had gone unreported. Second, since the other slaves would not be permitted to testify, there were no legal witnesses to the killing, and Lilburne could blame it on them.

Yet as the news of the crime spread abroad, public opinion stacked up, first against Lilburne and later against Isham as well. On Monday, March 16, the circuit court convened in nearby Salem. At 9:00 a.m., as the court opened session, the earth began a slight shaking that continued for an hour. In the absence of the court's two regular judges, two assistant judges, Jesse Ford and Dickson Given, presided. A grand jury was empaneled.

For the next two and a half days the earth continued to tremble as the grand jury made its way through the docket of cases, which included the usual assortment of charges of drunkenness, profanity, and assault and battery. (Coroner John Dorroh was found guilty of drunkenness and Sheriff Kirk of swearing; both were fined five shillings.) Late in the afternoon of Wednesday, March 18, John Gray, attorney for the Commonwealth of Kentucky, introduced the final case of the session, bringing "a presentment against Lilburn [sic] Lewis for murder."

It being too late in the day to proceed with the case, the court ordered Lilburne to appear the following day and "answer such charges as may be found against him by the grand Jury." He was released on $1,000 bail, which was guaranteed by five local men—his father-in-law, his commanding officer in the militia, and three of his brothers-in-law. Nowhere in the court documents was Isham Lewis mentioned.

But the next day—after a night that included a moderately strong shock at 9:00 p.m.—the Lewis brothers' situation changed dramatically. Commonwealth Attorney Gray had apparently learned something after the court adjourned the previous afternoon, and whatever it was, it totally changed the complexion of the commonwealth's case. Now, "Lilburn [*sic*] Lewis appeared in court . . . and the grand jury . . . found an indictment against him and Isham Lewis for murder a true bill . . . and ordered that the sheriff take them both in custody."

The phrase "a true bill" had profound meaning, indicating that the members of the grand jury regarded the evidence convincing enough to recommend that the brothers be bound over for trial. Equally important, the indictment was not for manslaughter but murder, which could mean the difference between a short term in the state penitentiary and death by hanging.

The implication of Isham in the killing introduced an entirely new aspect into the proceedings. When Lilburne had been the only one charged, there was no possibility that his wife, Letitia, could be called as a witness, Lilburne being protected by the age-old common-law principle that prevents a husband or wife from incriminating a spouse. Now, however, there was every likelihood that Letitia—who, from the proximity of the main house had no doubt heard the screams issuing from the kitchen cabin—would take the stand, and her testimony against Isham could very well damn both brothers. Lilburne and Isham were taken into custody and spent the night of March 19 in the Livingston County jail.

The record does not indicate why Gray had broadened his case, but it does make clear how serious that case had become. On Friday, March 20, as court began, the earth shook and continued in motion for the rest of the morning. Commonwealth Attorney Gray presented his indictment, charging that,

> *Lilbourn* [sic] *Lewis senior, farmer . . . and Isham Lewis yeoman . . . not having the fear of God before their eyes, But being moved & seduced by the Instigation of the Devil—on the fifteenth day of December Eighteen hundred and Eleven at the house of said Lilbourn Lewis senior . . . with force and arms in & upon the body of a certain Negroe Boy called George*

a slave the property of said Lilbourn Lewis senior . . . feloniously wilfully violently and of their malice aforethought an assault did make—and that he the said Lilbourn Lewis senior with a certain ax there & then had & held in both his hands of the Value of two dollars did strike cut and penetrate in and upon the neck of him the said Negro Boy George giving to the said Negro Boy George then & there with the ax aforesaid . . . one Mortal wound of the Breadth of four Inches and the Debth of three Inches of which said mortal wound he the said Negro Boy George instantly did die . . . and the said Isham Lewis then & there feloniously wilfully Violently and of his malice aforethought was present aiding helping abetting assisting and maintaining the said Lilbourn Lewis senior the felony and murder aforesaid in manner and form aforesaid to do and Commit, and so the Jurors aforesaid upon their oath aforesaid do say that the said Lilbourn Lewis and Isham Lewis feloniously wilfully Volentarily and of their malice aforethought him the said Negroe Boy George . . . did kill and murder, contrary to the statute in such case made and provided and against the peace and Dignity of the said Commonwealth of Kentucky.

No mention was made of the other slaves' work, dismembering the body and helping the brothers to burn the evidence, but the commonwealth's attorney had obviously somehow learned of the fatal axe blow.

The question of when Lilburne and Isham would stand trial now became an issue. There was only a day and a half left to the circuit court session, and the next session was not scheduled until June. The brothers' attorney, Henry F. Delaney, calculating his clients' chances to be better with the younger assistant judges than with one of the more experienced senior judges, petitioned the court for an immediate trial. Assistant Judges Ford and Given, however, wanted no part of it and ruled that the trial would take place during the circuit court's June session.

Bail was set at $1,000 for Lilburne and $500 for Isham. Tellingly, neither Lilburne's father-in-law nor any of his three brothers-in-law, all of whom who had guaranteed his earlier bail, would now sign for him. Neither would his commanding officer. Five new guarantors were found—four of whom, curiously enough, were witnesses for the commonwealth and would be testifying against the Lewis brothers in the coming trial.

The new evidence presented to the grand jury by John Gray had turned Lilburne's in-laws against him. Indeed, they no longer felt it safe for Letitia and her two-month-old son, James, to be at Rocky Hill, and soon after the Lewis brothers' release on bail, Letitia's father, brother, and two family friends went to the house to collect Letitia and the infant. A newspaper article in the *Kentucky Gazette* put it simply: "capt. Lewis's wife . . . made her escape to save her life." Lilburne was devastated by Letitia's flight and instructed his lawyer to bring trespassing charges against the four men who had rescued her. He would never see Letitia again.

Lilburne was now slipping fast, losing by the day his tenuous grasp on what little sense of self he had left. On April 2, the five guarantors of his bail bond appeared at Rocky Hill to demand a mortgage on his slaves as security against his and his brother's fleeing to avoid trial. Lilburne's future was closing in fast.

In an otherwise sensationalized account of the murder and its aftermath written thirteen years later, the Reverend William Dickey accurately characterized Lilburne's state of mind at this juncture: "Now he saw that his character was gone, his respectable friends believed that he had massacred George; but, worst of all, he saw that they considered the life of the harmless Letitia was in danger from his perfidious hands. It was too much for his chivalry to sustain. The proud Virginian sunk under the accumulated load of public odium."

Lilburne had lost everything. He was an outcast in his community and a failure in his home life. There was only one way out. Lilburne decided to end his life, but the courage to do it alone eluded him, so he talked his brother into a suicide pact.

On April 9, as the ground trembled almost imperceptibly, the older brother wrote his will, dividing his property and personal effects among his six children, his father, his three sisters, and his "beloved but cruel wife Letitia." He folded the will and on the outside wrote a short note to James McCawley, one of his designated executors (Richard Ferguson was another), that said, in part, "I have fallen a victim to my beloved but cruel wife Letitia I die in the hope of being united to my other wife in Heaven." It can be taken as a true reflection of his complete divorce from reality that Lilburne Lewis, murderer and prospective suicide, still believed he was going to heaven.

The next morning, April 10, at 11:00 a.m. there was, in Jared Brooks's words, "a tremulous shake . . . generally felt through the country and town." The tremor produced such a severe disturbance of the earth's magnetic field that Brooks's "compass would not act for nearly ten minutes."

At about this time, Lilburne—the disorder of his mind an inner reflection of the turmoil in the physical world about him—and Isham stood with their flintlock rifles in the fenced-in family burial ground at Rocky Hill, preparing to carry out their suicide contract. Before coming to the graveyard, Lilburne had scribbled a message to Letitia on the opposite side of the folded will where he had written the note to McCawley. "My beloved but cruel Letitia," he wrote, "receive this as a pledge of my forgiveness to your connections the day of Judgement is to come I bear you no Malice but die on account of your Absence & my dear little son James Adieu my love Lilburne Lewis." Now, flipping the paper over, he added a postscript to the message to McCawley: "NB Within this inclosure myself & brother request to be entered in the same coffin & in the same grave." Standing alongside the grave of his first wife, Elizabeth, Lilburne placed the papers on the ground beside where he would fall.

The brothers faced each across the thirty-foot by thirty-foot enclosure and raised their rifles. "Wait!" cried Isham before Lilburne could give the command to shoot. What if one of the flintlocks misfired?—a not-uncommon occurrence with that type of firearm. Lilburne considered the possibility and then instructed Isham to cut a piece of wood about two feet in length and bring it to him. When the younger brother brought the stick, Lilburne placed the butt of Isham's gun on the ground and leaned over, resting his chest against the muzzle. In the final irony of this broken man's life, he reached down, attempting to show Isham how the stick could be used to push the trigger and accidentally leaned too hard, causing the gun to fire. The ball entered his heart, and he fell to the ground, mortally wounded. As Isham stood by watching Lilburne bleed to death, he thought better of carrying out his part of the bargain, and instead fled the graveyard.

It did not take long for word of Lilburne's death to reach Coroner Dorroh, who lived twenty miles away. The following day, April 11, Dorroh rushed to Rocky Hill with a hastily gathered coroner's jury of twelve men to conduct an inquest. According to the coroner's report, Isham made a sworn statement, claiming "upon oath that him self and Lilbourn [*sic*] Lewis agreed to present a gun at each others breast and fire at a word with an intention of killing each other—but that Lilbourn in trying an experiment accidentally shot himself dead." The jury reached the conclusion "that Lilburn [*sic*] Lewis Did murder him self on the 10th Day of April 1812 on his own plantation and Isham Lewis present and acessary to the murder."

Under Kentucky law, Dorroh or a justice of the peace was now required to summon a court of inquiry to further investigate the circumstances of Lilburne's death. Until then, the law stipulated that Isham be taken into custody and held in jail. Dorroh took Isham directly to William "Baptist Billy" Woods, a justice of the peace—and an old friend of Thomas Jefferson's and the Lewis family's—for the court of inquiry. Woods had emigrated to Livingston County the previous year from Virginia's Albemarle County, the Lewises' former home turf. Perhaps not surprisingly, whether from old friendship, pity, or a combination of the two, Woods sprang Isham, acquitting him of accessory charges in Lilburne's death.

Another Livingston County justice of the peace, General Jonathan Ramsey, was appalled at Woods's action, however, and the very next day issued a warrant for Isham's rearrest. Deputy Sheriff Thomas Champion apprehended Isham and brought him before Ramsey and Justice of the Peace Joseph Reed, the senior member of the county court. After questioning Isham, the two justices crossed out Woods's acquittal and wrote a new order, stating that "Isham Lewis acknowledged in our presence that he was present when Lilburn [*sic*] Lewis killed himself and that he had consented to kill said Lilburn himself and went to the graveyard for that purpose and that he cut the stick and brought to said

Lilburn with which he pushed the trigger when he killed himself." Now charged with being an accomplice in both George's murder and Lilburne's suicide, Isham was taken to the log jail to be held for trial until the circuit court reconvened in June.

Monday, April 13 was, by Jared Brooks's count, "the 120th day of the continuance of the earthquakes," and he noted that "from the manner of moderating, it is to be hoped they will soon cease and let the earth repose again." The beginning and end of the Lewis murder case—from the killing of George to Lilburne's suicide—corresponds essentially to the beginning and end of the time frame during which the New Madrid fault system was in near perpetual motion.

Isham Lewis never stood trial. Less than a month later, on May 5, he escaped from the county jail—a common occurrence in Livingston County—and left Kentucky, never to return.

The wretched decline and fall of the once proud house of Lewis was complete.

SLAVERY, of course, would last half a century more, but the signs of its decline were already beginning to show. Fierce debates over the extension of slavery into the new territories had begun, and in 1807, Congress had passed a bill banning the importation of African slaves into the country. (Despite the law, about fifty thousand imported slaves were smuggled into the southern states during the next fifty years.) As the demand for new slaves grew, Kentucky became a breeding ground, exporting more than eighty thousand slaves downriver in the decades after the African slave trade was banned.

Lilburne Lewis's deed exemplified the worst excesses of the slave system, and it stands as a harbinger of the defining conflict to come. Lilburne's murder of George brought down the house of Lewis. Slavery itself would very nearly destroy the Union.

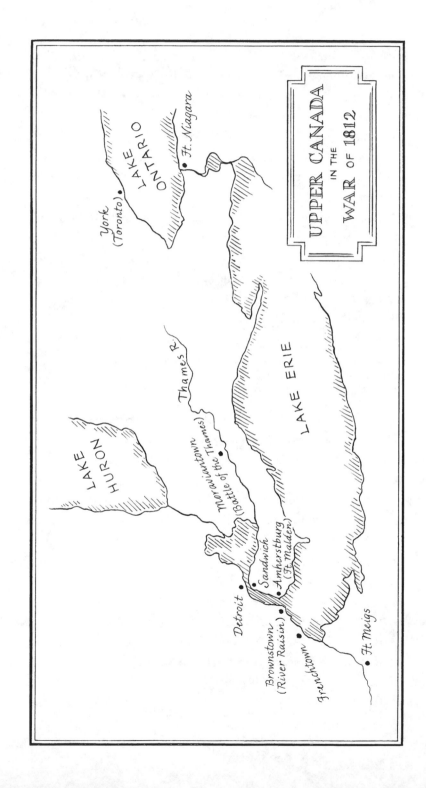

UPPER CANADA IN THE WAR OF 1812

LAKE ONTARIO

Ft. Niagara

York (Toronto)

Thames R.

LAKE HURON

Moraviantown (Battle of the Thames)

LAKE ERIE

Sandwich

Amherstburg (Ft. Malden)

Detroit

Brownstown (River Raisin)

Frenchtown

Ft. Meigs

Chapter Eleven

———

A WAR OF
EXTIRPATION

THE EARTHQUAKES that sealed the fate of Lilburne Lewis had
their most profound political effect on the fate of the pan-tribal
movement. As Tecumseh canvassed west of the Mississippi in late
December 1811 and January 1812, he put the earthquakes to good use in
his efforts to expand the confederacy. He pointed to the earth's tremors
as a confirmation of the Great Spirit's dissatisfaction with the tribes'
ceding of land to the United States and with the decline of traditional
native ways. As one of his biographers has written, "The significance of
these earthquakes, occurring just after Tecumseh had left the south and
while he toured the west, cannot be overstated. . . . The ensuing shocks
greatly advanced the cause of Tecumseh."

Sometime during this part of his trip, Tecumseh learned about
Harrison's destruction of Prophetstown. After visiting the Sac, Sioux,
and Iowa tribes, the Shawnee chief set out for home, stopping along the
way to see the Kickapoos, Potawatomis, Chippewas, and Ottawas.
Everywhere he went, Tecumseh found the mood turning increasingly
antagonistic toward the whites.

In late January, he reached the village on the Wabash. When he saw
the extent of the decimation, his heart sank. What had been a thriving,

vital community when he left was now a sparsely populated, burnt-out shell. The evidence that greeted Tecumseh was overwhelming. He saw, as he later related, the "great destruction and havoc, the fruits of our labor destroyed, the bodies of my friends laying in the dust, and our village burnt to the ground, and all our kettles carried off."

Those who had remained in the area after the Battle of Tippecanoe reoccupied the settlement when Harrison's troops left, and as Tecumseh now looked out at the charred and plundered village, he asked them for an account of how it had happened. They described to him how the battle had gone, and how, after the Indians' defeat, the Long Knives had torched the town, found and destroyed the caches of food that had been hidden in the woods, and desecrated the burial ground by disinterring bodies.

As the great warrior listened to their account, his sadness turned to anger at Harrison and his soldiers. They were not at hand to receive the brunt of his wrath, however, so he instead released his fury and frustration at his brother. Tecumseh grabbed The Prophet by the hair and berated Tenskwatawa for disobeying his orders to keep the peace. When Tenskwatawa tried to defend his actions, Tecumseh shook him roughly and through clenched teeth threatened to kill him if he ever again did anything to imperil the pan-tribal movement.

Tecumseh knew he would soon have to rebuild the shattered confederacy, but for the moment that would have to wait. A more immediate concern was getting through what was developing into a severe winter, and after the Battle of Tippecanoe, the remaining inhabitants of Prophetstown had no stores left.

In February, Tecumseh sent a delegation to Fort Malden to ask the British for food and other supplies, including ammunition. The British, already accused by the U.S. of arming the Indians, were wary of being drawn into a war with the United States on the natives' account. After the Battle of Tippecanoe, the British minister in Washington had gone to great pains to assure the American government that the British king had no desire for war. Accordingly, Tecumseh's request generated no shot and only a small amount of powder.

Despite Britain's efforts to mollify the U.S., the two nations seemed to be edging toward war. For one thing, American public opinion placed the blame for the Indian uprisings squarely on the British, and the Battle of Tippecanoe was a powerful stimulus for the war sentiment. Even more important, there was the still unresolved issue of Britain's maritime offenses, including the trade embargo of the continent, the seizing of American ships, and the impressment of U.S. sailors. (Between 1803 and 1812, the British had seized perhaps as many as one thousand U.S. cargo vessels and impressed over six thousand American citizens into the Royal Navy.) If the British could be defeated in a war, the sovereignty of the United States would be permanently established. Moreover, with the 1812 election on the horizon, President Madison saw a declaration of war as an opportunity to unify the Republican Party.

It is generally forgotten that the War of 1812 was every bit as much a war against the Indians as against the British. In President Madison's June 1 address to a Congress filled with War Hawks led by Henry Clay, he would list the United States' grievances against the British—in addition to the maritime offenses, there was the charge of arming and conspiring with the Indians of the northwest.

On the frontier, the sentiment was strongly for war. A victory over the British would end the blockade of American trade with Europe. The British blockade of the continent was seen as a major cause of the economic depression that had plagued the Ohio Valley for five years because it eliminated the European market as an outlet for American farm produce. In Congress and the press, an invasion of Canada, where the British were vulnerable, was advocated vigorously. If Canada were seized, it could be used as a bargaining chip to force the British to open Europe to American commerce. Equally important, a British defeat would mean a faster end to the ever-growing Indian threat.

In February 1812, however, there still appeared to be a slight chance that war could be avoided, as the three parties engaged in a complex, three-way dance of diplomacy. The British were not the only ones backing off; Harrison and Tecumseh were also trying to at least postpone a fight. Tecumseh needed to buy time in order to feed his people and restore the movement, while U.S. officials attempted to follow up the Tippecanoe engagement with a less belligerent policy. After the battle, Governor Harrison had boasted that Indian resistance in the Old Northwest was finished. At the end of December, he wrote to Secretary of War Eustis, "All the accounts that I have received from the Indian Country agree in stating the entire dispondence of the Prophets party and their disinclination for further hostilities." Eustis instructed Harrison to extend an invitation for Tecumseh, The Prophet, and other chiefs to travel to Washington and meet President Madison "to re-establish the relations of peace and friendship."

While the Fort Malden delegation was out, Tecumseh sent another group to Harrison, promising peace and stating that he was willing to go to Washington to see the president. Harrison, only too eager to believe that the pan-tribal movement was defeated, accepted Tecumseh's proposal.

But it was not to be. Hopes for peace were soon dashed by a spate of killings by hot-blooded Winnebago, Potawatomi, and Kickapoo warriors that broke out all across the frontier. Attacks on settlers in the state of Ohio and in the Illinois, Indiana, and Upper Louisiana territories sent a wave of terror and panic through the white communities. By June, forty-six whites had been killed, and hundreds of settlers had abandoned their homesteads, fleeing to nearby towns and forts. Governors Edwards of Illinois and Howard of Upper Louisiana reinforced their militias and appealed to Eustis to undertake an aggressive war against the western tribes.

By April, Harrison was forced to admit that he had misjudged the situation and that the Indians needed to be once and for all conquered. He asked Eustis rhetorically, "What other course is there left for us to pursue but to make a war of extirpation upon them?"

MEANWHILE, as Tecumseh began recruiting again in earnest, the earthquakes continued to be a determining factor in many tribesmen's thinking. The Potawatomi chief Gomo, known for his moderate and peaceful positions, expressed the opinion that the "Great Spirit is angry and wants us to return to ourselves, and live in peace. . . . You see many

Children have sold their Lands, the Great Spirit did not give them the Land to Sell—perhaps that is the Cause the Great Spirit is angry."

In May, Tecumseh and The Prophet attended an intertribal council on the Mississinewa River in eastern Indiana. Twelve tribes were represented, but most of the participants were not supporters of the pan-tribal movement. (Tecumseh's efforts to unite certain factions of various tribes under the pan-tribal banner was exacerbating the conflicts within those same tribes by creating tensions between those who supported the confederation and those who opposed it.) In addition to the tribesmen in attendance, the Mississinewa conference also had a number of U.S. government officials present.

The council began with an address by Isidore Chaine, a mixed-blood Wyandot also known as Shetoon. Chaine was a double agent. He led a delegation of U.S.-friendly Wyandots who opposed Tecumseh's confederation, but he had also been secretly engaged by British Indian agent Matthew Elliott, a staunch friend of Tecumseh. Publicly, Chaine was to inform Tecumseh that the Wyandots and the British wanted him not to go to war with the Americans; later, however, in private, Chaine would give Tecumseh a very different message from Elliott.

After Chaine's talk, Tecumseh rose to respond. Surveying the assemblage, including the U.S. officials, he began by thanking the Wyandots for their concern and then assured them that "our hearts are good, they were never bad. Governor Harrison made war on my people in my absence: it was the will of God that he should do so. We hope it will please God that the white people may let us live in peace; we will not disturb them, neither have we done it, except when they come to our village with the intention of destroying us. . . . I will further state, that had I been at home, there would have been no blood shed at that time."

Tecumseh then chastised the Potawatomis for allowing their warriors to attack white settlers, and a Potawatomi chief retorted that The Prophet was to blame for those attacks, having incited some of the younger men of their tribe to violence. Tecumseh responded by claiming that the positions of himself and his brother had constantly been misrepresented to the whites by "pretended chiefs of the Potawatomies and others, that have been in the habit of selling land to the white people that did not belong to them."

Finally, a Delaware chief pleaded, "Our white brethren are on their feet, their guns in their hands; there is no time for us to tell each other you have done this, and you have done that; if there was, we would tell the prophet that both the red and white people had felt the bad effect of his counsels. Let us all join our hearts and hands together, and proclaim peace throughout the land of the red people."

In public, Tecumseh reiterated to the Wyandots that had he been at Prophetstown when Harrison made his approach, there would have been no fighting, and he pledged to keep the peace as long as the Americans did the same. "If we hear of the Big Knives coming towards our villages to speak peace," Tecumseh said, "we will receive them; but if We hear of any of our people being hurt by them, or if they unprovokedly advance against us in a hostile manner, be assured we will defend ourselves like men. —And if we hear of any of our people having been killed, We will immediately send to all the Nations on or towards the Mississippi, and all this Island will rise like one man— Then Father and Brothers [i.e., the British and Wyandots] it will be impossible for You or either of You to restore peace between us."

In their secret meeting, Chaine presented Tecumseh with a black wampum belt from Elliott, signifying that war between Britain and the U.S. was at hand. He advised him to keep his warriors out of trouble, return to Prophetstown to stash food and ammunition, and then go north to Fort Malden to meet with Elliott.

In all, Tecumseh could not have been displeased with Mississinewa—with U.S. officials present, there had been no talk of war. In his report to the British, however, Isidore Chaine related that despite the restraint shown by the tribes at the council, "all the Nations are aware of the desire the Americans have of destroying the *Red people* and taking their Country from them."

Tecumseh followed Chaine's instructions. In mid-June, he prepared to leave the rebuilt Prophetstown, and as before, warned Tenskwatawa to prevent the inhabitants of the village from engaging the Long Knives in his absence.

Accompanied by a small entourage of ten warriors, Tecumseh set out for Fort Malden at Amherstburg, the British post that sat across the river from Detroit and twenty-five miles to its south. On his way to Canada, Tecumseh stopped at Fort Wayne on June 17 for what would be his last meeting with U.S. officials. For four days, he engaged in talks with the agent Benjamin Stickney. He insisted that he was going to Canada for two reasons: to obtain powder and shot from the British, and to try and negotiate a general peace with the Wyandots, Ottawas, and Chippewas. Stickney was not fooled by Tecumseh's pretense of innocence. The agent told the chief that with war looming between the United States and Britain, his traveling to Canada could only be construed as a hostile act.

While Tecumseh was at Fort Wayne, the news arrived that General William Hull was marching north toward Detroit with a large force. When Tecumseh left the fort on June 21, neither he nor Stickney could have known that Congress had declared war three days earlier.

IRONICALLY, as war fever had been rising in the U.S., the British— already in the throes of an economic depression and overextended in their conflict with Napoleon—had been trying to avoid a second war with the Americans. In November 1811, Britain had agreed to a settlement in the *Chesapeake* affair, which dated back to June 1807. The British consented to repudiate the attack, pay reparations to the U.S., and return the two surviving American sailors. Unfortunately, the intervening four and a half years since the incident made the British concessions appear hollow to the American public.

In a further conciliatory gesture, the Admiralty had issued orders to avoid encounters with American naval vessels and to steer clear of American commercial ships. In addition, during the 1811–12 session of Parliament, the opposition Whigs argued for lifting the continental blockade and restoring trade with the U.S. as a means of improving the country's economy. In May, the British offered the United States a share of the continental trade if American merchants would consent to operating under British license. The Madison administration rejected the proposal, not wanting to be required to go through the British to do business with the continent.

In June, in a final concession aimed at averting a war, the British canceled the licensing system altogether and lifted the blockade of the continent. Regrettably, when word of this decision reached the United States, it was weeks too late, for on June 18, Congress had declared war. Madison later acknowledged that the declaration of war would have been postponed if the news had been known in Washington.

On July 1, Tecumseh crossed into Canada, where he committed himself and his followers to the British side. "He has shewn himself to be a determined character," wrote Matthew Elliott, "and a great friend to our Government." Tecumseh's supporters at Fort Malden numbered between three and four hundred warriors, but his potential army of rebellious tribesmen was many times larger.

On July 6, Hull's army reached Detroit, giving the U.S. a total force of two thousand troops there. Six days later, he and his men crossed the river into Canada unchallenged, seizing the settlement of Sandwich, directly across from Detroit. The war was on.

The following day, July 13, Hull issued a menacing "Proclamation" to the inhabitants of Canada, warning them not to take part in the conflict. "In the name of my Country and by the authority of my Government I promise you protection to your *persons, property and rights.* Remain at your homes, Pursue your peaceful avocations . . . If contrary to your own interest & the just expectation of my country, you should take part in the approaching contest, you will be considered and treated as enemies and the horrors, and calamities of war will Stalk before you.

"If the barbarous and Savage policy of Great Britain be pursued, and the savages are let loose to murder our Citizens and butcher our women and children, this war, will be a war of extermination.

"*. . . No white man found fighting by the Side of an Indian will be taken prisoner.* Instant destruction will be his lot."

The British government had allied with Tecumseh, but the Americans knew that Canadian whites cared more about peace and prosperity than fighting for a distant crown. Hull's edict had its intended effect, as hundreds of Canadian civilians began asking him for safeguarding. Canadian militiamen deserted in great numbers until the force at Fort Malden was down to under four hundred troops. A general panic swept through Upper Canada. But Hull declined to press his advantage; instead of advancing further, he lost his nerve and his offensive stalled.

Events began to turn away from the Americans and toward the British–Native American alliance. First, two hundred miles north of Detroit, a combined force of four hundred warriors, fewer than fifty British soldiers, and a group of Canadian volunteers captured Fort Michilimackinac, where Lake Michigan and Lake Huron come together. Next, a group of Ohio volunteers under Major James Denny was ambushed and routed by a party led by Tecumseh in an encounter near Detroit. Then Tecumseh and his warriors captured the mail to and from Hull's camp, from which they gained valuable intelligence, including a letter to Eustis in which Hull expressed concern that a large number of Indians would soon be arriving to fight alongside the British. "Under these circumstances," he informed the secretary of war, "you will perceive that the situation of this army is critical."

These incidents, and his obsessive though hardly irrational fear of Indian atrocities, reduced Hull to a state of paralysis, which destroyed his troops' morale. On August 8, "in opposition to every officer of the army," as one of his officers wrote, he "Shamefully Retreated back to Detroit," leaving only 250 men in Sandwich. "Our commander is Dam^d forever in the estimation of this army," the officer continued, "they say he has completely disgrasced them. I fear we shall be in a few weeks, unless Reinforced in a desperate situation. . . . We are in as near a State of Mutiny at this time as is possible to be without Reality."

Three days later, after a fierce battle in which, though outnumbered, "The Indians . . . under the command of Tecumseh, fought with great obstinacy," as Hull later wrote, the remaining U.S. troops were recalled. The pan-tribal confederation's string of victories swelled the ranks of Tecumseh's warriors, as scores of recruits made their way to Fort Malden.

On August 13, General Isaac Brock, the lieutenant governor of Upper Canada and perhaps the most capable British officer in the war, transferred from the Niagara front to the Detroit theater with about three hundred men. Upon his arrival, Matthew Elliott sought out Tecumseh and brought him to Brock.

Tecumseh arrived at the meeting dressed in his signature fringed deerskin shirt and leggings, and moccasins adorned with porcupine-quill ornamentation. Around his neck he wore a large silver medallion with a likeness of King George III. He strode gracefully into the room, his "bright hazle eyes, beaming cheerfulness, energy, and decision," as Brock's aide-de-camp Captain John Glegg later wrote. As the chief entered the room, Brock immediately went to shake his hand. The tall, barrel-chested Guernsey Islander with the ruddy complexion, and the slender, lithe, copper-skinned Shawnee took an instant liking to each other.

The day after Brock's arrival, he held a council with the pan-tribal leaders in which they developed a plan to take Detroit. Tecumseh expressed tremendous satisfaction that the "great father beyond the great salt lake . . . had at length awoke from his long sleep" and sent his warriors to help the tribes regain their ancient lands.

Knowing of Hull's fear of the Indians from the captured mail, Brock sent him a letter on August 15 demanding "the immediate surrender of fort Detroit." Playing on Hull's dread of Indian atrocities, Brock warned, "It is far from my intention to join in a war of extermination, but you must be aware, that the numerous body of Indians who have attached themselves to my troops, will be beyond controul the moment the contest commences."

Although Hull replied, "I am prepared to meet any force which may be at your disposal," when the British and their Native American allies crossed the river on the 16th and advanced on the U.S. garrison as British artillery fire bombarded the fort from across the river, Hull surrendered the fort, the town (whose inhabitants were packed into the fort), his army of over two thousand men, their weapons and provisions, and the newly built warship *Adams* with barely a fight. Hull would later be court-martialed and sentenced to death for this, but the sentence would subsequently be commuted.

The capture of Detroit marked the high point of the pan-tribal movement's success. Brock wrote of Tecumseh, "a more sagacious or . . . gallant Warrior does not I believe exist. He has the admiration of every one who conversed with him."

Brock's return to the Niagara front soon after the capture of Detroit marked a turning point. Tecumseh not only lost a close friend and true ally, but Brock was replaced by Colonel Henry Procter, a man who had very little of his predecessor's leadership or communication skills.

For Tecumseh and his followers, two main problems in the prosecution of the war began to emerge. First, it became increasingly apparent that the British were not equipped to fight anything more than a defensive campaign, whereas the tribesmen were interested in attacking and regaining the land they had lost to the United States. Second, the natives were exceedingly skilled in warfare conducted out in the open, but when it came to assailing a fort, they had neither the firepower, the numbers, the training, nor the provisions to lay siege to a stronghold, as unsuccessful blockades of Fort Wayne and Fort Madison in September demonstrated.

A third siege, at Fort Harrison, undertaken by Tenskwatawa and the warriors of Prophetstown, once again in direct contravention of Tecumseh's orders, also proved ineffective. The tribesmen managed to set fire to the stockade and open a hole in the side of the fort, but U.S. reinforcements prevented them from taking it. Shortly after the failure at Fort Harrison, Tenskwatawa hid his remaining food supply in the woods and abandoned Prophetstown. His brother had been right; he was a prophet, not a war chief, and the time had come for the war chiefs to take the lead.

AFTER Hull's humiliating surrender of Detroit, William Henry Harrison, who had resigned as governor of Indiana to take the brevet commission of major general in the Kentucky militia, assumed command of the U.S. war effort in the northwest. One of his first orders was for U.S. forces to march out and burn Indian villages throughout the area. Twenty-nine villages, most of them deserted, were destroyed. On November 19, Kentucky militiamen discovered the hidden supplies left by Tenskwatawa's retreating group and appropriated them before set-ting fire to Prophetstown for the second time in a year.

The Prophet and what remained of his followers set out for Canada with the intent of seeking food and protection from the British, joining Tecumseh at Amherstburg. As winter settled in, the brothers instructed their followers to return to their own villages and themselves left the Detroit area for the Wabash country. The plan was to reassemble in Canada in the spring for a massive campaign against the United States.

There are conflicting reports of Tecumseh's activities during the winter of 1812–13. The most reliable information indicates that he was quite ill for some of the time and spent the season recuperating near Prophetstown, where seven hundred warriors were drawn to him.

During the time Tecumseh was convalescing, the United States suffered another devastating defeat at the River Raisin south of Detroit. Harrison had planned to assemble three armies and attack Fort Malden, but one of his generals, James Winchester, arrived early with 1,300 troops and took it upon himself to advance with nine hundred of his men. On January 22, a combined force of six hundred British sol-diers commanded by Procter and seven hundred tribesmen led by the Wyandot chief Roundhead, one of Tecumseh's most loyal followers, met and thrashed Winchester's badly positioned forces. Almost three hundred U.S. troops were killed and nearly six hundred taken prisoner. Compounding the disaster was the massacre, by a large group of drunken warriors, of eighty wounded Americans who had been left behind to await medical care. The defeat of Winchester's army forced Harrison to abandon his plans for a winter assault on Fort Malden, and he instead undertook construction of Fort Meigs, near present-day Maumee, Ohio, from which he planned to base a campaign to recapture Detroit. The new fort was completed by April.

When Tecumseh returned to Canada in mid-April, he and Procter plotted an attack on the well-designed and equally well-built Fort Meigs, intending that the strike would result in the capture or death of the bitterly despised Harrison. The siege began on May 1. For the next four days, British artillery pounded the stronghold from two sides of the Maumee River with over 1,600 cannonballs, but because of an ingenious earthen mound engineered by Fort Meigs designer Captain Eleazer Wood, the bulwark proved essentially impregnable to the bombardment.

However, early on the cold, wet morning of May 5, the battle took a dark turn. Reinforcements—eighteen flatboats carrying 1,400 Kentucky militiamen—neared Fort Meigs. The U.S. side now had the greater force, and Harrison sent a plan upriver: the fresh troops were to divide into two units, with eight hundred men under the command of Colonel William Dudley landing across the river and upstream from the fort, where they would attack one of the British artillery positions and disable the cannons before crossing the river and entering the garrison.

Dudley's troops easily overwhelmed the British battery, but some of the nearby native warriors began shooting at the Kentuckians from under cover of the forest. Flushed with their effortless success in seizing the battery, Dudley and his Kentucky men, many of whom had little more than a month's training, rushed impetuously ahead into the woods in pursuit of their attackers instead of retreating across the river as instructed. The tribesmen lured the green troops on, and as the skirmish continued, more and more warriors and British joined the fray. Soon the Kentuckians were caught in a deadly crossfire as, in American soldier George Carter Dale's account, "the bullits seemed to be flying thick as hail stones . . . the screams and groans of the wounded, crying for help at most every step."

The natives closed in, shrieking their bloodcurdling war whoops and brandishing their tomahawks and scalping knives. Up close they were a terrifying vision: "their fiendlike appearance was almost enough to kill a fellow, without shooting him," as Dale described them, "being painted with most every color, their heads tipped off with bird wings, huge bunches of feathers and skins of animals . . . their faces being blacked as black as cole and grease would make them, the upper and lower lips then marked with white stripes."

The Kentuckians stopped in their tracks, frozen with fright. "The men stood as if they could not help themselves," said a report to Harrison, "and got shot down very fast." Then the Americans broke ranks, turning and running back toward the river, many of them discarding their rifles as they went. In the stampede, wrote another survivor named Joseph Underwood, *"such confusion ensued* that the officers *lost all command. . . .* The *strongest & fleetest getting ahead,* leaving *the weaker & wounded far behind,* many of whom were *overtaken & tomahawked* by the Indians."

The slaughter was merciless. British infantryman Shadrach Byfield saw a militiaman "the Indians had met with and scalped, lying in a miserable plight and begging for water; while covering over his head with boughs . . . a party of the Indians came up and found fault with us for shewing any lenity to the dying man; and one of them instantly despatched him with his tomahawk." Colonel Dudley himself was killed in the mayhem.

In the meantime, the British had recaptured their artillery position—in their haste, the Kentuckians had neglected to push the cannons into the river—and when the militiamen emerged from the forest, they were forced to surrender. More than five hundred, many of whom were wounded, were captured; a mere 170 of Dudley's men made it across the river to the safety of Fort Meigs.

The battle was over, but now another round of hideous carnage was about to begin, as the captors marched the prisoners downriver to the ruins of the old Fort Miami, where there was a British camp. Soon they were intercepted by a large contingent of tribesmen, who began harassing the Kentucky men as they walked along, taking their clothing, wallets, money, watches, pocketknives, and anything else they fancied, all the while whipping and beating the prisoners. Captain Leslie Combs, "then a beardless boy of 19," had received a wound to his shoulder, which was dressed in bandages. An Indian came up to Combs and began stripping his jacket from him. "I showed him my wound," Combs later wrote. "'Twas vain; before I could unfasten the bandage, regardless of my pain, *he tore* my coat off from my shoulders."

All the while, as the young captain Thomas Christian later told it, "the tomahawk was busy along the entire route, leaving behind us a path of blood and scalped comrades. Matters growing worse and worse at every step, the savages becoming more and more enraged as we neared the fort."

When they reached their destination, a gauntlet of warriors lined the narrow lane that led into the dilapidated stockade. They were armed with "rifles pistols, war clubs, tomahawks & butcher knives" wrote Combs, "while on either side & under their feet, a number of dead bodies of white men were lying, perfectly naked & scalped."

"To hesitate was instant death," recalled Christian, "and without further orders each made his individual dash for life through the yelling savage lines with superhuman speed and agility. Many who were knocked down gained the entrance upon all-fours with astonishing speed. . . . The way was slippery with human blood and blocked in places by the slain."

As the Kentuckians hurried through the gauntlet, *the Indians employed themselves,"* related Underwood, *"in throwing their war clubs & tomahawks* at *the men & shooting them down with their guns."* Many more Americans were killed and wounded during this barbaric ritual.

Finally, the Kentucky men reached the safety of "the fort, or rather slaughter-pen," as Christian put it, where there was a British guard waiting. Hoping they were now safe, they sat on the ground, the able-bodied cradling the wounded in their laps. But when all the prisoners were inside the fort, the Indians, outnumbering the Kentuckians by two to one, suddenly came rushing in.

Then, in Underwood's words, *"An Indian painted black,* accoutered *with tomahawk, butcher knife, & rifle, mounted the delapidated earthen embankment of the old Fort . . .* & by his *infuriated looks, manners & gesticulation determined to commence a general massacre*—His *Indian dialect* we did not understand, but it was *manifest* from the *excited conduct of the British & Indians* that *something horrible was impending.* No one then present can forget the importunate exclamation which *the British and Canadian soldiers addressed to the Indian: 'Oh, Nichee wah!'* was repeated by them again & again—I was later informed that these words in *the Potowetamie dialect meant 'Oh brother desist, don't do so.' All their entreaties were of no avail*— The *Indian raised his rifle & Shot the man at the foot of the embankment through the body, killing him on the Spot."*

Now a wholesale spree of scalpings, shootings, and tomahawkings broke out, led by the black-painted warrior. The defenseless prisoners, wrote Christian, "like terror-stricken sheep hemmed in by dogs, or a parcel of hogs in a butcher's pen, were piled one upon another in one corner. Those at the bottom were being smothered, while those upon the top were being drenched with blood and brains." The stricken British soldiers stood helplessly by and watched the slaughter. One tried to intervene and was immediately slain by the rampaging warriors.

The British officers conferred urgently amongst themselves, and concluded that there was only one man who could put an end to the killing. A desperate message was sent to Tecumseh back on the battle-field, informing him of what was taking place and urging him to hurry to the camp. When Tecumseh received the message, he immediately set off at a gallop for Fort Miami, accompanied by Matthew Elliott.

More than any other event in Tecumseh's life, his behavior on this occasion proves his courageous nobility. Into the melee he rode and dismounted. He looked around in horror at what was taking place— over forty American prisoners were dead, and still the bloodbath con-tinued. Tecumseh leapt up onto a high point on the wall of the crumbling old fort.

The Shawnee raised his arms and called out. Almost immediately, the Indians stopped their shooting and hacking. When he had their attention, Tecumseh began to speak in the most emphatic way. As Combs recalled, "I could not understand his language, but his gestures and manner satisfied me that he was on the side of mercy." He did not speak for long, but whatever he said was effective, and the marauders began to disperse. "The Indian crowd generally showed assent by signif-icant grunts, while the black Murderer growled & shook his head & and upon receiving an evident personal rebuke, whirled on his heel & left."

Tecumseh's actions made no less of an impression on the Kentuck-ians than on his own people. Underwood mentioned his "intelligent look, and dignified demeanor." Dale said "he was the only man that acted like a gentleman, as an officer." And Combs wrote that Tecumseh was "more humane than his ally and employer." By some accounts, after the killing stopped and order was restored, Tecumseh turned to Procter, now a general, and roundly denounced him for allowing the massacre to occur.

Tecumseh also showed remarkable compassion for four Shawnees who had accompanied the Long Knives as scouts and been captured by the Wyandots. These four men were treated rather harshly; by their account, "the Wyandots took us and directly striped us of every thing we had, and tied us very close, and struck us several times and pulled our hair from all parts. . . . Walk upon the Water, a Wyandot War chief, he took a stick and struck us about the head as hard as he could. . . . They kept us two days at this place very close tied up so that our hands and arms were black. . . . The next evening *Tecumsey* came to us, and shook hands with us. . . . They then untied us after assurances that we would not run away." Knowing that his words would be reported to Harrison, Tecumseh told the four Shawnee scouts that "it was eight years since he was working to fix this war, and that he had everything accomplished, and that all Nations from the North were standing at his word." Thanks to Tecumseh, the four Shawnees were soon returned to their homes.

Despite the capture of over five hundred American troops, and the lopsided number of casualties and prisoners on the American side, the Battle of Fort Meigs was no more than a limited victory for the British and pan-tribal alliance. They failed to destroy the fort and seize or kill Harrison. Moreover, after the battle, most of the British militia returned to their homes to attend to planting their spring crops. Virtually all of Tecumseh's warriors, satisfied with the plunder of weapons, clothing, and provisions taken from the twelve captured flatboats, also left to celebrate their victory; fewer than two dozen remained with him. As a result, the siege of Fort Meigs was lifted on May 9.

Fort Meigs would be the last success of the war for the pan-tribal movement.

Chapter Twelve

———

THE FATAL BLOW

T HE UPHEAVAL in the earth's crust had subsided, but the after-shocks of war continued. They would bring down both the British–Native American alliance and the pan-tribal movement.

In the summer of 1813, a series of events sent the cause of the British and pan-tribal alliance in Upper Canada into a tailspin. A second unsuccessful attempt to take Fort Meigs in July was followed by a disastrous attack on Fort Stephenson (at current-day Fremont, Ohio). In late August or early September, Tecumseh's staunch ally Roundhead died. Perhaps most damaging, the British lost a decisive naval battle for control of Lake Erie in the middle of September, leaving the Americans in a position to cut off all incoming supplies to Fort Malden, which by now was populated by not only Procter's army but by 1,200 of Tecumseh's warriors and their families.

After the Battle of Lake Erie, and without so much as an enemy soldier in sight, Procter ordered the dismantling of Fort Malden. Tecumseh demanded a council with the British general. The Native Americans had staked everything on their alliance with the British; now, however, the Shawnee chief correctly discerned that these "allies" were not concerned with defending his people's homelands but merely with hanging on to their remaining colonial territory. They had already lost the United States, and at this point they simply wanted to retain Canada.

Tecumseh also began to suspect that Procter had no heart for fighting. At their meeting on September 18, Tecumseh gave a fiery speech in which he accused Procter of as much. When he said, "We must compare our father's conduct to a fat animal that carries its tail upon his back, but when affrighted, he drops it between his legs and runs off," he drew laughter from both the native warriors and the British soldiers. Tecumseh told Procter that if he intended to run, he should leave his ammunition with the tribesmen, who would put it to good use. "Our lives are in the hands of the Great Spirit. We are determined to defend our lands, and if it is his will, we wish to leave our bones upon them."

At a second council three days later, Procter persuaded Tecumseh to follow him to Chatham on the south bank of the Thames River and there make a stand. The British troops would proceed upstream and set up a position, and Tecumseh's warriors would join them there. The chief was reluctant, but he knew he had no alternative.

When Tecumseh arrived at Chatham on October 2, he was infuriated to find no Procter and no British entrenchment. The British troops were camped on the north side of the river, and no preparations had been made to defend against Harrison's army, which was closing in fast. Moreover, as the native forces had moved east, the attrition rate had been high; of the three thousand (including women and children) who marched from Amherstburg, half had left for home during the retreat to Chatham.

The following day, Procter sent word that he was further upriver, just downstream of Moraviantown, where a better defensive position could be established. On October 4, once again without options, Tecumseh's force followed the British retreat. As was his custom, Tecumseh rode rearguard to protect those ahead of him, and engaged in a skirmish with Harrison's troops in an attempt to slow their advance. During the fight, Tecumseh suffered a flesh wound as a rifle ball grazed his left arm.

Finally, on October 5, a force of about one thousand men—half British and half Native Americans—prepared to meet an army about three times its size on the north side of the river. The British, low on ammunition and with just one cannon, took up an exposed position across the road. Tecumseh, with only the most militant of his followers still beside him, stationed himself in the thicket behind.

By some accounts, Tecumseh had a premonition of his impending death before the battle. Notwithstanding any qualms he may have had, he went up and down the line of British soldiers, offering encouragement and pressing the hand of each officer. To Procter, he said, "Father, tell your young men to be firm, and all will be well." Then he joined his warriors.

The attack on the British line came in mid-afternoon and broke it almost at once. As the British soldiers fell into disarray, Procter galloped off, fleeing the battlefield and abandoning his troops to their own devices, an act for which he was later court-martialed. The Americans now swarmed forward to meet the Indians in the woods, and a fierce battle ensued.

A group of horsemen, led by Colonel Richard Mentor Johnson, commander of one third of Harrison's army, broke through. Johnson was wounded four times, but managed to remain in the saddle. Tecumseh, dressed in fringed deerskin leggings and shirt with a sash tied around his waist, rode in and out among his warriors, firing his rifle at the enemy and inspiring his men. With red and black war paint, Tecumseh's fierce countenance spurred the Indians, who fought valiantly against the larger, better-equipped American force.

On one of these forays into the thick of the fighting, as Tecumseh fearlessly charged forward to encourage his warriors, an American soldier raised his rifle and fired a shot into the Shawnee's chest. Mortally wounded, Tecumseh dropped to the ground. When he fell, wrote one of the American soldiers, his warriors "gave the loudest yells I ever heard from human beings and that ended the fight."

In the chaos of battle, exactly who killed Tecumseh was uncertain. Four candidates emerged, and ultimately, Colonel Johnson himself was most widely credited with the deed. Much later, Johnson would use this to his decided advantage.

After his death, the tributes to Tecumseh poured in from those who had fought against him. "TECUMSEH is certainly killed—I saw him with my own eyes," wrote Major Thomas Rowland; "it was the first time I had seen the celebrated chief. There was something so majestic, so dignified, and yet so mild in his countenance, as he lay stretched on his back on the ground where a few minutes before he had rallied his men to the fight. . . . He had such a countenance as I shall never forget."

John Reynolds said, "When Tecumseh fell in battle no other warrior was equal to the task to supply the place of this great man. Tecumseh was not blood-thirsty or brutal in his passions. His hatred to the whites governed all his actions, and this hostility arose entirely from his patriotism to preserve his nation and country from destruction. I have been always sorry that the war in which the Indians engaged against us made it necessary to destroy Tecumseh; as he was the greatest man in either of the armies in which he was slain."

Even his most dedicated adversary, William Henry Harrison, could not help but pay homage to Tecumseh's character in a letter to the Ohio governor Return Jonathan Meigs: "I enclose you Tecumseh's speech to Proctor [sic]; it is at once an evidence of the talents of the former, and the great defect of them in the latter."

THE GREAT MAN was dead, but his influence lived on. At the time of his death, the Creeks were already engaged in a desperate war against the United States, a war triggered at least in part as a result of the legend of Tecumseh's prediction of the New Madrid earthquakes.

The tribe's hunting grounds had been shrinking for decades, as white settlers moved into Alabama, then part of the Mississippi Territory. A residue of resentment against the federal government lingered over the roads that had been cut—for the most part against the tribe's wishes—through Creek lands. Despite the opinion expressed in The Weekly Register in September 1813—"this race of aboriginals have been treated with the utmost gentleness and generosity. They have no possible cause of complaint, (nor do they alledge any) against us"—many Creeks were seething with anger even before Tecumseh's prophecy ignited their fury.

The rebellion had actually started in 1812, when the earthquakes brought on a nativist religious revival among the Creeks. The Red Sticks, a faction of militant Creek warriors, began attacking whites on the roads that the U.S. had so brazenly cut. In March, a party of Red Sticks burst into a cabin on the Duck River and killed a family of settlers. Whites throughout Alabama and Tennessee were suddenly filled with dread. Enter Andrew Jackson.

THE WAR of 1812 would eventually help define the political careers of two presidents and a vice president. Richard Mentor Johnson would become Martin Van Buren's vice president in 1837, and William Henry Harrison would be elected president four years later. But both of them were preceded in office by the irrepressible "Old Hickory."

By late 1813, Jackson had risen to a place of prominence in Tennessee. He had started out in public life as a self-schooled backwoods lawyer and gone on to serve brief terms in both the U.S. House of Representatives and Senate. After leaving Congress, he was appointed to a judgeship on the Tennessee Supreme Court, a post he held for six years. He was known for his honesty and common sense in the courtroom and his violent behavior outside it. Jackson was a hot-tempered brawler who was involved in several duels during his lifetime, including an 1806 gunfight over a perceived slight to his wife in which Jackson, after having received a bullet in the chest, managed to take aim and kill his opponent.

Given his temperament, Jackson was best suited for military life. As a teenager, he had fought in the American Revolution and been taken prisoner by the British at age fourteen. After the war, Jackson joined the Tennessee state militia, and by 1802, he was its major general, a position he still held when the War of 1812 broke out.

In response to the Creek uprising, Jackson wrote to Tennessee governor Willie Blount in early June, asking for permission to head up an invasion of Creek country. The Creeks, wrote Jackson, *must be punished*—and our frontier protected . . . the fire of the militia is up, they burn for revenge, and now is the time to give the creeks the fatal blow, before the[y] expect it—as far as I can learn from the Cherokees, the Creeks are making every preparation for war."

The following day, Jackson wrote a follow-up letter to Blount in which he concluded that "the object of *Tecumpsies* visit to the creek nation is unfolding to us. That incendiary, the emissary of the *Prophet*, who is himself the tool of England, has caused our frontier to be stained with blood, and our peacefull citizens to fly in terror from their once happy abodes.

"The sooner we strike, the less we shall have to overcome; and a terrible vengeance inflicted at once upon the tribe may have its effect upon all others."

Indian agent Benjamin Hawkins—who had brought the news of the latest road through Creek land to the tribe the previous fall during the gathering at which Tecumseh made his legendary earthquake prophecy—now warned Big Warrior, to whom Tecumseh had made the prediction, that unless the Duck River murderers were caught and executed, the Creeks would suffer terrible retribution from the U.S. government. In response, Big Warrior's agents sought out and killed eight men from Upper Creek villages. Big Warrior carried out the work of government officials in order to gain their favor, and it would not be his last killing of fellow tribesmen at the government's behest. Not surprisingly, his actions caused tremendous animosity within the tribe.

In July 1812, Tecumseh's influence extended further south to Florida when a band of Seminoles, together with a group of escaped slaves and some Red Sticks, also took up arms. They began attacking settlers' homes, killing the residents and freeing their slaves. In September, they defeated a small detachment of Georgia volunteers, which brought down the full force of the government on them; in February 1813, an army of federal and Tennessee troops invaded Florida and put down the uprising.

The following month, a band of Red Sticks who had fought at the River Raisin and participated in the massacre of prisoners there, were returning home when—ignoring Tecumseh's instructions to keep the peace until he could return to the south and lead a rebellion—they went on a rampage, killing seven white families near the mouth of the Ohio River. Again, Hawkins demanded the execution of the murderers, and again Big Warrior complied, thereby sparking the outbreak of a full-scale civil war among the Creeks. Most of the Upper Creeks aligned themselves with the Red Sticks, while the majority of Lower Creeks sided with Big Warrior and the United States. Cherokee chief John Ross wrote to Ohio governor Meigs, "in consequence of those murderers being killed a civil war amongst themselves, have taken place. The intelligence recd from the Creek nation at this present crisis is very serious. The hostile party is said to be numerous & if assistance is not given to the Big Warrior & his party by the U.S. it is apprehensive that they will be conquered from the Superior force of the rebels."

In July 1813, a group of three hundred Red Sticks traveled to Pensacola to ask the Spanish, who still controlled Florida, for supplies,

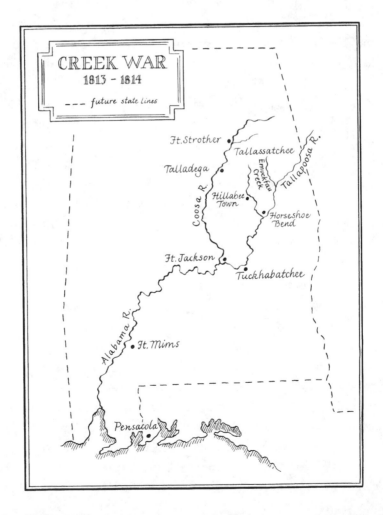

including arms. The Spaniards, anticipating a looming conflict with the U.S. and needing to keep the Creeks as allies, provided the Red Stick party with powder and shot. An observer wrote, "The league seems to be very formidable & I fear will daily gain much additional strength. They have all gone Stark mad & the fermentation will communicate like wildfire. They will spill much innocent blood with the Ammunition which the Govr . . . gave them."

As they were returning home, the party was engaged by a troop of Mississippi militia. They fought off their assailants, and in spite of losing some of their newly gained ammunition, considered the encounter a victory. Now, hostilities escalated quickly. On August 14, Blount wrote to Jackson "to order a campaign to be carried on against a portion of the creek Indians to punish them for their hostility."

On August 30, William Weatherford, a half-Scotsman, led a thousand Creek warriors against Fort Mims, north of Mobile. Surprising the garrison, the Creeks overwhelmed the inhabitants and a gruesome massacre ensued. Weatherford, whom General Samuel Dale considered "endowed . . . with a noble person, a brilliant intellect, and a commanding eloquence," tried to stop the slaughter, but as he later confessed, "my warriors were like famished wolves, and the first taste of blood made their appetites insatiable."

When a burial detail arrived several days later, they found almost 250 dead. "Indians, negroes, white men, women and children lay in one promiscuous ruin," wrote the head of the squad in his report. "All were scalped, and the females, of every age, were butchered in a manner which neither decency nor language will permit me to describe. The main building was burned to ashes, which were filled with bones. The plains and the woods around were covered with dead bodies. . . . The soldiers and officers, with one voice, called on Divine Providence to revenge the death of our murdered friends."

The cry for revenge was taken up from every direction. Jackson once again raised a militia in Tennessee, telling his officers, "the women and helpless children found therein [i.e., Fort Mims] call a loud for a retaliatory vengeance. Those distressed citizens of that frontier who have yet escaped the Tomahawk implored the brave Tennesseans for aid. They must not ask in vain." Jackson intended to exterminate the Creeks and then continue south and take Florida from the Spanish.

The Tennesseans moved, and by the end of October, Jackson had built Fort Strother on the Coosa River, near present-day Lincoln, Alabama. During the month of November, U.S. troops inflicted grave casualties on the Creeks.

On November 3, Jackson dispatched General John Coffee with nine hundred horse troops to attack the Creek village of Tallassatchee. There, another massacre ensued, but this time, it was the Indians who were on the receiving end. Every warrior in Tallassatchee, along with a number of women and children, was slain—about two hundred people in all. Coffee, who lost only five men, with forty-one wounded, also took eighty-four prisoners. Jackson wrote to his wife that Coffee carried out his mission "in elegant stile."

Next, Jackson proceeded with two thousand men against Talladega, where over a thousand Red Sticks had laid siege to the small village of Creeks friendly to the United States. Early on the morning of November 9, the Tennesseans attacked, killing three hundred and breaking the siege. Jackson's casualties came to seventeen killed and more than eighty wounded.

On November 18, a part of General John Cocke's army of East Tennesseans invaded the Creek village of Hillabee Town, which had already sent a message to Jackson offering surrender. Despite the Indians' offering no resistance, sixty were slain and 250 taken prisoner. The Tennesseans suffered no casualties.

Ten days later, General John Floyd's force of nearly one thousand Georgia militia attacked two villages near the junction of the Tallapoosa and Coosa rivers. Once more, the battle was lopsided—the Georgians killed two hundred Creeks, while losing eleven men, with fifty-four wounded.

In the course of one month, the Creeks had lost about 20 percent of their warriors. Now they were given a respite, for many of Jackson's enlistees had reached the end of their one-year term of duty and returned home. By January 1814, however, reinforcements began arriving—four thousand militia followed by the U.S. 39th Regiment of regulars. After two inconclusive encounters, one involving Jackson's troops and the other Floyd's, the decisive battle of the Creek War took place on March 27, 1814, at Horseshoe Bend.

Horseshoe Bend was a peninsula formed by an extreme bend of Alabama's Tallapoosa River. On the point end, 1,200 Creeks had gathered, about a quarter of whom were women and children. They built a breastworks for defense across the neck of the peninsula, keeping their canoes at the point in case an escape was necessary. Jackson marched with a force of three thousand, including several hundred friendly Creeks and Cherokees. Coffee and his warriors took up a position across the river from the point, and as Jackson's artillery began shelling the breastworks, some of the warriors with Coffee swam across the river to steal the canoes, which they then used to ferry two hundred men over to the point.

When they landed, Jackson made a frontal assault on the breastworks, and in the resulting crossfire, the Creeks were sitting ducks. As Jackson later wrote to his wife, "The *carnage* was *dreadfull.*" About 850 hostile Creeks were slaughtered, including three hundred who were drowned or shot in the river as they tried to escape. One soldier later reported that "the party detailed to count the dead warriors found on the battle field . . . so as to make no mistake in the count, cut off the tip of each dead Indian's nose so soon as the count was made." Three hundred and fifty prisoners were taken, only three of whom were warriors. Of Jackson's troops twenty-six died and 106 were wounded; the friendly Creeks had five killed and eleven wounded, and the friendly Cherokees lost eighteen, with thirty-six wounded.

It was upon slaughters such as Talladega and Horseshoe Bend that Andrew Jackson built his reputation.

A week after Horseshoe Bend, Jackson addressed his troops:

> You have . . . destroyed a confederacy of the enemy, ferocious by nature, & grown insolent by the impunity with which they had so long, committed their depredations. . . . Barbarians, they were ignorant of the influence of civilization & of government, over the human powers. . . . Stupid mortals! . . . So it must ever be when presumption & ignorance contend against bravery & prudence.

The fiends of the Tallapoosa will, no longer murder our women &
children, or disturb the quiet of our borders. . . . They have disappeared
from the face of the Earth. . . . How lamentable it is that the path to peace
should lead through blood & over the carcases of the slain!! But it is in the
dispensations of that providence which inflicts partial evil, to produce
general good.

Our enemy are not sufficiently humbled since they do not sue for
peace. A collection of their forces again await our approach & remain to
be dispersed. Buried in ignorance & seduced by their prophets, they have
the weakness to believe they shall still be able to make a stand against our
arms. We must undeceive them. They must be made to atone for their
obstinacy & their crimes by still farther suffering.

But soon after the Battle of Horseshoe Bend, before Jackson could
inflict "still farther suffering" on the Creeks, William Weatherford surrendered to Jackson. "My people are no more!!" he said. "Nothing is left
me but to weep over the misfortunes of my country. . . . Their bones
are bleaching on the plains of Tallushatches, Talladega, and Emuck-
fau . . . my warriors are no more! The miseries of my nation affects me
with deepest sorrow!"

On August 9, 1814, the Treaty of Fort Jackson was signed. The
Creeks ceded more than half their land, over 20 million acres, to the
U.S. government. "They [*sic*] hostile creeks has forfeighted all right to
the Territory we have conquered," wrote Jackson. In fact, despite
Jackson's qualifier, the Treaty of Fort Jackson made no distinction
between hostile and friendly Creeks—the former and the latter alike all
lost their land. The Creek nation, like the pan-tribal confederation in
the Old Northwest, was broken, its demise hastened, at least partly, by
the New Madrid earthquakes.

Chapter Thirteen

———

THE FIELD
OF SLAUGHTER

WITH THE CREEKS subdued, Jackson was free to proceed
south to take Florida from the Spanish and meet the British at
New Orleans. It was the last step in the process of conquering the river
valleys, controlling the waterways, pushing the British and Spanish out
of the United States forever, and setting the stage for the age of the
steamboat.

More than a year earlier, in March 1813, anticipating an assault on
the southwest by the British, President Madison had ordered the
annexation of West Florida, a piece of land that today forms the southeastern corner of Mississippi and the southwestern corner of Alabama.
Madison's justification for this blatant land grab was that it was part of
the Louisiana Territory, a specious claim at best. The commander of the
United States army that marched on Mobile and secured a bloodless
Spanish surrender was none other than George Morgan's old nemesis,
James Wilkinson.

Wilkinson had spent his time since the Spanish Conspiracy
becoming embroiled in other treacherous schemes, while at the same
time continuing to enjoy a position of power and prominence in the
west. He was one of two American officers who, in December 1803,

received the keys to New Orleans and raised the American flag in the French transfer of the Louisiana Territory to the United States. In 1805, Jefferson appointed him governor of the territory.

That same year, Wilkinson had become entangled in a conspiracy with Aaron Burr that ranks as one of the most infamous episodes in the history of the early republic. Burr was already notorious for the 1804 duel in which, while serving as the nation's vice president, he killed Alexander Hamilton. After leaving office, Burr made several trips down the Ohio River to explore possibilities on the frontier.

With Wilkinson as a co-conspirator and Kentucky as headquarters, Burr had enlisted the aid of a wealthy Irish immigrant named Harman Blennerhasset, whose chief talents were getting into trouble and squandering his inherited fortune. Blennerhasset had been forced to leave Ireland because of his association with revolutionaries and his marriage to his niece, a union that violated alike the laws of the Irish and English churches. Using Blennerhasset's funds, Burr raised a private army with the intent of seizing Mexico and the Louisiana Territory and establishing an empire reaching from the new state of Ohio down to Panama, with himself as emperor.

At the last moment, Wilkinson had thought better of the idea and written to Jefferson in November 1806, informing him of "a deep, dark, wicked and widespread conspiracy" to dismember the Union. In a curious coincidence, before leaving on one of his trips to the frontier, Burr had also called upon George Morgan, then residing in Pennsylvania, and hinted at the nature of his seditious venture, making veiled offers of recruitment to Morgan and his sons. His suspicions aroused, Morgan also wrote to Jefferson.

Acting on the letters from Morgan and Wilkinson, Jefferson issued a warrant for Burr's arrest, and though he was subsequently acquitted at trial, it was the resulting scandal—and not, as is commonly thought, his duel with Hamilton—that forced Burr into exile in Europe. Wilkinson, on the other hand, retained his office and Jefferson's continued good favor.

As commander of the army at New Orleans in 1809, Wilkinson's ineffectiveness as a leader had resulted in the deaths of hundreds of men from disease. Hundreds more deserted, and by January 1810, the force had been reduced by half, as more than a thousand men were gone.

In 1811, Wilkinson was court-martialed for conspiring with Burr and being on the Spanish payroll; he was acquitted of all charges, whereupon he resumed his army and political careers. But by the summer of 1813, Wilkinson had thoroughly alienated the Louisiana militia to the point where many enlistees simply refused to serve under him any longer. As a result, John Armstrong, who had replaced Eustis as secretary of war, sent Wilkinson north to oversee the attempt to regain superiority on the northern front, where the British had crossed the Niagara River and captured Fort Niagara.

Wilkinson's mismanagement of the campaign to take Montreal was a catastrophe. His military ineptitude, coupled with large doses of medicinal laudanum, resulted in two disastrous defeats in the fall and following spring, in between which a bitter winter caused high rates of illness and mortality among his troops. In April 1814, he was relieved of his command.

And so James Wilkinson, a villain whose treachery was matched only by his incompetence, made his ignominious exit from the national scene.

EXCEPT in the south, where Jackson was overpowering the Creeks, the war was not going well for the U.S. in the spring of 1814. The defeat of Napoleon had freed up British forces, and ten thousand veterans of the European campaign were shipped over to fight in the American conflict.

In the north, British troops invaded Maine and seized the territory down to the Penobscot River. A second force attacked Washington, burning the White House, the capital, and other government buildings. A third landed at Pensacola to join together with what was left of the native resistance, and a fourth sailed for New Orleans.

The British offered to negotiate a peace, and Madison accepted. At the negotiation table in Ghent, Belgium, the British proposed a settlement: they would retain the territory they had gained in New York and Maine and, in keeping with a promise they had made to Tecumseh, the United States would allow the establishment of an Indian buffer state between Canada and the United States. Under this proposal, one third of U.S. territory east of the Mississippi was up for grabs.

Suddenly, however, the whole complexion of the war changed. After sacking Washington in August, British ships attacked Baltimore but, in the battle that gave birth to "The Star Spangled Banner," the British could not prevail, and they retreated. The following month, at the Battle of Lake Champlain, U.S. warships defeated the British fleet. In the space of two months, the Americans had turned the tide.

H AVING written to Armstrong to inform him of his intention to take Pensacola, Jackson advanced into Florida. James Monroe, the new secretary of war, wrote back, warning Jackson that at "the directions of the President," he should "take no measures, that would involve this Government in a contest with Spain." Monroe's letter did not arrive, however, until after Jackson, acting on his own, had marched on Pensacola on November 7 with an army of four thousand, including militia, regulars, and friendly Indians. The Spanish governor of the city surrendered with hardly a fight, which led the British to destroy their forts and retreat.

Jackson returned to Mobile, then continued on to New Orleans, arriving on December 1 to defend the city against the anticipated British invasion. Between December 14 and the end of the year there were several battles, and though inconclusive, they were costly for both sides—British casualties amounted to 430 of their 6,500-man force, while Jackson's army lost 435 of his approximately 5,000 men, including 140 captured.

The encounter that history knows as the Battle of New Orleans was fought on January 8, 1815. Ironically, a peace accord, the Treaty of Ghent, had been signed two weeks earlier, on December 24, as the British, having lost their appetite to continue fighting, abandoned Maine, New York, and their Native American allies. Word of the agreement, however, had unfortunately had not reached the southwestern front, and on the 8th of January, a senseless bloodbath took place.

Leading up to the encounter, weather conditions had been foul—rainy during the day and freezing at night. By the time the battle arrived, the men on both sides were cold, wet, hungry, exhausted, and miserable.

The British troops, now numbering between eight and nine thousand, were seasoned, disciplined veterans of the Napoleonic wars—many had fought with Wellington, who would soon defeat Napoleon at Waterloo—while Jackson's ragtag army of four thousand was a patchwork of regulars, militia, frontiersmen, free blacks, slaves, Indians, citizens of New Orleans, and pirates led by Jean Laffite who, in exchange for their services, were granted immunity from prosecution for violating American trade laws. From Wellington's brother-in-law, British commander General Edward Pakenham, to his officers, to the ranks of the enlisted men, the British were supremely confident of defeating the outmanned and apparently overmatched Americans. They fully "expected to annihilate Jackson's force in an instant," as one British soldier wrote.

Except for a relatively minor encounter on the west bank of the Mississippi that was won by the British but had no effect on the total outcome, the Battle of New Orleans took place on a seven-hundred- by four-hundred-yard plain situated on the east side of the river, several miles below the city. Outnumbered more than two to one, Jackson knew a fight in the open was suicide, so he chose a defensive position. The Americans' front line, along which more than three thousand men were stretched, was strung out for the better part of a mile on the north side of a ten-foot-wide canal that ran perpendicular to the river but had very little water in it. Flanked by the river on their west and an impenetrable cypress swamp to the east, Jackson's men erected a four-foot parapet of earth on their side of the canal. Given the four-foot depth of the canal, the rampart had the effect of being an eight-foot-high wall to the British soldiers who would be faced with scaling it. The American artillery was placed at key locations along the rampart. Just before sunset on January 7, as Jackson reviewed the final preparations, he repeated the legendary Bunker Hill order, "Don't fire till you see the whites of their eyes."

Later that night, Colonel William Thornton, along with 1,300 soldiers, crossed the river to attack the American position under the command of General David Morgan, with his force of just over six hundred troops. The British attacks on the east and west banks the following morning were intended to be coordinated and under cover of darkness, but Thornton was delayed in embarking, and during the crossing, the strong current of the Mississippi carried his boats a mile and a half downstream. As a result, when Pakenham was preparing to launch his assault before dawn, Thornton and his men were still marching double-time up the west bank toward Morgan's position. Pakenham was further delayed when troops carrying the fascines and ladders for filling the canal and scaling the rampart were late in getting into place. An impetuous man by nature, Pakenham's impatience grew as he saw his opportunity for a surprise night attack slipping away.

When the sun rose on the 8th, a thick fog blanketed the battlefield. Pakenham could wait no longer, and he ordered the firing of the cannonball that was to signal the start of the attack. After a short pause, the air was rent by the thunder of artillery from the British side, returned directly by the Americans. As the British troops slogged forward in strict formation over the muddy, slippery ground toward the American line, the fog began to lift, and the advancing horde of brilliant red uniforms was suddenly fully exposed. "The Americans saw us," wrote one British officer, "and then opened upon us from right to left, a fire of musketry, grape, round-shot, and canister, than which I have certainly never witnessed any more murderous." Another similarly called the fire "the most murderous I ever beheld before or since."

A Kentuckian described the din as "a pretty considerable noise. There were . . . brass pieces on our right, the noisiest kind of varmints, that began blaring away as hard as they could, while the heavy iron cannon, toward the river, and some thousands of small arms, joined in the chorus and made the ground shake under our feet."

The redcoats were sitting ducks, as the Americans were hidden securely behind their parapet, taking target practice. John James Audubon's friend Vincent Nolte, who fought with Jackson's men, wrote that the British "were falling fast but . . . saw no enemy. The whole right of the British column were mowed down by these invisible riflemen.

. . . I called it the field of slaughter; for it really was slaughter, and not battle as on an open plain where foe meets foe; for here the British troops were perfectly exposed to the deadly and accurate bullets of our riflemen; and the latter were entirely invisible, being not only protected but absolutely hidden from view."

In a piece of strategic idiocy comparable to the British tactics at the Battle of the Somme a century later, the British officers allowed wave upon wave of their soldiers to advance and be cut down by Jackson's perfectly situated men. One American later related that whenever the British troops would reach the rampart, "the deadly rifles of the Americans poured a stream of fire into the British ranks, which soon, riddled through and through, fell back in disorder from the foot of the parapet." The British withdrew twice, regrouped and made two more advances, only to be met with the same deadly hail of bullets.

The plain became a killing field, and in a short time, the battleground was littered with red uniforms. "In the whole course of my military career," a British officer sadly observed, "I recollect no such instance of desperate and immediate slaughter as then." Even the Americans were affected by the carnage. One wrote, "The sight was a terrible one to see a field with dead and wounded laying in heaps." Another said, "I could have walked on the dead bodies of the British for one quarter of a mile without stepping on the ground."

The first charge lasted a mere twenty-five minutes, and the entire battle was over in less than two hours. When the shooting stopped, the Kentucky man who felt the ground shake from the noise looked out over the field and saw "individuals . . . in every possible attitude. Some laying quite dead, others mortally wounded, pitching and tumbling about in the agonies of death. Some had their heads shot off, some their legs, some their arms. Some were laughing, some crying, some groaning, and some screaming. There was every variety of sight and sound. Among those that were on the ground, however, there were some that were neither dead nor wounded. A great many had thrown themselves down behind piles of slain, for protection. As the firing ceased, these men were every now and then jumping up and either running off or coming in and giving themselves up."

Casualty figures for both sides vary, but the British lost at least two thousand men—nearly three hundred killed, over twelve hundred wounded, and almost five hundred captured. The British high command—including Pakenham, two other generals, seven colonels, and seventy-five other officers—was decimated. American casualties amounted to well under a hundred—no more than thirteen dead, fewer than forty wounded and twenty missing.

One of the handful of Americans killed in the Battle of New Orleans was Isham Lewis.

THE CONFLICT that many contemporaries saw as the second American War of Independence was over, and though in the end it was more of a stalemate than a victory since the Treaty of Ghent merely restored boundaries to where they had been before the war, the War of 1812 nonetheless signaled the advent of a new era for the young republic. The sovereignty and territorial integrity of the United States were now indisputable.

British attempts to reclaim territory below the Canadian border were ended. When the Spanish were driven from Florida less than five years later, the entire span of country between the Atlantic Ocean and the western boundary of the Louisiana Territory would be consolidated under the American flag—until the conflict over slavery temporarily tore the Union apart four decades later.

In the Old Northwest and the south, Indian resistance had been ruthlessly crushed (except for the Seminoles, who rebelled three more times in the next half-century). It was a policy that would be perpetrated on many more tribes in the republic's inexorable push westward.

In that movement, steamboats would become instrumental in opening up settlement west of the Mississippi, facilitating the passage of people and goods up and down the river.

With the end of the War of 1812, the future course of western expansion—the policy that would shortly come to be known as Manifest Destiny—was now set in stone.

EPILOGUE

NEW MADRID was rebuilt. As the shocks grew weaker and further apart, people gradually started making their way back to the town. "Strangers begin to move in," wrote a New Madrid resident on Christmas Day 1812, "and the Inhabitants are returning to their plantations and repairing their buildings." Between the normal erosion of riverbank and the land that crumbled into the Mississippi during the earthquakes, the river now flowed through the original town site, and New Madrid rose again on the new north bank.

Minor tremors continued sporadically for years. In 1820, a group of people going up the Mississippi on a steamboat stopped near New Madrid and went ashore. While in one of the houses, they were nearly knocked off their feet by a shock. Their host, perceiving her guests' fear, said, "Don't be alarmed . . . it is nothing but an earthquake."

PREDICTABLY, the New Madrid earthquakes made believers of many sinners, and itinerant preachers from all over the country rushed to the area to harvest the thousands of ripe souls. Throughout the region hit by the quakes, there was a rekindling of the great revival movement that had swept the south from 1797 to 1805. With ready-made sermon material at their disposal, zealous clergy seized upon the earthquakes as a means of instilling the fear of God in their flocks. The preachers who came to the New Madrid area exploited the circumstances, exhorting people to heed God's manifest warning and repent.

One frontier preacher, Rev. James B. Finley, was a master at using the shocks to turn people toward religion. Finley was positively sanguine about the effect of the earthquakes. "Although we had some favorable indications, before this event, of a revival," he related, "it contributed greatly to increase the interest on the subject of religion. Mul-

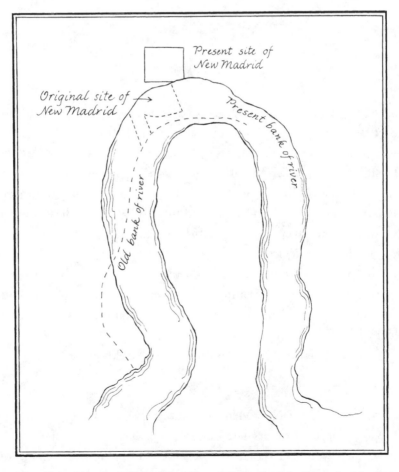

The original location of New Madrid and the bank of the Mississippi in 1811 compared with the town site and river bank ca. 1912 (adapted from Fuller, p. 93).

titudes who previously paid no attention to the subject of religion, now flocked out to meeting, and the power of God was manifested, not only in the earthquake . . . but in the small yet powerful voice. The number of converts was great, and the work extended almost every-where."

Another preacher who realized great success as a result of the quakes was Elder Wilson Thompson of Bethel Baptist Church in Cape Girardeau County, Missouri, where the membership jumped from eighty in 1812 to 186 the following year. "During the revival I baptized four or five hundred subjects," Elder Thompson wrote in his autobiography, "some old and some young, and some white and some black, but all professed to be sinners, and to trust in Christ as their Saviour."

Perhaps the most dramatic evidence of the renewed interest in religion came from the Western Conference of the Methodist Church, which covered present-day Tennessee, Kentucky, Arkansas, Illinois, Indiana, Ohio, West Virginia, and areas of Mississippi, all of which were affected to a greater or lesser degree by the quakes. In 1811, the membership of the Methodist Western Conference was 30,741; the following year, the membership catapulted to 45,983, a 50 percent increase. By comparison, in the same year, membership in the Methodist Church in the entire rest of the country increased by 7,197, an increase of only 5 percent.

The idea of an angry God warning people to repent, with its implicit eschatological overtones, was a theme that occurred over and over. In "A Call to the People of Louisiana [i.e., the Louisiana Territory]," an anonymous ballad discovered in an old hymnbook, a survivor of the quakes penned the following verses:

> *Come, my friends, and neighbors all,*
> *Come listen and I'll tell you,*
> *Concerning of the mighty call*
> *That took place in Louisiana,*
>
> *On Sunday night, you all may know,*
> *As we were all a sleeping;*
> *The Lord from heaven look'd down,*
> *And set the earth to shaking.*

The writer goes on to tell about the onset of the first quake, and the gathering of people in the dark night. After dawn:

Immediately the shake came on,
Which you will all remember;
The houses reeled to and fro;
The earth it split asunder.

The people gather'd all about,
In places there were many;
The Christians stood with lifted hands,
Lord, spare the Louisiana.

More than six months have past and gone,
And still the earth keeps shaking;
The Christians go with bow'd down heads,
While sinners' hearts are breaking.

The great event I cannot tell,
Nor what the Lord is doing;
But one thing I am well assur'd,
The scriptures are fulfilling.

After a couple of verses of general admonitions, the author concludes:

The prophets did foretel of old,
That great events are coming;
The Lord Almighty's bringing on
The days of tribulation.

Prepare, before it is too late,
To meet the Lord from heaven;
King Jesus stands with open arms,
To save your souls from ruin.

Unfortunately, as Peter Cartwright, "the backwoods preacher," observed, "though many were sincere, and stood firm, yet there were hundreds that no doubt had joined from fright." In all too many cases, when the shocks were over, large numbers of these "earthquake Christians" became backsliders. One preacher sadly noted that when the danger had passed, one third of his congregation left the church and returned to their old ways.

On January 12, 1814, the General Assembly of the Missouri Territory passed "A Resolution for the relief of the Inhabitants of the County of New Madrid." It was a plea for help from the federal government for those whose land had been ruined in the quakes, and it was signed by Governor William Clark, who a decade earlier had teamed with Meriwether Lewis to find the Northwest Passage, and had subsequently been appointed governor of the Missouri Territory in 1813.

The resolution read, in part:

> *Whereas in the Catalogue of miseries and afflictions, with which it has pleased the Supreme being of the Universe, to visit the Inhabitants of this earth, there are none more truly awful and destructive than earthquakes. . . . And whereas It is notorious to this general assembly, that the Inhabitants of the late District now county of New Madrid, in this Territory, have lately been visited with Several Calamities of this Kind, which have deluged large portions of their Country and involved the greatest distress, many families, whilst others have been entirely ruined, whole districts of country have been annihilated and many valuable farms utterly destroyed—Many of these our unfortunate felow-citizens are now wandering about without a home to go to or a roof to Shelter them from the pitiless Storms—Be it therefore resolved, by the General Assembly for the Territory of Missouri, that they do recommend the Inhabitants of the Said Country of New Madrid, who have thus suffered, to the consideration of the National Legislature, and that in the opinion of the Said General Assembly, provisions ought to be made by law, for granting to the Said Inhabitants, relief, either out of the public land, or in Such other way as may be consistent to the wisdom and liberality of the general government.*

A little more than a year later, on February 17, 1815, Congress passed the New Madrid Relief Act, the first federal disaster relief act in U.S. history. Unfortunately, the act itself turned out to be a disaster.

The legislation provided for residents whose land had been damaged in the earthquakes to trade their land titles for a certificate that would be good for any unclaimed government land for sale elsewhere in the Missouri Territory. The only restriction was that the new grants had to be between 160 and 640 acres, regardless of how much or little land a person had previously owned. Well-intentioned though the legislation was, it did little to help the residents of the New Madrid area.

Communications being what they were, word of the New Madrid Relief Act did not reach the New Madrid area for months. News did reach St. Louis and other places, however, and speculators were soon beating a hasty path to New Madrid and buying up land for a pittance from unsuspecting locals. Of the 516 certificates issued for redemption, only twenty were held by the original landowners. Three hundred and eighty-four certificates were held by residents of St. Louis, some of whom had as many as forty claims. Adding insult to injury, many banks in Missouri failed, making the Missouri banknotes used to pay for these claims worthless. Governor Clark himself was not above profiting from the situation, as he authorized two of his agents, Theodore Hunt and Charles Lucas, to purchase land in the New Madrid area. Meanwhile, opportunists in New Madrid caught on to what was happening and began selling their land titles many times over. Before too long, the term "New Madrid claim" came to be synonymous with fraud.

Litigation over the resulting land claims tied up the courts for over twenty years, with hundreds of fraudulent claims being pressed. Over the next three decades, Congress passed three more pieces of legislation to try and straighten out the mess. The last case stemming from the New Madrid Relief Act was finally settled in 1862, fifty years after the earthquakes of 1811–12—by which time the frontier had moved a thousand miles west.

*   *   *

WITH THE notable exception of Andrew Jackson, the characters in this story never again exerted profound influences on American history. Old Hickory was elected seventh president of the United States and served two terms, from 1829 to 1837. He died in 1845.

JAMES WILKINSON was court-martialed for the second time after his disastrous handling of the attempt to capture Montreal. As before, he was acquitted, but now his army career was over. Wilkinson spent the next two years writing his three-volume, two-thousand-page memoirs, after which he returned to the west. In 1822, he went to Mexico, where he died in December 1825.

NICHOLAS AND LYDIA ROOSEVELT remained in New Orleans as agents for the Ohio Steamboat Navigation Company following their successful conquest of the Mississippi. After a few months, however, Robert Fulton forced Nicholas out of the business, and the couple returned to New York. In 1814, Roosevelt was awarded the patent for the side-wheel design of steamboats, which quickly became the industry standard. In the next few years, however, the meteoric proliferation of steamboats made the likelihood of recovering damages a quixotic quest, and Roosevelt never filed suit for patent infringement. The Roosevelts had seven more children and retired to Skaneateles, New York, near Syracuse, when Nicholas was seventy-two. He died in 1854 at the age of eighty-seven; Lydia outlived him by twenty-four years, the difference in their ages, and died in 1878.

THE STEAMBOAT *New Orleans* ran a profitable, regular route, carrying passengers and cargo between her namesake port and Natchez. On July 13, 1814, she tied up for the night near Baton Rouge. It had been raining, and the river was swollen, but overnight the water fell a foot and a half, and when it did, the *New Orleans* got snagged on a stump, and the gallant boat sank.

RICHARD MENTOR JOHNSON was widely credited with having killed Tecumseh. After serving in Congress, he was elected vice president on

Martin Van Buren's ticket in 1836. His campaign slogan was "Rumpsey dumpsey, Rumpsey dumpsey, Colonel Johnson killed Tecumseh." Johnson died in 1850.

WILLIAM HENRY HARRISON ran for president in 1836 and lost to Van Buren. Four years later, campaigning under the slogan "Tippecanoe and Tyler Too!," Harrison was elected. On March 4, 1841, he and Vice President John Tyler were inaugurated on a bitterly cold Washington day. Despite the frigid wind blowing off the Potomac, Harrison refused to wear an overcoat, and in the course of his hour-and-forty-minute inauguration address, he caught a cold that quickly developed into pneumonia. A month later to the day, Harrison was dead, his tenure as president the shortest in U.S. history.

THE PROPHET stayed in Canada until 1824, supported by the British. When he returned to the United States, he became an advocate of the land cessions that he and Tecumseh had so bitterly opposed, and helped the government move the remaining Ohio Shawnees to Kansas. He died in poverty in 1836.

OVER THE COURSE of the next century and more, the New Madrid earthquakes gradually receded from public awareness, as the New Madrid fault system produced just two shocks greater than magnitude 6.0 in the 180 years following the 1811–12 sequence—a 6.5 in 1843 and a 6.8 in 1895. An occasional magazine article would appear and several epic poems and novels using the quakes as a setting were written, but in general, the largest series of earthquakes ever to hit the North American continent faded from memory—until 1990, when a prediction by Dr. Iben Browning suddenly brought the New Madrid fault system to the forefront once again.

Browning was a climatological and business consultant who claimed to have predicted the magnitude 6.9 Loma Prieta quake that struck northern California during the 1989 World Series, causing extensive damage in the San Francisco Bay area. Browning also claimed to have predicted other large earthquakes and volcanic eruptions, including the 1980 explosion of Mount St. Helens in Washington.

Addressing a business seminar in Atlanta in February 1988, Browning told his audience that an earthquake could strike the Memphis area in early December 1990. More than a year and a half later, on November 27, 1989, a short Associated Press story made the prediction public, and the following day, a longer story appeared in the *Memphis Commercial Appeal.* Two weeks later, speaking to the Missouri Governor's Conference on Agriculture, Browning repeated his prediction that there was a 50 percent probability that a magnitude 6.5–7.5 earthquake would hit the New Madrid area on December 3, 1990. Browning's prognostication was based on tidal forces, which were going to be extraordinarily high on December 2 and 3.

Suddenly, people were interested in the New Madrid fault system again. The Loma Prieta quake in October 1989 had received widespread television coverage, and the repeated viewings of the worst of the damage had created a climate in which Browning's prediction was taken seriously by the media and the public. Despite the fact that the connection between tidal forces and earthquakes has never been proven, and despite the refutation of Browning's prediction by several seismologists, including the Center for Earthquake Research and Information director Arch Johnston, media outlets all over the country began picking up the story and running with it.

The issue was given further apparent credence in June 1990 when David Stewart threw his support behind the Browning forecast. Stewart, a geophysicist, was then the director of the Center for Earthquake Studies at Southeast Missouri State University and one of Missouri's leading earthquake preparedness experts. On July 21, in an article in the *St. Louis Post-Dispatch* entitled, "Quake Prediction Taken Seriously," Stewart was quoted as saying that Browning's "methodology does seem to be promising and worthy of serious and thorough consideration."

In fact, Browning's methodology was highly questionable—he had no physical model for his prediction and showed no verifiable evidence to back up his prediction. Moreover, it turned out that his "predictions" of the Loma Prieta quake and the Mount St. Helens eruption were also suspect. Browning's doctorate was in zoology; he was a self-taught climatologist with no scientific expertise in seismology or earthquake prediction. After Stewart joined Browning, a number of seismologists made efforts to debunk the prediction, but the cow was already out of the barn.

The Associated Press picked up the *Post-Dispatch* piece, and it was reprinted in newspapers throughout the New Madrid Seismic Zone region. Stories then ran in major newspapers all across the country, including the *New York Times, Wall Street Journal, Chicago Tribune,* and *Miami Herald.* Soon the national media jumped in. *Time* and *Newsweek* published articles and *USA Today* ran close to a dozen stories. Browning appeared on *Good Morning America.* Johnston was interviewed for the *Today* show. *World News Tonight* and *NOVA* planned segments on the New Madrid fault system.

Earthquake and natural disaster agencies, together with organizations like the Red Cross, unwittingly exacerbated the crisis by sending out literature on earthquake preparedness without also providing a disclaimer regarding Browning's prediction. Throughout the New Madrid Seismic Zone, agencies were inundated with requests for information. National Guard units in Missouri and Arkansas conducted earthquake drills. Department stores passed out survival-tip literature and stocked up on blankets, bottled water, and first-aid kits. Many school districts announced that schools would close on December 3. A minor 4.6 tremor near Cape Girardeau, Missouri, on September 26, made the situation that much worse, as many people interpreted the event to be a foreshock of the anticipated December quake.

Except for Stewart, the entire scientific community was aligned against the Browning prediction. "Earthquake experts across the country consider this 'prediction' ridiculous and unscientific," wrote Douglas A. Wiens, a professor of earth and planetary sciences at Washington University of St. Louis, in an op-ed piece for the *Post-Dispatch* on September 30. "The public should disregard all predictions about the specific date that an earthquake will occur. No one can make such predictions. Though scientists have investigated many different factors that could signal an impending quake, none has proved reliable." Nevertheless, the media continued to treat the Browning prediction as genuine news.

In mid-October, the National Earthquake Prediction Evaluation Council (NEPEC) released a study that thoroughly refuted Browning's prediction, but still the media hype went on. By the beginning of December, the New Madrid Seismic Zone region was in a state of near-hysteria.

On the weekend of December 1–2, a carnival-like atmosphere prevailed in New Madrid. More than thirty satellite trucks from television and radio networks worldwide were parked in downtown New Madrid, with its population of just over 3,300. Church marquees advertised sermons with earthquake-inspired themes like, "Preparing for the Big One? Are You Prepared for the Last One?" Cars prowled the town displaying homemade signs along the same lines: "NEW MADRID SAVE YOUR CITY FAST AND REPENT." Rev. Frank McRae of the St. John's United Methodist Church cheerfully admitted, "You don't get breaks like this often." Tourists roamed the streets, and the Chamber of Commerce sold "official" earthquake T-shirts and sweatshirts. Tom's Grill offered quake burgers that were served divided down the middle by a jagged line, while McDonald's advertised free coffee, "a price you can shake & rattle about." Near the Mississippi River, the Faultline Express Band played earthquake songs. A California psychologist featured an Iben Browning doll that children were encouraged to pummel as a way of dealing with their fears about the earthquake prediction.

December 3 came and went with no earthquake, of course. The tourists and media crews quickly left, and after several months in the limelight, New Madrid went back to being an ordinary Mississippi River town.

The Browning prediction underscored the fact that there is only one thing certain about the New Madrid fault system, and that is that it will go off again. It could be in two hundred years. Or it could be tomorrow.

Notes

Chapter One: A TIME OF EXTRAORDINARIES

4   Much of this territory: As Nobles indicates in *American Frontiers,* one of the essential characteristics of the "frontier" was that no nation could claim sovereignty.

5   "Tecumseh, at the head": Pickett, *History of Alabama,* Vol. 2, pp. 242–43.

6   "in a very dignified": This description of Tecumseh's manner and the quotations that follow are from Hunter, *Memoirs of a Captivity Among the Indians of North America* (pp. 28–31), a book that was originally discredited as fraudulent for political reasons, but has more recently been shown to almost certainly be authentic. This talk was delivered several months later to the Osage, among whom Hunter lived, but there can be little doubt that the talk given in Tuckhabatchee would have been very close to the rhetoric and language quoted here. See Goltz, "Tecumseh, The Prophet and the Rise of the Northwest Indian Confederation," p. 260, fn.

       Claiborne's *Life and Times of Gen. Sam Dale, The Mississippi Partisan* contains another version of Tecumseh's address to the Creeks that is of dubious authenticity (pp. 59–61). The tone of this version is extremely strident: "Burn their dwellings! Destroy their stock! Slay their wives and children! . . . War now! War forever! War upon the living! War upon the dead! Dig their very corpses from the grave. Our country must give no rest to a white man's bones." Not only is this type of language and rhetoric anomalous to Tecumseh's style of oratory, it is moreover extremely unlikely that he would have spoken in such a manner with whites present, as Claiborne reports to have been the case.

7   He also implored his listeners: This paragraph and the next are based on Pickett, *History of Alabama,* Vol. 2, pp. 243–44, whose informants included several eyewitnesses.

8   The Great Spirit: This paragraph is based on Sugden, *Tecumseh: A Life,* p. 246.

8   And was his name not Tecumseh: For a fuller explanation, see Gatschet, "Tecumseh's Name," pp. 91–92.

9   "Your blood is white": Thomas L. McKenney and James Hall, *The Indian Tribes of North America,* Vol. 1, p. 94.

9   As the legend has it: There is another version of Tecumseh's prophecy, in which he vows that in about four months he will climb a mountain and stamp upon the ground three times until the earth shakes. As Sugden points out in his biography of the Shawnee leader, "The significant fact is not whether Tecumseh did or did not predict the earthquakes, but that the Creeks believed that he had done so. That belief was crucial, for it established Tecumseh's credibility. . . . There were extensive standing grievances against the United States; Tecumseh had sharpened that hostility, outlined a strategy, and claimed supernatural support; and the earthquakes proved that he was right. These were the three linked factors that took the [Creeks] into one of the most desperate Indian revolts in American history." (Sugden, *Tecumseh*, p. 251)

11   he raised the axe above his head: There are only two contemporaneous accounts of George's murder and its aftermath. The Livingston Circuit Court documents are the most informative and reliable. The other, a newspaper article in the *Kentucky Gazette* of May 12, 1812, contains no details of the murder itself. There are two other nineteenth-century sources. Thirteen years after the murder, Reverend William Dickey, a passionate abolitionist, wrote a letter luridly describing the event. (In *American Slavery As It Is,* Theodore D. Weld, comp., pp. 93–94) William Watts's 1897 book, *Chronicles of a Kentucky Settlement,* coyly changes all the names of the people involved. Both the Dickey and Watts versions contain some flagrant inaccuracies.

12   In North America: The proliferation of natural phenomena was most abundant in, but not strictly limited to, North America. On the last three days of January, the island of São Miguel in the Azores was shaken by a series of earthquakes. Then on February 1, a thunderous marine volcano erupted a mile offshore, spewing forth, in the words of an observer, "continually immense bodies of sparkling fire, beautifully variegated with every colour of the rainbow, intermixed with rising volumes of smoke, at the same time very large rocks are seen ascending to an astonishing height, till, their force being spent, they return with ever increasing velocity, to . . . their former watery station." The eruptions lasted about six days, and when the smoke cleared, a new island, about a mile in circumference, was seen at latitude 37°45', longitude 25°58', (*Lexington American Statesman,* Oct. 5, 1811, reprinted from the *Boston Palladium*).

12   The year was ushered in: *Pennsylvania Gazette,* Jan. 1, 1812.

12   "Between St. Louis and New Madrid": Drake, *Natural and Statistical View, or Picture of Cincinnati and the Miami Country,* p. 239. In *The Rambler in North America, 1822–23,* English traveler Charles J. Latrobe places the flood earlier in the year. "During the earlier months," Latrobe writes, "the waters of many of the great rivers overflowed their banks to a great extent, and the whole country was in many parts covered from bluff to bluff. Unprecedented sickness followed." (Vol. 1, p. 102) No doubt Drake, who witnessed the flood firsthand and wrote his account in 1815, is the more accurate source.

12   "In the summer months": *Kentucky Gazette,* May 12, 1812.

12   "more violent and destructive": *Lexington American Statesman,* Nov. 9, 1811.

13   In early September: The comet had first been discovered in Europe in March.

Napoleon took it as a sign that he was meant to invade Russia, which he did—with notoriously disastrous results.

13 "Anciently these sideral erratics": *Kentucky Gazette*, Oct. 15, 1811, italics in original.

13 "The day was remarkably serene": Ibid., May 12, 1812.

13 "A spirit of change and a restlessness": Latrobe, *Rambler in North America*. In *The New Madrid Earthquakes*, Penick, having found no contemporary corroboration of the squirrels' lemming-like migration, regards it as a tall tale. (pp. 12, 161) However, there is evidence that before the great forests disappeared, these migrations occurred periodically. In writing about the northern gray squirrel in *The Viviparous Quadrupeds of North America*, Audubon and Bachman state, "This species of squirrel has occasionally excited the wonder of the populace by its wandering habits and its singular and long migrations." (p. 200) They point out that these migrations usually occur in autumn. Similarly, Robert Kennicott, in "The Quadrupeds of Illinois," wrote, "The most interesting feature in the habits of this animal is the remarkable migration performed by large bodies of them. . . . Immense numbers congregate in autumn, and move off together, continuing their progress in the same general direction, whatever it may be, not even turning aside for large streams." (p. 64) From eyewitness accounts, Kennicott places the migrations at five-year intervals. The migration of 1811, therefore, while not unique, was significant enough to have been remembered by Latrobe's informants and associated with the many other singular events of the annus mirabilis.

13 "On the 30th of November, 1811": Pierce, *The Year: A Poem in Three Cantoes*, Appendix, p. 17.

13 "These are no common events": *Kentucky Gazette*, May 12, 1812.

14 "The great scale upon which Nature is operating": *Lexington American Statesman*, Dec. 17, 1811, italics in original.

14 "Whether these things are ominous or not": Carrigan to the Hon. Israel Pickens, quoted in Mitchill, "A Detailed Narrative of the Earthquakes," p. 300.

18 "The novel appearance of the vessel": Latrobe, *Rambler in North America*, Vol. 1, pp. 105–6.

18 somewhere around twelve miles per hour: Cincinnati's *Liberty Hall*, Oct. 30, 1811.

20 "the boisterous gaiety of the hands": Flint, *Recollections of the Last Ten Years*, pp. 103–5.

20 "The arrival of such a squadron": Hall, *Letters from the West*, p. 229.

20 One western traveler witnessed: The dialogue is from Schultz, *Travels on an Inland Voyage*, pp. 145–46, italics in original.

21 "the citizens, roused to indignation": Hall, *Letters from the West*, p. 229.

Chapter Two: A COUNTRY EQUAL TO OUR MOST SANGUINE WISHES
Page

26 George Morgan was a distinguished patriot: In April 1775, Morgan was in Philadelphia when news of the fighting at Lexington and Concord reached the city. He and his friends immediately formed themselves into a volunteer infantry

battalion, naming themselves "The Greens," presumably for their green uniform jackets. (Savelle, *George Morgan: Colony Builder*, p. 128) According to another of the company, however, the group was "sneeringly styled, *The silk-stocking company*, ... branded as an aristocratic assemblage. ... There were about seventy of us. We met morning and evening, and from the earnest and even enthusiastic devotion of most of us to learn the duties of soldiers, the company, in the course of a summer's training, became a truly respectable militia corps. When it had attained some adroitness in the exercises, we met but once a day. This was in the afternoon, and the place of rendezvous the house of our captain, where capacious demijohns of Madeira, were constantly set out in the yard where we formed, for our refreshment before marching out to exercise." (Graydon, *Memoirs of His Own Time*, pp. 122–23, italics in original)

When the company was dispatched to Boston the following spring, Captain Morgan stayed behind—with his knowledge of the west and expertise in commerce, as well as his familiarity with native languages and customs and the high esteem in which he was held by the Delaware people, the Continental Congress appointed Morgan Indian agent at Fort Pitt, where he was posted in April 1776. His instructions were to size up the attitudes of the western tribes toward the U.S.-Britain conflict and to enlist their neutrality for the remainder of the war, for any outbreak of hostilities with the native tribes in the west would seriously dilute the war efforts against the British in the east.

In January 1777, Morgan's duties were expanded to include management of the Fort Pitt commissary, and he was promoted to the rank of colonel. As commissariat, he was responsible for outfitting expeditions departing from the fort, for supplying the Continental troops garrisoned at forts scattered over nearly 350 miles of frontier, and for improving regional transportation to aid the war effort, which included building roads and boats. It was Morgan who, in the spring of 1776, first suggested that the revolutionaries could ship arms and supplies up the Mississippi and Ohio rivers from New Orleans. When Congress asked General Benedict Arnold to explore the possibility of an expedition against Pensacola in 1777, he in turn consulted George Morgan, and the following year, Congress solicited Colonel Morgan's opinion about the possibility of a projected expedition against Detroit.

In "George Morgan, His Family and Times," Julia Morgan Harding, a descendant, claimed that "Colonel Morgan was with Washington and his army during the terrible winter at Valley Forge as deputy commissary general." (*Washington* (Pa.) *Observer*, May 21, 1904) Similarly, in *History of Beaver County* (Pennsylvania), Bausman wrote that George Morgan "served throughout the Valley Forge campaign, and was at the siege of Yorktown." (p. 67, fn) However, Savelle's biography of Morgan contains no reference to Valley Forge, and Morgan is not mentioned in Reed's "Valley Forge Commissariat." Moreover, none of Morgan's letters from the winter of 1777–78 were written from Valley Forge.

26   "a man of education and refinement": Cuming, *Sketches of a Tour to the Western Country*, in Thwaites, *Early Western Travels: 1748–1846*, Vol. 4, p. 240.

26   "the first in America": Cutler, *Life, Journals and Correspondence of Rev. Manasseh Cutler, LL.D.*, Vol. 1, p. 246. Cutler gave a detailed description of Morgan's farm:

"His house stands . . . in a situation which commands a complete view of his whole farm, consisting of about 200 acres. Here I saw verified what I had before often heard observed, that the boundaries of his farm might be easily distinguished from his neighbors', from its high state of cultivation.

" . . . His garden consists of three acres, and is principally employed for making experiments, which appeared to be well judged and critically attended to. . . . In his garden he had Indian corn growing, in long rows, from different kinds of seed, collected from the different latitudes on this Continent, as far north as the most northern parts of Canada, and south as far as the West Indies. His Apiary struck me with astonishment. On the southern side of his garden he had 64 swarms of bees in a line, which I judged extended more than 15 rods. He takes the honey when he pleases, without destroying the bees."

Morgan's most significant contribution to agriculture was his study of the life cycle of the Hessian fly, an imported pest that had devastated the wheat crops of New York and Connecticut since 1778. Morgan spotted the fly in his vicinity in the spring of 1786; by the following autumn it had caused widespread damage in the area. Morgan began a series of experiments, breeding the fly and observing its life cycle to discover its habits, and he published his findings in several articles that aided in the effort to defeat the destructive insect. His papers on the Hessian fly were published in *The American Museum* (July 1787; Sep. 1787; July 1788). He also published articles on "bee-culture, the cultivation of flax, manures, the selection of seeds and the breeding of sheep and cattle." His essay for the Philadelphia Society on the organization of a barnyard was awarded a gold medal, and he wrote a paper for the Philadelphia Society for the Promotion of Agriculture in which he made "recommendations for a model and experimental farm which that society proposed to establish. He insisted that, contrary to popular belief, farming could be made profitable, and . . . he concluded that the chief reason for the failure of the American farmer lay in faulty organization and inefficiency." (Savelle, *George Morgan*, pp. 192–93)

27 George Washington, Benjamin Franklin: For a discussion of land speculation in early America, see Miller, *The Founding Finaglers*, pp. 59–73.

In the eighth edition (1814) of *The Navigator*, Zadok Cramer writes about some of the victims of land speculators. "GALLIOPOLIS, Is finely situated on a high second bank of the Ohio, in a fertile and extensive bottom, commanding a handsome view of the river. About twenty-five years ago, Galliopolis was settled by 100 French families, who had been lured here from favorable representations of the country, and the cheapness of the land they had purchased for settlement. Their titles proving bad, the inhabitants, reduced and mortified, were obliged to abandon their establishment of an intended city." (p. 101) He further notes, "THE honest and unsuspecting French inhabitants of Galliopolis are not the first victims to the wiles of land speculators. Our country presents a most lamentable history of the misfortunes of an honest, industrious people, willing to risk their lives and every thing they possessed, to enter the forest with axes on their shoulders, to clear fields and make improvements, as a home for themselves and a patrimony for their children after them. And after having exhausted, by labor and toil, incident to the settlement of a new country, the prime and vigor of life, what do they see enter their peaceful, and as they thought, secure doors, but *the sheriff with a writ of ejectment,* issued by a powerful land company, who, if they cannot frighten the settler off his land, frighten him into a compromise, by which he yields at least one-half his tract, and a great proportion of his labor, rather than be turned out of house and home altogether, by expensive lawsuits. The north-eastern part of Pennsylvania is a grievous witness of this, and Kentucky no better, if not still worse." (pp. 235–36, italics in original)

27   "Grimly," as one historian has written: Whitaker, *The Spanish-American Frontier: 1783–1795,* p. 32.

28   Before long, Gardoqui in New York: Among those submitting colonization proposals to the Spanish was Baron von Steuben, the Prussian mercenary who had served as a volunteer under George Washington at Valley Forge and was instrumental in developing the training manual for the Continental Army. Von Steuben wrote to Miró, "A combination of facts and reasonings, which has been amply unfolded to Don Diego de Gardoqui, the Minister from your Court, leaves me without a doubt, but that with the instruments and materials now in my choice and direction, I shall be able to form a barrier, on the Northern frontier of Louisiana and Florida, which shall be impenetrable to any assaults which may be expected to be made upon it." (Letter of March 16, 1788, *legajo* 3894, in the Papeles de Estado at the Archivo Histórico Nacional [hereafter AHN] in Madrid)

Another application came from Revolutionary War hero and famed Indian fighter George Rogers Clark, whose proposed site was a hundred-square-mile piece of land opposite the mouth of the Ohio River. In his letter of March 15, 1778, Clark wrote, "No property or person is safe under a government so weak and infirm as that of the United States, and as a result I have been induced to put into practice what I have for so long a time contemplated, of offering myself to the King of Spain with a numerous colony of desirable subjects." In James, *The Life of George Rogers Clark,* p. 393, original in the *Gardoqui Papers,* Vol. 1, pp. 269–72, in the Durrett Collection at the University of Chicago.

28   "Would it be consistent": Morgan to Gardoqui, Aug. 16, 1788, AHN, *legajo* 3894.

29   in the fall of 1767: Julia Morgan Harding incorrectly places the voyage in 1763. ("George Morgan") From the surviving fragment of a journal Morgan kept during the trip, it is clear that he set out on September 30, 1767. (Col. James Morgan, "Morgan's Journey Down the Mississippi in 1767," in *Report of the Eighth International Geographic Congress, 1904,* pp. 952–55)

29   "Permit me": Gardoqui to Morgan, Sep. 2, 1788, AHN, italics in original, legajo 3894.

30   The immigrants: While Morgan had remarkably advanced ideas with regard to Native Americans, he appears to have shared the prevailing attitudes of the ruling class of his day toward African-Americans. Early in his career, when he was the western agent for the Philadelphia firm of Baynton, Wharton and Morgan, one of the "articles" Morgan imported for sale in Illinois was slaves.

30   "As you seem anxious": Gardoqui to Morgan, date unknown, quoted in Houck, *The Spanish Regime in Missouri,* Vol. 1, p. 275, fn.

31   He printed and distributed handbills: The handbill was circulated widely and ruf-
      fled feathers in the U.S. corridors of power. When Gardoqui wrote to Count
      Floridablanca, the Spanish minister of state, "The sensible people of the United
      States are beginning to fear Morgan's colony, and there have been many, who in
      confidence have told me that I have been able to take advantage of an opportu-
      nity to alienate one of the most important and most loved men in the country," he
      may have been inflating his own importance, but there is no denying that
      Morgan's venture caused varying degrees of concern among prominent Ameri-
      cans. (Dec. 24, 1788, AHN *legajo* 3894)

         In January 1789, one J. Dawson wrote to Governor Beverly Randolph of Vir-
      ginia that Morgan's colony was situated in "a country as fine in soil and superior
      in trade to any in America," and that if the project went ahead, the United States
      would lose "many thousands of her best citizens. We have certain information
      that Morgan has already entered into engagements with the most reputable
      characters and the most useful farmers and tradesmen to go to New Madrid
      with him." (Palmer, *Calendar of Virginia State Papers*, Vol. 4, p. 555) Dawson
      pointed out that although the lands on the Ohio were rich, farmers there lacked
      a market, and this lack of commercial potential would cause many of the "best
      inhabitants on these waters" to emigrate. Worst of all, it would increase discon-
      tent in Kentucky, eventually leading to separation of the territory from the
      Union.

         James Madison mentioned Morgan's project to President-elect Washington,
      observing that some people were of the opinion "that emigrations to the Spanish
      territory will be enticed from Kentucky, as rapidly, as the allurements of the latter
      place have obtained them from the Atlantic States." *(The Writings of James Madi-
      son*, Hunt, ed., Vol. 5, p. 329) Madison later sent Washington a copy of Morgan's
      handbill, calling it "the most authentic & precise evidence of the Spanish project
      that has come to my knowledge." (Ibid., p. 331)

         In a letter to Thomas Jefferson, Madison called the scheme "silly . . . on the
      part of Spain. . . . But it clearly betrays the plan . . . of making the Mississippi the
      bait for a defection of the Western people. Some of the leaders in Kentucky are
      known to favor the idea of connection with Spain." (Ibid., p. 333)

         For his part, Jefferson was pleased with Morgan's idea: "I wish a hundred
      thousand of our inhabitants would accept the invitation. It will be the means of
      delivering to us peaceably [i.e., free access to the Mississippi] what may otherwise
      cost us a war." (Jefferson to Washington, *The Writings of Thomas Jefferson*, Ford,
      ed., Vol. 5, p. 316)

         And General Josiah Harmar, Commander of the U.S. Army in Ohio,
      ridiculed it outright: "The people are all taken with Colonel Morgans New
      Madrid—They are in my opinion Mad-rid indeed." (Harmar to Arthur St. Clair,
      May 8, 1789, in the Peter Force Collection, Library of Congress Manuscript
      Division [hereafter LC MSS])

32   "voyage on the Mississippi": Chevalier, *Society, Manners, and Politics in the United
      States*, p. 213.

32   one ill-fated boat carrying flour: Jordan, ed., "Notes of a Journey from Philadel-

phia to New Madrid, Tennessee, 1790," pp. 209–16, original in the Manuscript Division of the Historical Society of Pennsylvania.

32   In *The Navigator:* Cramer, *Navigator,* pp. 276, 37.

32   Johann Heckewälder: Heckewelder, "Narrative of John Heckewelder's Journey to the Wabash in 1792," p. 183.

33   Violent storms: A boat that Timothy Flint was on had already run aground, "narrowly escaped wreck" on a group of sawyers, and almost sank from a leak when it "encountered the severest storm of thunder, hail, and wind," that the writer had ever experienced:

> *Wherever the full force of the thundergust passed the river, it twisted the cotton trees in all directions, as though they had been rushes. No person, who is unacquainted with the Mississippi, can have an adequate idea of the roughness and agitation occasioned by a tempest, especially when the wind blows in a direction opposite to the current. Storms on it are at least as dangerous as they are on the sea. The waves came in on the running-boards, as they are called, of the boat, at times two feet deep. We were heavily laden, our boat an hundred feet keel, old and frail; the water gained upon us, notwithstanding all our efforts to bail and pump; and such was the violence of the wind and current, that it was all in vain to attempt to give the boat headway in any other direction, than to let her float before the wind, making no exertion, only to keep her bow across the waves. Two very large boats, that came in company with us from the mouth of the Ohio, that had been lashed together before the storm, unlashed as the storm commenced. The one went on a sawyer, and was dashed in pieces. She had been loaded with four or five hundred barrels of flour, porter, and whiskey, and the barrels were floating by us in all directions. The hands left the other, that was loaded in the same way, and she floated by us, sunk to the roof. We made every effort to run her on shore in vain. Nor did we ever ascertain what became of the hands of either boat. They probably all perished. For the water was over the banks from ten to twenty feet, and the width of this overflow was probably forty miles.* (Flint, *Recollections,* pp. 218–19)

Another harrowing account of a storm on the Mississippi is given by Collot in *A Journey in North America,* an account of his 1796 trip (Vol. 1, pp. 57–59).

33   "so heavy that we could not see": Col. James Morgan, "Morgan's Journey," p. 953.

34   A boat that got sucked into: Boatmen told a joke about a Kentucky flatboat that was drifting downriver at night when it passed a brightly lit plantation mansion where a grand ball was taking place. After a half hour of floating, the boat passed another magnificent party, and half an hour later, yet another. After a number more of these, the Kentuckian remarked, "Well, this is the beatenest country for frolicking I ever seed. The whole river is one universal jubilee." When dawn broke, the boatman discovered he'd spent the night in an eddy and gone around in circles seeing the same party all night (Shields, *Natchez: Its Early History,* p. 29).

34   "tore away all the frame-work": Forman, *Narrative of a Journey Down the Ohio and Mississippi in 1789–90,* p. 25.

34   "I think Jonas": In Hulbert, *The Ohio River: A Course of Empire,* pp. 237–38, location of original unknown.

35   "The inclemency of the season": *Legajo* 202, in the Papeles Procedentes de Cuba

at the Archivo General de Indias (hereafter AGI) in Seville. The letter is signed by George McCully, John Dodge, Peter Light, David Rankin, John Ward, Israel Shreve, John Stuart, and James Rhea, and transcribed by Samuel Stillman, Jr. ("A true copy of the original taken by me New Madrid April 14th 1789 Saml. Stillman Junr.). The letter was published in the *Virginia Gazette and Weekly Advertiser,* Aug. 27; Col. Shreve's name was omitted from the list of signers, and Samuel Stillman was called "Samuel Sellman."

36   "after maturely considering every circumstance": Ibid.

36   The site had first been settled: The entire region had been inhabited by indigenous people for thousands of years, as evidenced by the mounds that exist throughout the area. The mounds were built for ceremonial purposes by the Mississippian culture that flourished in the area from about A.D. 1000–1600. Legend has it that de Soto encountered these people in the New Madrid area on his trip up the Mississippi. Author Henry Brackenridge, wrote that about four miles from New Madrid was "one of the largest Indian mounds in the western country . . . twelve hundred feet in circumference, and about forty in height, level on the top, and surrounded with a ditch five feet deep and ten wide." *(Views of Louisiana,* p. 130) Today, two mounds still exist adjacent to the town.

36   They named the place L'Anse à la Graisse: In 1796, Pierre La Forge, civil commandant of New Madrid, wrote that the early traders "found abundance of game, and especially bears and buffaloes, hence the name, l'anse a la graisse." (Quoted in Billon's *Annals of St. Louis in Its Early Days Under the French and Spanish Dominations, 1764–1804,* p. 264) In *A Tour Through the Southern and Western Territories of the United States of North-America,* John Pope claimed that the name came from the "great Quantities of Bear-Meat [that] were stored up for the Use of the Garrison and the *French* and *Spanish* Navigators up and down the *Mississippi,* which Meat is of a very oleose Quality, though in my Opinion the greasiness of the Soil, with the Devexity of the River, sufficiently justify the Epithet." (pp. 21–22, italics in original)

36   "The country rises gradually": Letter of April 14, 1789, *legajo* 202, AGI.

37   "General Directions for Settlement at New Madrid": Houck, in *The Spanish Regime in Missouri,* writes that "Morgan's plan for the survey of the lands of his supposed colony is highly interesting, because in 1796 it was in effect adopted by the United States in making a survey of the lands north of the Ohio. The second section of the act follows the exact words of Morgan's instruction. . . . In fact the whole system of a rectangular survey of the public lands as developed in the act can be traced to Morgan's plan of surveying the lands of his supposed colony as outlined in these instructions." (Vol. 1, pp. 300–301, fn)

37   His directions to surveyors: "General Directions for Settlement at New Madrid," Apr. 6, 1789, George Morgan Papers, LC MSS.

Chapter Three: DISAPPOINTMENTS AND SUFFERINGS

Page

41   "ever saw who was": John Randolph to Joseph Nicholson, June 25, 1807, in Nicholson Papers (LC MSS).

41   "unprincipled imbecile": Scott, *Memoirs of Lieut.-General Scott, LL.D,* Vol. 1, p. 94, fn.

41   "the worst of all bad men": Anthony Wayne, quoted in Knopf, ed., *Anthony Wayne, A Name in Arms,* p. 506.

41   "Some men are sordid": Wilkinson to Gardoqui, Jan. 1, 1789, in Fortier, *A History of Louisiana,* Vol. 2, p. 142, location of original unknown.

43   The following day: "Memorial," *legajo* 2373, AGI, italics in original.

44   Wilkinson also submitted to Miró a "Declaration": *Legajo* 2373, AGI.

45   It did not take very long: For two contemporary accusations against Wilkinson, see Daniel Clark, *Proofs of the Corruption of Gen. James Wilkinson;* and Bodley, ed., *Littell's Political Transactions in and Concerning Kentucky.*

45   The depths of Wilkinson's treachery: For two good discussions of Wilkinson's motives in this affair, see Bodley, Introduction to *Littell's Political Transactions in and Concerning Kentucky,* and Christian, "General James Wilkinson and Kentucky Separatism, 1784–1798."

46   "It was the usual practice": Charles Wilkins to Judge Harry Innes, in Verhoef, *The Kentucky River Navigation,* pp. 224–25. The letter goes on to state, "Various modes were adopted to evade the payment of duties by adventurers to New Orleans, and it was practiced by others as well as myself, to petition the Governor for a grant of land under the pretense of becoming an inhabitant & I was induced to believe that the mildness of his Catholic Majesty's Colonial government was always spoken of with praise."

46   some of it in cipher or code: In *legajo* 2373, AGI, there are three lengthy dictionaries of code containing a total of approximately six thousand entries including words, proper names, place names, days of the week, and months of the year. There is also a cipher alphabet employed by Wilkinson in communications to Miró.

46   where conditions continued to be volatile: In one letter to Miró, Wilkinson told of his role in foiling a plot involving Dr. John Connolly in October 1788. Connolly was an American who had fought for the British during the Revolutionary War and had been captured and imprisoned by the Americans. In his letter, Wilkinson wrote about gaining Connolly's confidence to discover that Great Britain was willing to assist western Americans in wrestling Louisiana from Spain. British forces in Canada were not strong enough, so Connolly had been empowered by Lord Dorchester, the British governor of Canada, to raise an army and confer commissions in Kentucky. Connolly reportedly told Wilkinson that Dorchester would "furnish implements of War, pay & cloathing for ten thousand men if we [i.e., Kentuckians] would undertake the Enterprize." Wilkinson informed him that it would not be easy to enlist Americans into an alliance with England, given the history of relations between the two countries. Wilkinson then engaged a hunter to feign an attempt on Connolly's life, after which he pretended to have the hunter arrested. Frightened for his safety, Connolly begged Wilkinson for an escort out of Kentucky, which the latter provided once Connolly promised to keep him informed of any further plotting on Dorchester's part. (Wilkinson to Miró, Feb. 12, 1789, *legajo* 2373, AGI)

46   "I must proceed with caution": Ibid.

47 "I can solemnly assure you": Ibid, italics in original.

47 "The traitor's scheme": Bodley, *Littell's Political Transactions*, p. xli.

47 "goes north of the Ohio": Dunn to Wilkinson, Nov. 1788, in the James Wilkinson Papers, Chicago Historical Society.

48 "has hurried": Wilkinson to Miró, Feb. 12, 1789, *legajo* 2373, AGI.

48 "This Colonel Morgan": Wilkinson to Miró, Feb. 14, 1789, *legajo* 2373, AGI.

49 "Now you will see": Miró to Morgan, May 23, 1789, *legajo* 202, AGI, italics in original.

50 "The name given to the Settlement": Morgan to Miró, May 23, 1789, *legajo* 202, AGI.

51 "I do not believe his Excellency": Morgan to Gardoqui, Aug. 20, 1789, George Morgan Papers, LC MSS.

51 it contained several provisions: Never one to give up easily, Wilkinson continued to connive with Miró for a couple of years, tapping the Spaniard's largesse for whatever he could finagle. He continued to draw his $2,000 annual pension, and also demanded and received a $7,000 "loan" to finance his continued efforts to promote Kentucky's secession. All the while, Wilkinson played out the cloak-and-dagger affair as far as it would go. "I have the best authority to say," he wrote Miró early in 1790, "that my connexion with you is strongly suspected by the Congress, & they have spys on my motion in this country. . . .

"[B]e certain to write every word in Cipher as you may be assured I am narrowly watched by the servants of General Washington." (Wilkinson to Miró, Jan. 26, 1790, *legajo* 2374, AGI.)

But by 1791, when Miró was replaced as governor, he had tired of Wilkinson's game and was no longer supporting his opportunistic schemes, although Wilkinson continued to receive his $2,000 per year. A series of disastrous commercial ventures had brought Wilkinson to the brink of bankruptcy, and now he was forced to sell his house and land to pay off his considerable debts. Faced with ruin—aside from the $7,000 loan from Miró, the $2,000 annual pension from Spain had been his only income—Wilkinson once again accepted a commission in the U.S. army. On October 22, 1791, George Washington appointed him to the rank of lieutenant colonel commandant of the Second United States Infantry. The fact that Wilkinson was still collecting his $2,000 annual pension from Spain did not stop him from accepting the commission as commander of the western army; conversely, his new post—the assumption of which included an oath of allegiance to the United States—did not induce him to renounce his Spanish pension. No doubt, Wilkinson saw his new situation as the best of both worlds. With his new duties, however, Wilkinson lost interest in the Spanish Conspiracy for the time being (see note, Chapter 13, p. 272, "Wilkinson had spent his time since the Spanish Conspiracy."). But the damage to George Morgan's dreams had already been done.

52 the Spaniards' liberal immigration policy: In Harmar's May 8, 1789, letter to St. Clair, written from Fort Harmar on the Ohio River, he said, "The Emigration continues if possible more rapid than ever—Within these 20 days not less than one hundred souls have passed daily." (Peter Force Collection, LC MSS)

52   "two or three hundred houses": Baily, *Journal of a Tour in Unsettled Parts of North America, in 1796 & 1797*, p. 136.

52   In 1796, an eight-page promotional tract: de Hault Delassus, *An Official Account of the Situation, Soil, Produce, &c. of that part of Louisiana which lies between the mouth of the Missouri and New Madrid, or L'Anse a la Graise, and on the west side of the Mississippi*, in Library of Congress Rare Book Room.

53   "inhabitants were the first along the river": Alliot, *Historical and Political Reflections on Louisiana*, p. 133.

53   the Treaty of San Lorenzo: In addition to opening the Mississippi to U.S. citizens, the Treaty of San Lorenzo also established the 31st parallel as the southern border of the United States.

53   "Col. Morgans settlement on the mississippi": Hawkins to Madison, Aug. 27, 1789, in *The Papers of James Madison*, Rutland, et al., eds., Vol. 12, pp. 358–59.

53   "putrid fevers and agues": Collot, *Journey in North America*, Vol. 2, p. 18.

54   "Nothing can hinder": Ibid., pp. 17–18.

54   "at least three hundred yards": Brackenridge, *Views of Louisiana*, p. 129.

54   "the cheerful little town": Hildreth, "History of a Voyage from Marietta to New Orleans, in 1805," p. 128.

54   "I must give you": Ashe, *Travels in America Performed in 1806*, p. 296.

55   "It is the residence": Brackenridge, *Views of Louisiana*, p. 129.

55   The New Madrid area: There were also a number of Native Americans living around New Madrid. At Cape Girardeau, fifty miles north, there was a sizable settlement of Shawnee and Delaware who had accepted the Spanish government's invitation to relocate after the American Revolution. It was probably delegates from this group that accompanied George Morgan on his visit to the Spanish commandant at St. Louis.

55   "I have heard particulars": Flint, *Recollections*, p. 221.

Chapter Four: ONE OF THOSE UNCOMMON GENIUSES

Page

60   Indiana Territory governor William Henry Harrison: In 1800, the Old Northwest Territory had been divided into the Ohio Territory and the Indiana Territory.

60   "Your father invites you to be seated": Joseph McCormick interviewed by Lyman Draper, Tecumseh Papers, State Historical Society of Wisconsin: Lyman Draper Manuscripts (hereafter SHSW:LDM), 3YY109 (indicates Vol. 3, series YY, p. 109).

60   "Governor Harrison is not my father": Augustus Jones to Draper, Feb. 4, 1885, Tecumseh Papers, SHSW:LDM, 3YY107.

61   "The effect": Law, *The Colonial History of Vincennes*, p. 84.

61   "under a clear sky, and in an open path": Ibid., p. 85.

62   "with a freedom and sense": Badollet to Gallatin, Sep. 25, 1810, in *The Correspondence of John Badollet and Albert Gallatin, 1804–1836*, Thornbrough, ed., p. 168.

62   "There are unfortunately too many of them": Harrison to Eustis, Aug. 22, 1810, in *Messages and Letters of William Henry Harrison*, Esarey, ed., Vol. 1, p. 460.

62   "the great man of the party": Ibid.

62   *Brother,* I wish you": Ibid., pp. 463–67.

63   "Those fellows intend mischief.": Dawson, *A Historical Narrative of the Civil and Military Services of Major-General William H. Harrison,* p. 156.

64   "I am alone the acknowledged head": Harrison to Eustis, Aug. 22, 1810, in Esarey, *Messages and Letters,* Vol. 1, p. 469.

64   "Well," he said: Dawson, *Historical Narrative,* p. 159.

65   "one of the finest looking men I ever saw": Floyd to his wife, Aug. 14, 1810, Tecumseh Papers, SHSW:LDM, 2YY118.

65   "This great chief": Anon., *The History of Madison County, Ohio,* p. 287.

65   "His house was always supplied": Anthony Shane interviewed by Benjamin Drake, 1821, Tecumseh Papers, SHSW:LDM, 2YY58.

65   "Tecumtheth was always remarkable": Stephen Ruddell narrative, Jan. 1822, Tecumseh Papers, SHSW:LDM, 2YY122.

65   "The implicit obedience": Harrison to Secretary of War Eustis, Aug. 7, 1811, in Esarey, ed., *Messages and Letters,* Vol. 1, p. 549.

66   "when prisoners fell into his hands": Ruddell narrative, p. 123.

66   "About dark": James Galloway to Drake, Jan. 29, 1841, Frontier War Papers, SHSW:LDM, 7U84[2] (superscript numbers indicate subsidiary pagination). As this incident indicates, Tecumseh spoke and understood some English.

66   "a great publick speaker": Statement of Johnston, Tecumseh Papers, SHSW:LDM, 11YY17.

66   "naturally eloquent": Ruddell narrative, p. 132.

66   "Arrogance, impulsiveness": Sugden, *Tecumseh,* p. 96.

67   Tecumseh's younger brother Tenskwatawa: The two brothers could not have been more different. Unlike the handsome Tecumseh, Tenskwatawa was an unattractive man whose homeliness was heightened by a childhood accident that left him blind in his right eye, which was thereafter permanently closed. Tecumseh was the embodiment of Shawnee manhood—a skilled hunter, courageous warrior, and eloquent orator, a born leader who exemplified the Shawnee virtues of generosity, dignity, and integrity. Tenskwatawa, at least before his vision, was a failure, an object of disdain, a man with no standing in the tribe. He was a loud-mouthed braggart, a poor hunter, an inadequate warrior, and a shameless, incorrigible alcoholic. His only positive aspect was the training given him by an old, well-respected medicine man and prophet.

67   The brothers were heirs: For a discussion of earlier pan-tribal movements, see Dowd, *A Spirited Resistance: The North American Indian Struggle for Unity, 1745–1815.*

68   "Brothers," wrote Wells in a letter: Wells to the Shawnees residing at Greenville, Apr. 22, 1807, National Archives (hereafter NA), Secretary of War/Letters Received/Registered (hereafter SoW/LR/R), Record Group 107, Microfilm M 221, Reel 14.

69   "I really fear": Harrison to Dearborn, July 11, 1807, in Esarey, *Messages and Letters,* Vol. 1, p. 223.

69   "entirely devoted": Harrison to Dearborn, Aug. 29, 1807, ibid., p. 243.

69   "My children it must be stopped": Harrison to Shawnees, Aug. 1807, ibid., pp. 249–51.

69   "The discontent of the Indians": McKee to William Halton, June 11, 1807, Canada/Indian Affairs Papers, Record Group 10, Vol. 2, p. 627, National Archives of Canada, Ottawa; quoted in Sugden, *Tecumseh*, p. 157, original not seen.

70   "This is the first reguest": JOURNAL OF THE PROCEEDINGS at the Indian Treaty at Fort Wayne and Vincennes, Sep. 1 to Oct. 27, 1809, in Esarey, *Messages and Letters*, Vol. 1, p. 368.

71   "yet but very little harm done": Harrison to The Prophet, July 19, 1810, in ibid., p. 448.

72   "The Great Spirit said": Harrison to Eustis, Aug. 6, 1810, in ibid., p. 457.

72   "This brother": Ibid., p. 456.

Chapter Five: THE IMPENDING DESTRUCTION

Page

73   "there is not at present": Harrison to Eustis, Dec. 24, 1810, in Esarey, *Messages and Letters*, Vol. 1, p. 497.

74   "the time is drawing near": "Part of Several Speeches Delivered to Gen. Clark at St. Louis by the Ioways," May 1811, NA, SoW/LR/R, Record Group 107, Microfilm M 221, Reel 35.

74   "Do you really think": Harrison to Tecumseh, June 24, 1811, in Esarey, *Messages and Letters*, Vol. 1, p. 522. Despite his tough talk, Harrison recognized the potential threat of Tecumseh's efforts to unite the nations. A week after writing to Tecumseh, he told Eustis, "If some decisive measures are not speedily adopted we shall have a general combination of all the Tribes against us." (Ibid., p. 526)

75   "with difficulty": Badollet to Gallatin, Aug. 6, 1811, in *The Correspondence of John Badollet and Albert Gallatin, 1804–1836*, p. 187.

76   "would put his warriors in petticoats": Harrison to Eustis, Aug. 6, 1811, in Esarey, *Messages and Letters*, Vol. 1, p. 545.

76   "The more I think of that man": Badollet to Gallatin, Aug. 6, 1811, *Correspondence*, p. 184.

76   "one of those uncommon geniuses": Harrison to Eustis, Aug. 7, 1811, Esarey, *Messages and Letters*, Vol. 1, p. 549.

76   "If the prophet should commence": Eustis to Harrison, July 17, 1811, ibid., p. 536.

76   "been particularly instructed": Ibid., p. 537.

77   "There can be no doubt": Harrison to Eustis, Aug. 7, 1811, ibid., p. 549.

77   "expedition about the 20th. of Sept.": Harrison to Bissell, Aug. 19, 1811, ibid., p. 552.

77   Ninian Edwards of Illinois: The Illinois Territory had been created out of the Indiana Territory in 1809.

77   "I consider peace": Edwards to Eustis, July 6, 1811, in *American State Papers, Indian Affairs* (hereafter *ASPIA*), Vol. 1, p. 800.

77   "the President may rest assured": Harrison to Eustis, Aug. 13, 1811, in Esarey, *Messages and Letters*, Vol. 1, p. 554.

78   "extirpation or forcible removal": Badollet to Gallatin, Aug. 6, 1811, *The Correspondence of John Badollet and Albert Gallatin, 1804–1836*, p. 187.

78   *"My Children.":* Harrison to the Miami, Eel River and Wea Tribes, enclosed in Harrison to Eustis, Sep. 17, 1811, in Esarey, *Messages and Letters*, Vol. 1, pp. 576–77.

78   *"Father* Your speech": Speech of Laprusieur, ibid., pp. 578–79.

79   "the war that may be waged": Harrison to Johnston, no date, ibid., p. 584.

79   "I had always supposed": Harrison to Eustis, Oct. 13, 1811, ibid., p. 599.

79   "A few companies more": Ibid.

79   "lay aside his hostile designs": Harrison to Eustis, Oct. 29, 1811, ibid., pp. 604–5.

81   "on their arms": Col. John Boyd to Richard Cutts, Dec. 16, 1811, W. H. Smith Memorial Library, Collection No. M11, Bx. 2, Indiana Historical Society.

83   "the Indians have never sustained": Harrison to Eustis, Dec. 4, 1811, in *ASPIA*, Vol. 1, p. 789.

83   "I think upon the whole": Harrison to Eustis, Nov. 18, 1811, in Esarey, *Messages and Letters*, Vol. 1, p. 629.

83   "a gentleman in Vincennes to his friend": "Extract of a letter from a gentleman in Vincennes to his friend in this place," *Lexington American Statesman*, Nov. 16, 1811.

84   "not come there to ask their permission": *Republican and Savannah Evening Ledger*, Oct. 17, 1811.

Chapter Six: THE BLOODY GROUND

Page

88   By the time of the Louisiana Purchase: The following year, New Jersey also outlawed slavery.

88   "the enjoyment of all the rights": Louisiana Purchase treaty in Kukla, *A Wilderness So Immense*, p. 351.

89   the Lewises of Albemarle County: The definitive book on the Lewis case is *Jefferson's Nephews* by Boynton Merrill, Jr. Robert Penn Warren's verse dialogue, *Brother to Dragons*, is also based on the case.

90   "C. L. Lewis my brother in law": Jefferson to Philip Mazzei, Jan. 7, 1792, "The Unpublished Correspondence of Jefferson and Adams to Mazzei," *The Virginia Magazine of History and Biography* 51, p. 119, original in Mazzei Archives, Pisa, Italy.

90   these men were an easygoing: An idea of the general character of this class of men may be gained from a description by Lieutenant Thomas Anburey, who, as a British prisoner during the Revolution, was permitted to travel freely provided he stayed within a hundred miles of Charlottesville. In *Travels Through the Interior Parts of America*, Anburey referred to Virginia planters as "abominably lazy," noting that most of them hired overseers to take care of their business affairs because they considered the supervision of such matters "beneath their dignity." Anburey went on to

describe a day in the life of a typical Virginia plantation owner: "He rises about eight o'clock, drinks what he calls a julep, which is a large glass of rum, sweetened with sugar, and then walks, or more generally rides around his plantation, views his stock, inspects his crops, and returns about ten o'clock to breakfast on cold meat, or ham, fried hommony, toast and cider. . . . He then saunters about the house, sometimes amusing himself with the little negroes who are playing round the door, or else scraping on a fiddle; about twelve or one he drinks toddy, to create him an appetite for dinner, which he sits down to at two o'clock; after he has dined, he generally lays down on the bed, and rises about five, then perhaps sips some tea with his wife, but commonly drinks toddy till bed time; during all this he is neither drunk nor sober, but in a state of stupefaction; this is his usual mode of living, which he seldom varies, and only quits his plantation to attend the Court-House on court days, or to some horse race or cock fight; at which times he gets so egregiously drunk, that his wife sends a couple of negroes to conduct him safe home."

Despite their vices, Anburey did concede that Virginians were "hospitable, generous, and friendly." (Vol. 2, pp. 328–30)

91   "extremely fond of society": Burnaby, *Travels Through the Middle Settlements in North-America*, pp. 22–25. In a footnote, Burnaby acknowledged that his characterization of Virginia's ruling class was not universal: "General characters are always liable to many exceptions. In Virginia I have had the pleasure to know several gentlemen adorned with many virtues and accomplishments, to whom the . . . description is by no means applicable."

91   "I have studied their character": Jefferson to Chastellux, Sep. 2, 1785, in *The Papers of Thomas Jefferson*, Boyd, ed., Vol. 8, p. 468.

91   "It is a culture": Jefferson, *Notes on the State of Virginia*, Peden, ed., pp. 166–68.

91   "The unprofitable condition": Jefferson to Mary Jefferson Eppes, in Randolph, *The Domestic Life of Thomas Jefferson*, p. 208.

92   "taciturn, moody": Pool, "Tragedies in Livingston."

92   "to say the least": Watts, *Chronicles*, p. 224.

92   "hypochondriac affections": Jefferson, "Memoir of Meriwether Lewis," in Clark and Lewis, *The History of the Lewis and Clark Expedition*, Vol. 1, p. xxxix.

92   "simple-minded": Schachner, *Thomas Jefferson: A Biography*, p. 65.

92   "The Randolphs were all strange people.": Pierson, *Jefferson at Monticello: The Private Life of Thomas Jefferson*, in *Jefferson at Monticello*, Bear, ed., p. 90.

94   "the bloody Ground": *Calendar of Virginia State Papers*, Palmer, ed., Vol. 1, p. 283.

94   "Here many refugees": Cartwright, *Autobiography of Peter Cartwright, the Backwoods Preacher*, W. P. Strickland, ed., pp. 24–25.

94   "did unlawfully make": Livingston Circuit Court Bundles, Sep. 1810.

94   "being a wicked and evil disposed person": Ibid.

95   "A frightfully cruel practice": Nolte, *Fifty Years in Both Hemispheres*, p. 179, italics in original.

95   "not now so common as formerly": Melish, *Travels Through the United States of America*, Vol. 2, p. 180, italics in original.

95   "an exceeding bad wound": Coroner's jury report, Dec. 9, 1804, Livingston Cir-

cuit Court Bundles, Dec. 1804, quoted in Merrill, *Jefferson's Nephews*, p. 239, original not seen.

95 "No slave shall go": Littell and Swigert, *A Digest of the Statute Law of Kentucky*, Vol. 2, p. 1150.

96 "receive, on his or her back": Ibid., p. 1160.

96 "with hands, fists": Livingston Circuit Court Bundles, June 1810.

96 "wholly lost the services": Ibid.

98 "hawked about the streets": Beverly L. Clarke, speaking at the Kentucky constitutional convention of 1849, *Report of the Debates and Proceedings of the Convention for the Revision of the Constitution of the State of Kentucky, 1849*, p. 387.

98 "committing a riot": Livingston Circuit Court (Court of Quarter Sessions) Order Book B, Feb. 25, 1801, pp. 10–11.

98 "A more miserable looking place": Evans, *Evans's Pedestrious Tour of Four Thousand Miles—1818*, p. 176.

99 Elizabeth, his wife of twelve years: There is no record of what caused her death. Childbirth is a reasonable surmise.

99 "our commerce is embarrassed": *Journal of the House of Representatives of the Commonwealth of Kentucky*, p. 72.

101 "a very beautiful young lady": Watts, *Chronicles*, p. 194.

101 "accomplished": Pool, "Tragedies in Livingston."

101 "cold, proud": Ibid.

102 "brought on not from my own imprudences": Isham Lewis to Jefferson, Apr. 27, 1809, Thomas Jefferson Papers, Massachusetts Historical Society.

102 "The public lands": Jefferson to Isham Lewis, May 1, 1809, Missouri Historical Society.

102 "shipwreck of the fortunes of his family": Jefferson to Gideon Fitch, May 23, 1809, Thomas Jefferson Papers, Massachusetts Historical Society.

Chapter Seven: THE MONSTER OF THE WATERS

Page

105 "directions for navigating": Cramer, *Navigator,* title page.

106 "must open to view": Ibid., p. 32.

106 "immensity of country": Ibid., p. 33.

106 "ere long have steam boats": Ibid., p. 31.

107 "of pieces of shingle": J. H. B. Latrobe, *A Lost Chapter in the History of the Steamboat*, p. 15.

108 "a double steam Engine": Patent papers and application are in the Franklin D. Roosevelt Presidential Library, Hyde Park, N.Y.

110 "Mr. Stevens mentioned to me": J. H. B. Latrobe, *Lost Chapter,* p. 17.

110 "recommend that we throw": Ibid., p. 35.

111 "I hope to hear your opinion": Ibid., p. 38.

111 "I say nothing": Ibid., p. 39.

111   "be contrasted with paddles": Ibid., pp. 40–41.

111   "as for vertical wheels": Ibid., p. 41.

113   "a broken man": Ibid., p. 33.

114   "a fine sensible young woman": Benjamin Latrobe to Christian Latrobe, Feb. 6, 1805, quoted in Hamlin, *Benjamin Henry Latrobe,* p. 225.

114   "an excellent housekeeper": Benjamin Latrobe to Roosevelt, July 1, 1805, in *The Papers of Benjamin Henry Latrobe,* Carter and Jeffrey, eds.

114   "a man of exceptionally good moral character": Benjamin Latrobe to Christian, May 18, 1805, in *The Correspondence and Miscellaneous Papers of Benjamin Henry Latrobe,* Van Horne, ed., Vol. 2, p. 76.

114   "talk over all our matters": Benjamin Latrobe to Roosevelt, Dec. 17, 1804, in Carter and Jeffrey, eds., *Papers of Benjamin Henry Latrobe,* italics in original.

115   "to break off the connexion": Benjamin Latrobe to Christian, May 18, 1805, *Correspondence and Miscellaneous Papers,* Van Horne, ed., Vol. 2, p. 76.

115   "he was not to be compared": Benjamin Latrobe to Isaac Hazlehurst, no date given, quoted in Hamlin, *Benjamin Henry Latrobe,* p. 230.

116   "Fulton I respect and love": Benjamin Latrobe to Lydia, May 11, 1809, in Van Horne, ed., *Correspondence and Miscellaneous Papers,* Vol. 2, p. 715.

117   "enveloped in thick clouds of smoke": Cramer, *Navigator,* p. 49.

117   "descends in fine dust": Ibid., p. 69.

119   "necessary comforts": J. H. B. Latrobe, *The First Steamboat Voyage on the Western Waters,* p. 7.

119   "comfortable bed room": Letter from Lydia Roosevelt to J. H. B. Latrobe, quoted in ibid., p. 7, fn.

120   "cooked & baked": Benjamin Latrobe to Robert Fulton, Feb. 1, 1813, in Carter and Jeffrey, eds., *Papers of Benjamin Henry Latrobe.*

121   "they would have gone to the bottom": Ibid.

121   "refused all applications": Lydia Roosevelt to J. H. B. Latrobe, *First Steamboat Voyage,* p. 10, fn.

121   "pouring rain came up": Ibid., pp. 10–11, fn.

122   "fancying every moment": Ibid., p. 11, fn.

123   "the largest vessel I had ever seen": Melish, *Travels Through the United States,* Vol. 2, p. 60.

123   "built with the best materials": *Pittsburgh Gazette,* Oct. 18, 1811.

123   "fully answers the most sanguine expectations": Ibid.

124   "a captain, an engineer named [Nicholas] Baker": J. H. B. Latrobe, *First Steamboat Voyage,* p. 14.

124   "built after the fashion of a ship": *American Railroad Journal,* July 26, 1851 (reprinted from the *Cincinnati Chronicle*).

124   "elegant, and accommodations for passengers not surpassed": *Pittsburgh Gazette,* Oct. 18, 1811.

125   fear of an engine explosion: Steam engines were notorious for their tendency to blow up. When Benjamin Latrobe and Roosevelt were engaged in building the water delivery system for the city of Philadelphia, an irate citizen wrote to the

Philadelphia Gazette to protest the recklessness of the project, complaining that "steam engines . . . are machines of all machinery the least to be relied on, subject to casualties and accidents of every kind." (July 31, 1800) Three decades later, when steamboats had become the primary mode of transportation on the western waters, French traveler Michel Chevalier found, "Explosions of the boilers are frequent, either on account of the ignorance and lack of skill of the engineers, or on account of the defective nature of the boilers themselves, and they are always attended with serious injury." (Chevalier, *Society, Manners and Politics*, p. 213) Of the nearly two thousand deaths from steamboat accidents before 1840, two thirds were caused by fire.

125 "The regular working of the engine": J. H. B. Latrobe, *First Steamboat Voyage*, pp. 14–15.

125 "in fine stile": *Liberty Hall*, Oct. 30, 1811.

125 "Her appearance was very elegant": *Western Sun*, Nov. 30, 1811, reprinted from *"Cincin. pap."*

126 "The British are coming": Philip Bush to Orlando Brown, July 9, 1862, in the Orlando Brown Papers, Filson Historical Society Library.

128 single most perilous obstacle: In 1797, Kentucky passed an act creating the office of Falls Pilot, to be appointed by the Jefferson County Court. As stated in the Preamble, the law was created, "Whereas great inconveniences have been experienced and many boats lost in attempting to pass the rapids of the Ohio for want of a Pilot, and from persons offering their services to act as Pilots, by no means qualified for this business." (quoted in Leahy, *Who's Who on the Ohio River and Its Tributaries*, p. 61) The regulation established the Falls Pilot's fee at $2, and assessed a penalty of $10 against any other person offering to act as a pilot. In March 1802, Falls Pilot James Patten, licensed by Kentucky to guide boats through the rapids, placed the following "Notice" in Pittsburgh's *Tree of Liberty* alerting the unsuspecting about another pilot who resided on the other side of the river. "THIS is to caution all persons who navigate the river Ohio," warned Patten, "that a certain ANTON BOMAN living in the Indiana Territory has undertaken to Pilot Boats through the Rapids without any authority and damages many Boats—and as I am authorized by the State of Kentucky, to prevent impositions on strangers, I hope every person who wishes to pass the Rapids will land on this side of the River, where the greatest attention shall be given to their safe passage." (*Tree of Liberty*, May 1, 1802)

128 "Frequent experiments of her performance": *Liberty Hall*, Nov. 21, 1811.

129 "an object of much curiosity": *Liberty Hall*, Dec. 4, 1811.

129 Today, a canal on the Kentucky side: As early as the beginning of the eighteenth century, there was talk of building a canal to make the Falls more passable. Yet the first canal and lock, on the Kentucky side of the river, would not be opened until December 1830, and it has had to be widened, with larger locks, ever since, in order to accommodate changes in the shipping industry. In the 1920s, a hydroelectric dam was added to the canal works, and even today, improvements and updates to the canal continue to be made.

Chapter Eight: ALL NATURE WAS IN A STATE OF DISSOLUTION

Page

137   "a balmy Indian summer": Quoted in Dudley, "The Earthquake of 1811 at New Madrid, Missouri," p. 423.

137   "the discharge of heavy artillery": Quoted in Korn, "Major Benjamin Holliday, 1768–1859," p. 18.

137   "complete saturation of the atmosphere": Bryan, letter to Lorenzo Dow, in *History of Cosmopolite*, p. 344. The strong "sulphurious" odor, which many eyewitnesses mention as having pervaded the air, almost certainly came from buried organic matter, including lignite, that was ejected from the depths of the earth. Some commentators have speculated that the smell may have been petroleum, an unfamiliar odor in the early nineteenth century, but whatever petroleum exists in the area is buried far too deep to have been expelled during the earthquakes.

138   "determined to rescue it": Musick, *Stories of Missouri*, p. 147.

138   "pale, sickly flashes of lightning": The question of lightning flashes is problematic. No satisfactory explanation has been produced for the frequently reported phenomenon of "earthquake lights." Most theories that attempt to account for the occurrence of earthquake lights—piezoelectric effect (certain types of crystal and quartz luminesce when deformed), ignition of swamp gas (methane), exoelectrons (electrons are released by the stress perturbation and they ionize)—do not match the observations because they are all dependent on the earthquake fault being at the surface of the ground and the observations of earthquake lights being at or near the surface trace of the fault. But most earthquake light observations are far removed from the fault, some of them more than fifty miles away, and many are near or over water, even out at sea.

   In 1990, Arch Johnston, director of the Center for Earthquake Research and Information at the University of Memphis, speculated that earthquake lights could be a result of sonoluminescence, a poorly understood phenomenon in which sound energy is transformed into light energy. In sonoluminescence, bubbles in a fluid are bombarded by a massive sound wave, and the tremendous concentration of energy sets off a flash of light. Recent developments in research have increased the plausibility of sonoluminescence as a possible explanation for earthquake lights.

138   "where the cries": Musick, *Stories of Missouri*, p. 148.

138   "solemn supplication": Account of A. N. Dillard in J. W. Foster, *The Mississippi Valley*, p. 20.

138   "no sun shone on us": Musick, *Stories of Missouri*, p. 148.

139   "confusion, terror and uproar presided": Pierce, *An Account of the Great Earthquakes*, p. 11.

139   "[T]he earth seemed convulsed": "Extracts from a letter to a gentleman in Lexington from his friend at N. Madrid," *The Reporter* (Lexington, Ky.), Feb. 1, 1812.

139   "rolling in waves": Campbell, *Campbell's Gazetteer of Missouri*, p. 395. Lesieur's claim brings up an interesting issue. There are several phenomena associated with earthquakes that struggle for a scientific explanation, and visible earth waves are

one of them. Although this phenomenon is frequently reported by earthquake witnesses around the world, there simply is no explanation for it. In fact, in later examining the site of an earthquake where earth waves have been reported, there is often no evidence of deformation. This is true even where the waves have been observed in concrete pavement. So earth waves join earthquake lights as anecdotal phenomena associated with earthquakes that are reported so often there must be some substratum of truth to them, but getting good, hard data to explain them has thus far proved elusive.

140   "The earth was, in the course of 15 minutes": *Western Sun,* Feb. 15, 1812. According to Lesieur, the water was "lukewarm—so warm, indeed, as to produce no chilly sensation while swimming and wading through it." (Campbell, *Campbell's Gazetteer of Missouri,* p. 396)

140   "like a great loaf of bread": Smyth-Davis, *History of Dunklin County, Mo., 1845–1895,* p. 15.

141   "the inhabitants had fled": "More of the Earthquake," *Farmer's Repository,* Feb. 28, 1812.

142   "those who did not see": Campbell, *Campbell's Gazetteer of Missouri,* p. 396.

143   major earthquakes along the New Madrid fault system: There is at least one report of Native American lore referring to a devastating earthquake before 1811. The first recorded earthquake in the New Madrid Seismic Zone occurred on Christmas Day 1699. A French missionary on his way down the Mississippi was camped south of present-day Memphis, when he and his party "were greatly astonished to see the earth tremble about one clock in the afternoon, and although this earthquake did not last long, it was violent enough for all to perceive it easily." ("Letter of J. F. Buisson St. Cosme, Missionary Priest, to the Bishop [of Quebec]," *Early Voyages Up and Down the Mississippi,* Shea, ed., p. 70)

143   "The Convulsions were so extreme": *Boston Weekly News-Letter,* Nov. 20, 1755.

144   "The temblor came lightly": *San Francisco Chronicle,* May 6, 1906.

145   "The sound was in the ground": Letter from Firmin La Roche in "A Sailor's Record of the New Madrid Earthquake," p. 270.

146   "quivered like the flesh": Haywood, *The Natural and Aboriginal History of Tennessee,* p. 31.

146   "It seemed as if the surface": McMurtrie, *Sketches of Louisville and Its Environs,* p. 233.

148   "it was a sure sign": J. H. B. Latrobe, *First Steamboat Voyage,* p. 27.

149   Assuming an Indian attack: An abortive Indian attack had, in fact, occurred when a group of Chickasaw canoes attempted to approach the boat in a hostile manner. The engineer turned up the fire in the boiler. For a short time, the paddling Chickasaws managed to stay abreast of "Penelore" or "Fire Canoe," as they called the *New Orleans,* but the steamboat soon easily outstripped its pursuers.

149   an engine explosion: See note, Chapter 7, p. 260, "fear of an engine explosion."

150   "there was no choice": J. H. B. Latrobe, *First Steamboat Voyage,* p. 26.

150   Firmin La Roche, a sailor by trade: La Roche, "Sailor's Record," pp. 268–70.

151   "if my flatboat load": Account of John Weisman, in Street, "The Historical Seismicity of Central United States: 1811–1928," Appendix A, p. A279.

152   "to become merciless enemies of navigation": Van Tramp, *Prairie and Rocky Mountain Adventures, or, Life in the West,* p. 101.

154   "30 or 40 acres": Cramer, *Navigator,* p. 305.

154   John Bradbury, a Scottish naturalist: Bradbury, *Travels in the Interior of America,* in Thwaites, *Early Western Travels,* Vol. 5, pp. 203–11.

155   "The river was covered with foam and drift timber": At this point on the river—downstream of the uplifted land that caused the current to run backwards—the rise in water level was attributable to two factors. The first, of course, would be the masses of riverbank that had caved in; the other was liquefaction, which expelled great volumes of groundwater into the river.

157   "it is doubtful if the earth": McMurtrie, *Sketches of Louisville,* p. 233.

157   "The Philanthropic emotions": Barker, "The Austin Papers," pp. 206–7.

158   "The Last Night of Island Ninety-Four": *St. Louis Globe-Democrat,* Mar. 9, 1902, p. 8.

160   "boil, bubble, and foam": Witherell, Letter in *Pioneer Society of the State of Michigan,* 1906, p. 111, in Street, "Historical Seismicity," p. A65.

160   John Dunn Hunter: Hunter's account, *Memoirs of a Captivity Among the Indians of North America,* was discredited for political reasons in the nineteenth century, but more recently, it has been accepted as genuine. See Drinnon, *White Savage: The Case of John Dunn Hunter.*

160   "filled with terror": Hunter, *Memoirs of a Captivity,* p. 25.

160   "in long, eloquent, and pathetic strains": Ibid., p. 28.

161   *"Brothers*—The Great Spirit is angry": Ibid., p. 31.

Chapter Nine: A REAL CHAOS

Page

164   "as violent as the severest": Bryan, in Dow, *History of Cosmopolite,* p. 344. The January 23 quake is the most difficult of the major events to assess because there is only one near-site eyewitness account other than Bryan's, and it is suspect.

The report was written by Louis Bringier. Bringier was a living tall tale. After gambling away the family fortune in the vice dens of New Orleans, he left town in disgrace and went up the Missouri River, where he was adopted into an unspecified Native American tribe, eventually becoming a chief. Bringier may have crossed the continent during this period, for he later claimed to have discovered gold on the Pacific coast. Afterwards, he went to Mexico, where he accumulated a fortune in silver mines, got mixed up in a revolution, lost his property, and was lucky to get out alive. He finally returned to New Orleans and became city surveyor, as well as surveyor-general of Louisiana.

A decade after the New Madrid earthquakes, Bringier wrote an account as part of a longer article in *The American Journal of Science and Arts,* in which he gave a graphic account of experiencing a quake that occurred as he was traveling in the vicinity of New Madrid. Bringier described water "blowing up the earth with loud explosions. It rushed out in all quarters, bringing with it an enormous quantity of carbonized wood, reduced mostly into dust, which was ejected to the height of from ten to fifteen feet, and fell in a black shower, mixed with the sand which its rapid motion had forced along." Bringier went on to describe the usual falling trees, and most dramatic of all, "the surface was sinking, and a black liquid was rising up to the belly of my horse, who stood motionless, struck with a panic of terror." (Bringier, "Notices of the Geology . . . ," pp. 20–22)

Bringier's account cannot be entirely trusted. He places it on January 6, a date that is not reported by anybody else as having had a quake strong enough to produce the severe types of liquefaction effects Bringier describes. More likely—if it is a genuine report—it refers to the January 23 shock, which was the only one of the three principal events to take place during the day, and a decade after the fact, Bringier simply got the dates confused. But given his penchant for mischief, the possibility that the report is bogus cannot be ruled out. In fact, elsewhere in this article, Bringier made such an exaggerated claim in describing another matter that the editor of the publication felt obliged to refute it in a footnote.

164 "vast forest": Nolte, *Fifty Years*, p. 180.

164 Audubon was on his horse: Maria Audubon, *Audubon and His Journals*, Vol. 2, pp. 234–35. Audubon incorrectly gives the month as November. He was notoriously inaccurate with dates.

165 wild animals temporarily lost their fear: Perhaps the most amazing tale of animal behavior during the New Madrid quakes was reported in the personal journal of one Samuel McDaniel, whose grandparents lived in New Madrid at the time of the earthquakes: "One morning grandpop and grandmother, after having spent a sleepless night, in watching for the Coming of Death, which they hourly expected, as the grim dawn came down on the troubled world, beheld great wild animals in his yard and garden. There were great bears, panthers, wolves, foxes etc. side by side with a number of wild deer, with their red tongues hanging out of their mouths. There was no signs of enmity, but all seemed animated by a common danger, that of the disturbance of nature.

"Later in the day there came a regular migration of wild things fleeing towards the hills. Great rattle snakes, black snakes and innumerable rats, coons, groundhogs, etc. etc. No one was at enmity towards another, nor did they seem to fear man." (McDaniel, "This Book by S. McDaniel," unpublished ms., Missouri Historical Society, pp. 5–6)

166 "the warning by animals": Quoted in Tributsch, *When the Snakes Awake*, p. 15.

166 "until the 4th of February": Bryan, in Dow, *History of Cosmopolite*, p. 344.

166 "a concussion": Ibid.

167 One of those on Tywappety Hill was Colonel John Shaw: Account of John Shaw, *Second Annual Report and Collections of the State Historical Society, of Wisconsin for the Year 1855*, Vol. 2, pp. 202–4.

167 "New Madrid had been designed": Dow, *History of Cosmopolite*, p. 346.

168 "The agitated water": Nolte, *Fifty Years*, pp. 182–83.

169 The best account of the February 7 earthquake comes from Matthias Speed: *Western Spy*, Mar. 28, 1812.

170 An old French trapper named Pierre Nichol: Joseph S. Williams, *Old Times in West Tennessee*, pp. 227–28.

171   Reelfoot Lake is the largest area of sunklands: Much has been made of a legend attributed to the Chickasaw that tells how Reelfoot Lake got its name. According to the legend, a chief named Reelfoot—so named for his clubfoot and awkward gait—stole a Choctaw princess away from her tribe and was intending to marry her. In a dream, he was warned that if he carried out his plans, the earth would shake with fury. Ignoring the dream, Reelfoot went ahead with the marriage, and during the wedding ceremony, the ground trembled and sank, and the Mississippi River ran backwards, flooding the area and drowning all the people. As fetching as this tale is, it is not a Chickasaw legend at all, but rather a story that was made up by whites and ascribed to the tribe.

171   "So severe a shock": *Augusta Herald,* reprinted in *Poulson's Daily American Advertiser,* Jan. 2, 1812, in Street, *Historical Seismicity,* p. A8.

171   "I felt an unusual sensation": Witherell, Letter, in Street, *Historical Seismicity.* Witherell's reaction is not atypical. People in earthquakes often experience feelings of disorientation, vertigo, nausea, and other similar affects. Audubon wrote, "I became bewildered in my ideas" during the January 23 quake. (Maria Audubon, *Audubon and His Journals,* p. 234)

172   "several hunting Indians": *The Western Intelligencer,* Feb. 21, 1812, in Street *"Historical Seismicity,"* p. A76.

173   "All of the crew were sleeping": La Roche, "Sailor's Record," pp. 269–270.

174   *Table 1.* The Modified Mercalli Intensity Scale: Adapted from Bolt, *Earthquakes,* pp. 283–95, and http://neic.usgs.gov/neis/general/mag_vs_int.html.

178   The three major events have been estimated: Otto Nuttli was the first seismologist to estimate the magnitudes of the three largest New Madrid earthquakes. In 1973, he calculated the body-wave magnitudes at 7.2 for December 16 (the 2:15 a.m. shock), 7.1 for January 23, and 7.4 for February 7. In 1981, using the surface-wave magnitude scale, he put them at 8.6, 8.4, and 8.7 for December 16, January 23, and February 7, respectively. However, the body-wave scale is not accurate above 6.5, and the surface-wave scale is not exact above 8.0, which leaves Nuttli's figures open to question. In 1996, Arch Johnston, director of the Center for Earthquake Research and Information in Memphis, who has devoted the major part of his career to studying the New Madrid earthquakes, determined the moment magnitudes of the three major events to be 8.1, 7.8, and 8.0 (with a variable range of ±0.3).

More recently, Susan Hough, of the United States Geological Survey office in southern California, reinterpreted the Modified Mercalli Intensity values, and on the basis of her scaled-down numbers, assigned moment magnitudes of 7.2–7.3 for December 16, 7.0 for January 23, and 7.4–7.5 for February 7. The size of an earthquake is very much dependent on the size of the fault on which it occurs, and in her very readable book, *Earthshaking Science: What We Know (and Don't Know) About Earthquakes,* Hough argues that the length and area of the faults involved in the New Madrid sequence are not capable of producing earthquakes with magnitudes greater than the ones she assigned.

Johnston's magnitude figures were partly based on the hypothesis that although the faults are short, they may also be wide (that is deep), going down perhaps twenty miles—a hypothesis not supported by seismicity data for the small earthquakes that continue to occur today along the New Madrid fault system. Johnston's conjecture gained a lot more plausibility, however, after the 2001 earthquake in Bhuj, India, which had a moment magnitude of 7.7. Bhuj is in a very similar geologic and tectonic setting to New Madrid—on a failed continental rift, with ancient crustal rock about twenty-five miles thick, very much like the central United States. After Bhuj, the magnitudes Johnston assigned to the New Madrid earthquakes appear rather more plausible.

178   Adding up the victims: Godfrey Lesieur identified a Mrs. Lafont, who died of fright, and a Mrs. Jarvis, who was hit by a falling cabin log and died a few days later. He also mentioned, "A man . . . who was moving from Tennessee with his family, a wife and seven children, and a young married man to help on the flat-boat, to Arkansas, were all lost but himself. . . . A man named Glasscock, and family, six or eight in number, were all lost at Island No. 16." (This is in a slightly different account than the one previously cited for Lesieur—see Rozier, *Rozier's History of the Early Settlement of the Mississippi Valley,* p. 206.) According to *Lloyd's Steamboat Directory,* "a flat boat belonging to Richard Stump was swamped, and six men were drowned." (p. 320) The letter from the man in New Madrid to his friend in Lexington related that "seven Indians were swallowed up; one of them escaped." ("Extracts from a letter," *The Reporter* [Lexington, Ky.], Feb. 1, 1812). Eliza Bryan's account told of one boat that was "wrecked in which there was a lady and six children, all of whom were lost." (Dow, *History of Cosmopolite,* p. 325) Captain John Davis mentioned several boats that were lost, but "the people were all saved except one man." (Cramer, *Navigator,* p. 306) James Ritchie reported, "A family of the name of Curran were moving from New Madrid to an old French town on the Arkansas river, called the Port; had passed the St. Francis swamps and found some of their cattle missing; Le Roy, the youngest son . . . rode back to hunt them, and was in the swamp when the first shock took place, was never seen afterwards, and was supposed to have been lost in some of those fearful chasms." (Dudley, "Earthquake of 1811," p. 422) If the tale of the disappearance of Island 94 is accurate, fifteen river pirates lost their lives. ("The Last Night of Island Ninety-Four) Bradbury assigns an indefinite number of deaths to the drifting canoes. (*Travels in the Interior,* p. 206) Hildreth's informant said, "Many boats were overwhelmed . . . and their crews perished with them." ("History of a Voyage," p. 130) Similarly, in Stephen F. Austin's account, "There were a number of Boats lost . . . and many lives." (Barker, "The Austin Papers," p. 207) Finally, Fr. Joseph wrote, "We made no effort to find out how many people had been killed, although it was told us that many were. We saw the dead bodies of several and afterwards drowned persons we saw floating in the river." ("Sailor's Record," p. 270)

178   Jared Brooks recorded, counted: McMurtrie, *Sketches of Louisville,* p. 255.

179   "One gentleman, from whose learning": "Extracts from a letter," *The Reporter,* Feb. 1, 1812 (Lexington, Kentucky), italics in original.

179   "Several authors have asserted": Bringier, "Notices of the Geology . . ." .

180   "steam was the more immediate": Pierce, *Year,* Appendix, p. 17.

180   "no doubt, but that": Nutall, *A Journal of Travels into the Arkansas Territory During the Year 1819*, p. 61.

180   "a subsidence": Macfarlane, "The 'Earthquake' at New Madrid, Mo., in 1811, probably not an Earthquake," *Proceedings of the American Association for the Advancement of Science, Thirty-second Meeting*, p. 247.

180   "faulting in the hard Paleozoic rocks": Fuller, *The New Madrid Earthquake*, pp. 104–5.

181   "the Great Spirit": Hunter, *Memoirs of a Captivity*, p. 25.

181   "the Shawanoe Prophet": "Extracts from a letter," *The Reporter* (Lexington, Kentucky), Feb. 1, 1812.

182   Some weeks later, probably around the middle of March: In *Jefferson's Nephews*, Merrill points out that Livingston County coroner John Dorroh never held an inquest to investigate George's death, as he was required by law to do. Given the fact that there was a penalty of £90 for neglecting to conduct such an inquiry, it is unlikely that Dorroh would have ignored this duty. Since the Livingston County grand jury was scheduled to convene on Monday, March 16, Merrill concludes that the skull must have been discovered close to that time, and Dorroh simply handed the matter to the grand jury.

182   a neighbor happened along: Two different men, Jonah Hibbs and Dick Hurley, have been credited with finding the skull and bringing it to the authorities.

Chapter Ten: THE ACCUMULATED LOAD OF PUBLIC ODIUM

Page

185   "moderate correction": Section 12 of the Georgia state constitution of 1798, for example, held: "Any person who shall dismember or deprive a slave of life shall suffer punishment as would be inflicted in case the like offence had been committed on a free white person, and on the like proof, except in case of insurrection by such slave, and unless such death should happen by accident in giving such slave moderate correction." (Thorpe, *Federal and State Constitutions*, Vol. 2, p. 801)

186   "would not convict the defendant": Catterall, ed., *Judicial Cases Concerning American Slavery and the Negro*, Vol. 2, p. 343. See also Hindus, *Prison and Plantation*, p. 135.

186   "malice aforethought": See note, Chapter 6, p. 258, "an exceeding bad wound."

187   "a presentment against Lilburn": Livingston Circuit Court Bundles, March 1812, p. 290.

187   "answer such charges": Ibid.

188   "Lilburn [*sic*] Lewis appeared in court": Ibid., pp. 300–301.

188   a short term in the state penitentiary: The average term for manslaughter in Kentucky was three years, nine months. Arson (of public property), counterfeiting, forgery, stealing a slave, horse stealing, breaking and entering, polygamy, rape, and selling a free person as a slave all carried heavier sentences than manslaughter. That both Lilburne and Isham faced capital punishment upon conviction was clear from the Kentucky law that stated, "Any person, his or her aiders, abettors

or counselors, who shall be guilty of murder . . . shall be punished with death."
(Littell, *The Statute Law of Kentucky*, Vol. 2, p. 467)

188   "Lilbourn [*sic*] Lewis senior, farmer": Livingston Circuit Court Order Book,
       1810–1814, Mar. 19, 1812, p. 288.

190   "capt. Lewis's wife": *Kentucky Gazette*, May 12, 1812.

190   "Now he saw that his character was gone": Letter from Rev. William Dickey to
       John Rankin, in *American Slavery*, Weld, comp., p. 94.

190   "beloved but cruel wife Letitia": Livingston County Will Book A, p. 34; original
       in Livingston Court Bundles, May 1812.

191   "a tremulous shake": McMurtrie, *Sketches of Louisville*, p. 252.

191   "My beloved but cruel Letitia": Livingston County Will Book A, p. 34.

192   "upon oath that him self": Coroner's inquest summons and jury report, Apr. 11,
       1812, Livingston Circuit Court, unmarked bundle.

192   "Isham Lewis acknowledged in our presence": *Commonwealth vs. Lewis & Lewis*,
       Livingston Circuit Court Bundles, Mar. 1815.

193   "the 120th day": McMurtrie, *Sketches of Louisville*, p. 252.

Chapter Eleven: A War of Extirpation

Page

195   "The significance of these earthquakes": Sugden, "Early Pan-Indianism: Tecum-
       seh's Tour of the Indian Country, 1811–1812," p. 290.

196   "great destruction and havoc": Canada/Indian Affairs Papers, Record Group 10,
       Vol. 28, p. 16512, National Archives of Canada, Ottawa; quoted in Sugden,
       Tecumseh, p. 257, original not seen.

197   a war against the Indians: The author of the earliest history of the War of 1812,
       published in 1816, gives the causes of the war as being the conflicts with the Indi-
       ans. (McAfee, *History of the Late War in the Western Country*, Chapter 1)

197   a Congress filled with War Hawks: In the congressional debate leading up to the
       war, John Randolph of Virginia argued against war, invoking the "character of the
       times" and offering the opinion that the nation was "on the brink of some dread-
       ful scourge—some great desolation—some awful visitation from the Power,
       whom, I am afraid, we have as yet, in our national capacity, taken no means to
       conciliate." (*Annals of Congress, 12th Congress, 1st Session*; pp. 1383–84) In response,
       John Calhoun of South Carolina ridiculed Randolph, mocking the "comets,
       earthquakes, eclipses, or the whole catalogue of omens which I have heard the
       gentleman from Virginia enumerate." (Ibid., p. 1399)

198   "All the accounts that I have received": Harrison to Eustis, Dec. 24, 1811, in
       Esarey, *Messages and Letters*, Vol. 1, p. 685.

198   "to re-establish the relations": Eustis to Harrison, Jan. 17, 1812, ibid., Vol. 2, p. 14.

198   "What other course is there": Harrison to Eustis, Apr. 22, 1812, in Esarey, ibid., p. 41.

198   "Great Spirit is angry": Speech of Gomo, Apr. 16, 1812, Ninian Edwards Papers,
       Chicago Historical Society.

199   "our hearts are good": This and the speeches that follow are from "Speeches of

Indians at Massassinway," May 15, 1812, in Esarey, *Messages and Letters,* Vol. 2, pp. 50–52.

200   "If we hear of the Big Knives": "Speeches of Indians on the Wabash in reply to message of Colonel M. Elliott, S.I.A.," ibid., p. 35.

200   "all the Nations are aware": Letter of Claus to Brock, June 16, 1812, in *Documents Relating to the Invasion of Canada and the Surrender of Detroit, 1812,* Cruikshank, ed., p. 33, italics in original. In a footnote, the editor incorrectly identifies the *"Red people"* as "the English," perhaps confusing the common reference to British soldiers as "redcoats."

202   "He has shewn himself": Elliott to Claus, July, 15, 1812, in Cruikshank, ed., *Documents,* p. 63.

202   "In the name of my Country": "Proclamation of Brig.-General Hull," in ibid., pp. 58–59, italics in original.

203   "Under these circumstances,": Hull to Eustis, Aug. 4, 1812, ibid., p. 116.

203   "in opposition to every officer": T. Berry to James T. Eubank, Aug. 8, 1812, James Taylor Papers, Burton Historical Collection, Detroit Public Library.

203   "The Indians . . . under the command of Tecumseh": Hull to the Secretary of War, August 13, 1812, in Cruikshank, ed., *Documents,* p. 140.

204   "bright hazle eyes": Tupper, *The Life and Correspondence of Major-General Sir Isaac Brock, K.B.,* p. 243.

204   "great father beyond the great salt lake": Ibid., p. 244.

204   "the immediate surrender of fort Detroit": Brock to Hull, Aug. 15, 1812, in Cruikshank, ed., *Documents,* p. 144.

204   "I am prepared to meet any force": Hull to Brock, Aug. 15, 1812, ibid., pp. 144–45.

205   "a more sagacious": Brock to the Earl of Liverpool, Aug. 29, 1812, ibid., p. 192.

205   Brock's return to the Niagara front: Brock was killed less than two months later in the Battle of Queenstown Heights.

207   "the bullits seemed to be flying": George Carter Dale Manuscript, SHSW, p. 10.

207   "their fiendlike appearance": Ibid.

207   "The men stood": "Narrative of four Shawnoe Chiefs relative to the capture of 4 of their young men at Colonel Dudley's Defeat," May 19, 1813, with letter from Wingate to Harrison, June 15, 1813, William Henry Harrison Papers, LC MSS.

208   *"such confusion ensued":* Account of Joseph R. Underwood, Tecumseh Papers, SHSW:LDM, 6YY23[2–3], italics in original. (See note, Chapter 4, p. 254, "Your father invites you to be seated.")

208   "the Indians had met with and scalped": Byfield, "A Narrative of a Light Company Soldier's Service in the Forty-first Regiment of Foot," p. 70.

208   "then a beardless boy of 19": Account of Leslie Combs, Mar. 1869, Tecumseh Papers, SHSW:LDM, 6YY21[2].

208   "I showed him my wound": Comb's report to Gen. Green Clay, May 6, 1815, Tecumseh Papers, SHSW:LDM, 6YY20[4], italics in original, later published as *Col. Wm. Dudley's Defeat Opposite Fort Meigs* (Cincinnati, 1869).

208   "the tomahawk was busy": Christian, "Sortie at Fort Meigs, May 1813," p. 6.

209   "rifles pistols, war clubs": Account of Leslie Combs, Feb. 1863, Tecumseh Papers, SHSW:LDM, 6YY22[1–2]

209 "To hesitate was instant death": Christian, "Sortie at Fort Meigs," p. 6.

209 *"the Indians employed themselves"*: Account of Joseph R. Underwood, p. 23³, italics in original.

209 "the fort, or rather slaughter-pen": Christian, "Sortie at Fort Meigs," p. 6.

209 *"An Indian painted black"*: Account of Joseph R. Underwood, p. 23³, italics in original.

210 "like terror-stricken sheep": Christian, "Sortie at Fort Meigs," p. 6.

210 "I could not understand his language": Account of Leslie Combs, Feb. 1863, p. 22³.

210 "intelligent look, and dignified demeanor": Account of Joseph R. Underwood, p. 23⁴.

210 "he was the only man": George Carter Dale Manuscript, p. 14.

210 "more humane than his ally and employer": Combs's report to Gen. Green Clay, p. 20.

211 "the Wyandots took us": "Narrative of four Shawnoe Chiefs," Harrison Papers, LC MSS, italics in original.

Chapter Twelve: THE FATAL BLOW

Page

213 "We must compare our father's conduct": *The Weekly Register* (Baltimore), Vol. 5, No. 10, Nov. 6, 1813, p. 175.

214 "Father, tell your young men to be firm": Proctor, *The Lucubrations of Humphrey Ravelin, Esq.*, p. 357.

214 "gave the loudest yells I": "Kentucky at the Thames, 1813: A Rediscovered Narrative by William Greathouse," Fredriksen, ed., p. 103.

214 exactly who killed Tecumseh was uncertain: Nor was it ever determined what became of his body. Some claimed it was mutilated, others that it was removed from the battlefield and buried in a secret place.

214 "TECUMSEH is certainly killed": "Death of Tecumseh: Extract of a letter from Maj. Thomas Rowland," Oct. 9, 1813, in *The War*, Nov. 9, 1813.

215 "When Tecumseh fell in battle": Reynolds, *My Own Times*, p. 131.

215 "I enclose you Tecumseh's speech": Harrison to Meigs, Oct. 11, 1813, in Esarey, *Messages and Letters*, Vol. 2, p. 576.

215 "this race of aboriginals": *The Weekly Register*, Vol. V, No. 3, Sep. 13, 1813.

216 *"must be punished"*: Jackson to Blount, June 4, 1812, in *The Papers of Andrew Jackson*, Moser et al., eds., Vol. 2, p. 300, italics in original.

217 "the object of *Tecumpsies* visit": Jackson to Blount, June 5, 1812, ibid., p. 301, italics in original.

218 "in consequence of those murderers": Ross to Meigs, July 30, 1813, in *The Papers of Chief John Ross*, Moulton, ed., Vol. 1, p. 19.

219 "The league seems to be very formidable": James Innerarity quoted in "A Prelude to the Creek War of 1813–1814," West, ed., p. 257.

219 "to order a campaign": Blount to Jackson, Aug. 14, 1813, in *The Correspondence of Andrew Jackson*, Bassett, ed., Vol. 1, p. 315.

219 "endowed . . . with a noble person": Claiborne, *Life and Times*, pp. 128.

219 "my warriors were like famished wolves": Ibid., pp. 128–29.

219   "Indians, negroes, white men": Maj. Kennedy's report to Gen. Claiborne, quoted in Pickett, *History of Alabama*, Vol. 2, pp. 282–83, original not seen.

219   "the women and helpless children": General Orders, Sep. 19, 1813, in Bassett, ed., *Correspondence*, Vol. 1, p. 320.

220   "in elegant stile": Jackson to Rachel Jackson, Nov. 4, 1813, in Moser et al. eds., *Papers of Andrew Jackson*, Vol. 2, p. 444.

221   "The *carnage* was *dreadfull*":Jackson to Rachel Jackson, Apr. 1, 1814, ibid., Vol. 3, p. 54, italics in original.

221   "the party detailed to count the dead warriors": Halbert and Ball, *The Creek War of 1813 and 1814*, p. 277.

221   *"You have . . . destroyed a confederacy of the enemy":* To Tennessee troops in Mississippi Territory," Apr. 2, 1814, in Moser et al., eds., *Papers of Andrew Jackson*, Vol. 3, pp. 57–58.

222   "My people are no more!!": Royall, *Letters from Alabama, 1817–1822*, pp. 91–92.

222   "They [*sic*] hostile creeks has forfeighted all right to the Territory": Bassett, ed., *Correspondence*, Vol. 3, p. 2.

Chapter Thirteen: THE FIELD OF SLAUGHTER

Page

223   Wilkinson had spent his time since the Spanish Conspiracy: In 1794, Wilkinson was involved in a second brief Spanish Conspiracy. He wrote to the new governor of Louisiana, Hector, Baron de Carondelet, suggesting that it was he who had saved Louisiana from an aborted invasion the previous year by an alliance of Frenchmen and Americans using Kentucky as a launching pad. He further advised that future attacks could be averted by engaging leading citizens to pacify the frontiersmen and stir up a secessionist movement in Kentucky, which had been admitted to the Union as a slave state two years earlier. De Carondelet hired Wilkinson to put the plan into effect and paid him $16,000 on top of his $2,000 annual pension.

In truth, most of the Kentucky leaders whom Wilkinson enlisted were only interested in the movement as a way of putting pressure on the federal government. Kentuckians were dissatisfied with President Washington for failing to open the Mississippi and for generally favoring the northeastern states in his governance of the country, and they saw Wilkinson's scheme as a strategy to leverage their interests with the government.

So, when de Carondelet sent an agent to New Madrid in July 1795 to arrange for the delivery of ten thousand rifles and twenty cannons to set the rebellion in motion, nobody showed up to meet him, and the second Spanish Conspiracy died on the vine. (See note, Chapter 3, p. 253, "it contained several provisions.")

224   "a deep, dark, wicked": Wilkinson, *Memoirs of My Own Times*, Appendix C.

226   "the directions of the President": Monroe to Jackson, Oct. 21, 1814, in Moser et al., eds., *Papers of Andrew Jackson*, Vol. 3, p. 171.

226 Word of the agreement: There were even a couple of battles after the Battle of New Orleans. In mid-January, the British took over the Georgia town of St. Marys, and early in February, they captured Fort Bowyer and Mobile. On the seas, there were encounters as late as June 1815.

227 slaves: According to *The Narrative of James Roberts*, before the Battle of New Orleans, Jackson canvassed the plantation owners of the area, enlisting slaves to fight against the British in the upcoming battle. After consulting with the owner of Roberts's plantation, "Jackson came into the field, chose out the ones he wanted, and then addressed us thus: 'Had you not as soon go into the battle and fight, as to stay here in the cotton-field, dying and never die? If you will go, and the battle is fought and the victory gained on Israel's side, you shall be free.'" Five hundred slaves, including Roberts, jumped at the chance. Following the battle, the slaves were instructed to return their guns to the ammunition house, "and Jackson ordered them to be unloaded, to serve a wicked end he had in view." The next morning, the guns were returned to the men to carry in a parade through New Orleans, after which Jackson turned to his "colored soldiers" and said, "Now, behave yourselves well, and go home to your masters." Roberts reminded the general of his promise, to which Jackson replied, "You are not my property, and I cannot take another man's property and set it free." Roberts asked Jackson to use his influence with their master and have them set free, but the answer was the same as before. "At that moment," wrote Roberts, "I cocked my gun; but there being no priming in it, I bit of a piece of cartridge, and, going to prime it, I for the first time discovered it was not loaded. Had my gun been loaded, doubtless Jackson would have been a dead man in a moment." Roberts claimed that "some sixty or seventy or more of the colored men were killed, of whom no account was ever taken in the details of the war." Of Jackson's motives, he wrote, "Such monstrous deception and villainy could not, of course, be allowed to disgrace the pages of history, and blacken the character of a man who wanted the applause and approbation of his country." (pp. 13–18)

227 "expected to annihilate Jackson's force in an instant": Letter from C. J. Forbes to James Cobb, in "Unpublished Letters Relative to the Battle of New Orleans," *Louisiana Historical Society Publications,* Vol. 9, 1917, p. 78.

227 "Don't fire till you see the whites of their eyes": Nolte, *Fifty Years,* p. 221.

228 "The Americans saw us": Gleig, *A Subaltern in America,* p. 260.

228 "the most murderous": *The Autobiography of Lieutenant-General Sir Harry Smith,* G. C. Moore Smith, ed., p. 247.

228 "a pretty considerable noise": Anon., "A Contemporary Account of the Battle of New Orleans by a Soldier in the Ranks," p. 11.

228 "were falling fast": Nolte, *Fifty Years,* pp. 221–22.

229 "the deadly rifles of the Americans": Anon., "New Orleans: From the Ms. of an Eye-witness," p. 41.

229 "In the whole course of my military career": Gleig, *Subaltern,* p. 262.

229 "The sight was a terrible one to see": "A Letter from Mr. A. Henderson," *The Weekly Register,* Vol. 7, No. 24, Feb. 11, 1815, p. 378.

229   "I could have walked": Lawrence, "An Eye-Witness of the Battle of New Orleans," p. 160.

229   "individuals ... in every possible attitude": Anon., "A Contemporary Account," p. 15.

230   except for the Seminoles: In the Seminole War of 1817–18, the U.S. side was commanded by Andrew Jackson and led to the U.S. taking Pensacola from the Spanish. The second Seminole war, from 1835 to 1842, was the most expensive of all U.S. Indian wars, costing $30 million and claiming thousands of lives. From the Everglades, the Seminoles waged a guerrilla campaign led by Osceola, who was arrested during truce negotiations in 1837 and died in prison the following January. The conflict dragged on, but by 1842, the tribe had been nearly eradicated. Over four thousand Seminoles surrendered and were deported to Oklahoma Territory. A few hundred avoided capture, however, and remained in the Everglades. In 1855, a third war broke out, led by Seminole chief Billy Bowlegs. It was a war of attrition, and in 1858, with only forty warriors left, the Seminoles surrendered.

Epilogue

Page

231   "Strangers begin to move in": Irwin, "A Reminder of the Earthquake of 1811," p. 85.

231   "Don't be alarmed": James, *Account of an Expedition from Pittsburgh to the Rocky Mountains*, p. 326.

232   "Although we had some favorable indications": *Autobiography of Rev. James B. Finley*, W. P. Strickland, ed., p. 239.

233   "During the revival": Thompson, *The Autobiography of Elder Wilson Thompson*, p. 135.

233   "A Call to the People of Louisiana": Hudson, "A Ballad of the New Madrid Earthquake," pp. 147–50.

235   "though many were sincere": Cartwright, *Autobiography*, W. P. Strickland, ed., p. 181.

235   "A Resolution for the relief": *The Territorial Papers of the United States*, Carter, ed., pp. 729–30.

236   The last case stemming: That same year, New Madrid played a minor role in the Civil War. In the Battle of New Madrid/Island No. 10, fought from March 2 to April 8, Union soldiers laid siege to the town and, by capturing Island No. 10, just upstream, gained control of the Mississippi south to Fort Pillow, Tennessee, about forty miles north of Memphis.

241   "You don't get breaks like this often": Quoted in Bailey, "Climatologist's Predicted Act of God Aids Church," *Memphis Commercial Appeal*, Dec. 1, 1990.

Bibliography of Works Consulted

Newspapers

Argus of Western America (Frankfort, Ky.)
Bardstown Repository (Ky.)
Boston Weekly News-Letter
Connecticut Mirror
Farmer's Repository (Charleston, W. Va.)
Kentucky Gazette (Lexington)
Lexington American Statesman (Ky.)
Lexington Reporter (Ky.)
Liberty Hall (Cincinnati)
Louisville Courier-Journal
Louisville Gazette
Memphis Commercial Appeal
Mississippi Messenger (Natchez)
National Intelligencer (Washington)

Pennsylvania Gazette (Philadelphia)
Philadelphia Gazette
Pittsburgh Gazette
Raleigh Register
Republican and Savannah Evening Ledger
San Francisco Chronicle
St. Louis Globe-Democrat
Tree of Liberty (Pittsburgh)
Virginia Gazette and Weekly Advertiser
    (Richmond)
Weekly Register (Baltimore)
Western Spectator (Marietta, Oh.)
Western Spy (Cincinnati)
Western Sun (Vincennes, Ind.)

Unpublished Manuscripts

Bruce, William. "Memoirs of the Bruce Family." Typescript, Manuscript Section, Indiana State Library.

Christian, Percy Willis. "General James Wilkinson and Kentucky Separatism, 1784–1798." Ph.D. dissertation, 1935.

Daughters of the American Revolution, Lucy Jefferson Lewis Chapter, New Madrid. "This Material All Came from the New Madrid County Archives in New Madrid County Courthouse, New Madrid, Mo." Typescript, Missouri Historical Society.

Goltz, Herbert Charles Walter, Jr. "Tecumseh, The Prophet and the Rise of the Northwest Indian Confederation." Ph.D. dissertation, 1973.

Latrobe, Benjamin Henry. "Letterbooks of Benjamin Henry Latrobe." Maryland Historical Society.

McDaniel, S. "This Book by S. McDaniel." Typescript, Missouri Historical Society.

McRaven, William Henry. "Tennessee Prodigies." Typescript, 1966. The McRaven Collection, Tennessee State Library and Archives.

Otero, Michael A. "The American Mission of Diego de Gardoqui, 1785–1789." Ph.D. dissertation, 1948.

Street, R. "The Historical Seismicity of Central United States: 1811–1928: Appendix A." Bound typescript, USGS Contract No. 14-08-0001-21251, 1984.

Viitanen, Wayne John. "The Winter the Mississippi Ran Backwards." Ph.D. dissertation, 1972.

COLLECTIONS

John Parker Boyd Papers, Indiana Historical Society.

Orlando Brown Papers. Filson Historical Society Library, Louisville.

George Carter Dale Manuscript, State Historical Society of Wisconsin.

Lyman Draper Manuscripts, State Historical Society of Wisconsin.

Ninian Edwards Papers, Chicago Historical Society.

Peter Force Collection, Manuscript Division, Library of Congress.

William Henry Harrison Papers, Manuscript Division, Library of Congress.

Thomas Jefferson Papers, Massachusetts Historical Society.

Thomas Jefferson Papers, Manuscripts Department, Univ. of Virginia Library.

Livingston County Court records, Livingston County Courthouse, Smithland, Ky.

John Lucas Collection, Missouri Historical Society.

Letters from Polly Wilson McGee to Joshua Lacy Wilson, online at "First American West: The Ohio River Valley, 1750–1820," http://memory.loc.gov/ammem/award99/icuhtml//fawhome.html

George Morgan Papers, Manuscript Division, Library of Congress.

National Archives and Records Administration.

Joseph Nicholson Papers, Manuscript Division, Library of Congress.

Papeles de Estado, Archivo Histórico Nacional, Madrid.

Papeles Procedentes de Cuba, Archivo General de Indias, Seville.

Franklin D. Roosevelt Presidential Library, Hyde Park, N.Y.

James Taylor Papers, Burton Historical Collection, Detroit Public Library.

James Wilkinson Papers, Chicago Historical Society.

WEB SITES

The New Madrid Compendium: www.ceri.memphis.edu/compendium/

The Nicholas Heinrich Crist Account Book (George Heinrich Crist account): free-pages.genealogy.rootsweb.com/~ptsonline/stories/cristaccountbook2.html

USGS Earthquake Hazards Program: neic.usgs.gov/

ARTICLES

Anderson, Robert. "Letter of Maj. Gen'l. Robert Anderson (of Fort Sumter Fame) to Benjamin Drake." *Pennsylvania Magazine of History and Biography,* Vol. 16, No. 2 (1917).

Andrews, Edward Deming. "The Shaker Mission to the Shawnee Indians." *Winterthur Portfolio* 7 (1972).

Anon. "The Battle of New-Orleans." *De Bow's Review* 16 (June 1854).

Anon. "A Contemporary Account of the Battle of New Orleans by a Soldier in the Ranks." *Louisiana Historical Quarterly* 9 (Jan.–Oct. 1926).

Anon. "New Orleans: From the Ms. of an Eye-witness." *Graham's Magazine* 28 (July 1845).

Barker, Eugene C. "The Austin Papers." *Annual Report of the American Historical Assoc. for the Year 1919* (1919).

Beall, William K. "Journal of William K. Beall, July–August, 1812." *American Historical Review* 17 (Oct. 1911–July 1912).

Beckwith, Hiram W., ed. "The Ft. Wayne Manuscript." *Fergus Historical Series* 26 (1883).

Bedinger, Daniel. "Extract from the Journal of Daniel Bedinger." *National Intelligencer,* Mar. 14, 1812.

Berry, Daniel. "The Illinois Earthquake of 1811 and 1812." *Transactions of the Illinois Historical Society* 12 (1911).

Bringier, Louis. "Notices of the Geology . . ." *American Journal of Science and Arts* 3 (1821).

Broadhead, Garland C. "The New Madrid Earthquake." *The American Geologist* 30 (Aug. 1902).

Brown, S. "Old Kaskaskia Days and Ways." *Transactions of the Illinois State Historical Society for the Year 1905.*

Brunson, Alfred, Rev. "Death of Tecumseh, at the Battle of the Thames in 1813." *Report and Collections of the State Historical Society of Wisconsin, for the Years 1857 and 1858* (1859).

Byfield, Shadrach. "A Narrative of a Light Company Soldier's Service in the Forty-first Regiment of Foot." *The Magazine of History with Notes and Queries* 11 (1910).

Carlson, Richard G., ed. "George P. Peters' Version of the Battle of Tippecanoe (November 7, 1811)." *Vermont History* 45 (1977).

Cates, Lorraine C. "Americanizing of New Madrid, Mo., by Col. George Morgan While Spanish Controlled Upper Louisiana." *St. Louis Genealogical Quarterly* 7 (Dec. 1974).

Christian, Thomas. "Sortie at Fort Meigs, May 1813." *Western Reserve and Northern Ohio Historical Society* 23 (Oct. 1874).

Cook, D. B. "The Death of Tecumseh." *The Century* 30 (June 1885).

Davidson, James. "Who Killed Tecumseh?" *Historical Magazine* 10 (July 1886).

Dawson, Henry B. "Who Killed Tecumseh?" *Historical Magazine* 10 (Oct. 1886).

"Death of Tecumseh: Extract of a letter from Maj. Thomas Rowland." *The War,* Nov. 9, 1813.

Dekay, J. E. "Notes on a Fossil Skull." *Annals of the Lyceum of Natural History of New-York* 2 (1828).

Din, Gilbert C. "The Immigration Policy of Governor Esteban Miró in Spanish Louisiana." *The Spanish Presence in Louisiana, 1763–1803*. Gilbert C. Din, ed. Lafayette, La.: Center for Louisiana Studies, 1996.

Dudley, Timothy. "The Earthquake of 1811 at New Madrid, Missouri." *Annual Report of the Board of Regents of the Smithsonian* (1859).

"Earthquakes." *The Panoplist and Missionary Magazine United* 4 (Apr. 1812).

Evans, Nelson W. "The First Steamboat on the Ohio." *Ohio Archaelogical and Historical Publications* 16 (1907).

"The First Steamboat on the Ohio River." *American Railroad Journal,* July 26, 1851.

Flugel, Felix, ed. "Pages from a Journal of a Voyage Down the Mississippi to New Orleans in 1817." *The Louisiana Historical Quarterly,* July 1924.

Fredriksen, John C. "Kentucky at the Thames, 1813: A Rediscovered Narrative by William Greathouse." *The Register of the Kentucky Historical Society* 83 (Spring 1985).

Gatschet, A. S. "Tecumseh's Name." *American Anthropologist* 8 (1895).

"Grouseland." *Chicago Tribune,* Mar. 6, 1886.

Hamilton, Robert M. "Quakes Along the Mississippi." *Natural History* 89 (1980).

Harding, Julia Morgan. "George Morgan, His Family and Times." *Washington* (Pa.) *Observer,* May 21, 1904.

Harrison, Lowell H. "Nat Crain and the Battle of the Thames." *Filson Club Historical Quarterly* 64 (July 1990).

Hay, Thomas Robson. "Some Reflections on the Career of General James Wilkinson." *Mississippi Valley Historical Review* 21 (Mar. 1935).

Heckewälder, John. "Narrative of John Heckewelder's Journey to the Wabash in 1792." *The Pennsylvania Magazine of History and Biography* 11 (1887).

Hedges, John P. "Early Recollectons of John P Hedges." *Indiana Magazine of History* 8 (1912).

Higginbotham, Don, and William S. Price, Jr. "Was It Murder for a White Man to Kill a Slave? Chief Justice Martin Howard Condemns the Peculiar Institution in North Carolina." *William and Mary Quarterly* 36 (Oct. 1979).

Hildreth, Samuel. "History of a Voyage from Marietta to New Orleans, in 1805." *American Pioneer* 1 (1844).

Hough, Susan, and Stacey Martin. "Magnitude Estimates of Two Large Aftershocks of the 16 December 1811 New Madrid Earthquake." *Bulletin of the Seismological Society of America* 92 (Dec. 2002).

Hudson, Arthur Palmer. "A Ballad of the New Madrid Earthquake." *Journal of American Folklore* 60 (1947).

Hulbert, Archer. "Western Shipbuilding." *The American Historical Review* 21 (July 1916).

Ireland, Robert M. "Aristocrats All: The Politics of County Government in Antebellum Kentucky." *The Review of Politics* 32 (July 1970).

———. "The Sale of Public Office in America." *Mid-America: An Historical Review* 52 (Oct. 1970).

Irwin, Ray W. "A Reminder of the Earthquake of 1811." *Missouri Historical Review* 31 (Oct. 1936–July 1937).

Johnston, Arch C. "A Major Earthquake Zone on the Mississippi." *Scientific American* 246 (Apr. 1982).

———, and Eugene S. Schweig. "The Enigma of the New Madrid Earthquakes of 1811–1812." *Annual Review of Earth and Planetary Sciences* 24 (1996).

Jones, James P. "Audubon and the New Madrid Earthquake." *The Register of the Kentucky Historical Society* 67 (July 1969).

Jordan, John W., ed. "Notes of a Journey from Philadelphia to New Madrid, Tennessee, 1790," *The Pennsylvania Magazine of History and Biography* 36 (1912).

Kennicot, Robert. "The Quadrupeds of Illinois." *Agricultural Report.* Washington: U.S. Patent Office, 1857–59.

Kingston, John T. "Death of Tecumseh." *Report and Collections of the State Historical Society of Wisconsin, for the Years 1857 and 1858* 4 (1859).

Klinck, Carl F. "Some Anonymous Literature of the War of 1812." *Ontario History* 49 (1957).

Korn, Anna Lee Brosius. "Major Benjamin Holliday, 1768–1859." *Missouri Historical Review* 4 (1919).

La Roche, Firmin. "A Sailor's Record of the New Madrid Earthquake." *Missouri Historical Review* 22 (1928).

Lawrence, Wm. P. "An Eye-Witness of the Battle of New Orleans." *Boston Public Library Quarterly* 9 (July 1957).

Lingel, Robert, ed. "The Manuscript Autobiography of Gordon Callie MacDonald." *New York Public Library Bulletin* 34 (Mar. 1930).

Macfarlane, James. "The 'Earthquake' at New Madrid, Mo., in 1811, probably not an Earthquake." *Proceedings of the American Association for the Advancement of Science* 32 (August 1883).

"Major Howell Tatum's Journal." *Smith College Studies in History* 7 (Oct. 1921–Apr. 1922).

Marraro, Howard R. "Unpublished Correspondence of Jefferson and Adams to Mazzei." *The Virginia Magazine of History and Biography* 51 (April 1943).

Mateker, Emil J. "Earthquakes in Missouri." *Washington University Magazine* 39 (1968).

McBride, James. "Brief Accounts of Journies in the Western Country." *The Quarterly Publication of the Historical and Philosophical Society of Ohio* 5 (Jan.–Mar. 1910)

McDaniel, Mary Jane. "Tecumseh's Visit to the Creeks." *The Alabama Review* 33 (1980).

McGee, J. W. "A Fossil Earthquake." *Bulletin of the Geological Society of America* 4 (Dec. 1892).

McHenry, Francis. "The Indian Prophet." *The Halcyon Luminary, and Theological Repository* 1 (1812).

McLoughlin, William G. "New Angles of Vision on the Cherokee Ghost Dance Movement of 1811–1812." *American Indian Quarterly* 5 (Nov. 1979).

Mitchill, Samuel L. "A Detailed Narrative of the Earthquakes." *Transactions of the Literary and Philosophical Society of New-York* 1 (1815).

Morgan, James, Col. "Morgan's Journey Down the Mississippi in 1767." *Report of the Eighth International Geographic Congress, 1904* (1905).

Neville, Morgan. "The Last of the Boatmen." *The Western Souvenir,* James Hall, ed. Cincinnati: N. and G. Guilford, 1828.

Nunez, Theron A. "Creek Nativism and the Creek War of 1813–1814." *Ethnohistory* 5 (1958).

Nuttli, Otto W. "The Mississippi Valley Earthquakes of 1811 and 1812." *Bulletin of the Seismological Society of America* 63 (Feb. 1973).

Parish, John C., ed. "The Robert Lucas Journal." *Iowa Journal of History and Politics* 4 (1906).

Penick, James, Jr. " . . . I Will Stamp on the Ground With My Foot and Shake Down Every House . . ." *American Heritage* 27 (Dec. 1975).

Pool, Atlanta H. Taylor. "Tragedies in Livingston." *Louisville Courier-Journal,* June 10, 1894.

Posey, Walter Brownlow. "The Earthquake of 1811 and Its Influence on Evangelistic Methods in the Churches of the Old South." *Tennessee Historical Magazine* (1931).

Pusey, Wm. Allen. "The New Madrid Earthquake—An Unpublished Contemporaneous Account." *Science* 71 (Mar. 14, 1930).

Reasenberg, Paul. "Unusual Animal Behavior Before Earthquakes." *Earthquake Information Bulletin* 10 (1978).

Reed, John F. "Valley Forge Commissariat." *The Picket Post* (1980).

Reps, John W. "New Madrid on the Mississippi." *Society of Architectural Historians Journal* 18 (March 1959).

Rothert, Otto A. "The Tragedy of the Lewis Brothers." *Filson Club History Quarterly* 10 (Oct. 1936).

Sachs, Janet Somerville. "Some Aspects of the Early History of Seismology." *Earthquake Information Bulletin* 11 (Mar.–Apr. 1979).

Sampson, F. A. "The New Madrid and Other Earthquakes of Missouri." *Proceedings of the Mississippi Valley Historical Assoc.* 6 (1912–1913).

Sargent, Winthrop. "Account of Several Shocks of an Earthquake in the Southern and Western Parts of the United States." *Memoirs of the American Academy of Arts and Sciences* 3 (1815).

Savage, James E. "Spaniards, Scoundrels, and Statesmen: General James Wilkinson and the Spanish Conspiracy, 1787–1790." *Hanover Historical Review* 6 (Spring 1998).

Savelle, Max. "The Founding of New Madrid." *Mississippi Valley Historical Review* 19 (June 1932).

Schulteis, Rose. "Harrison's Councils with Tecumseh." *Indiana Magazine of History* 27 (1931).

Shaler, N. S. "Earthquakes of the Western United States." *Atlantic Monthly* 24 (Nov. 1869).

Shaw, John. "Personal Narrative." *Second Annual Report and Collections of the State Historical Society of Wisconsin* 2 (1856).

Shen, Ling-huang. "Can Animals Help to Predict Earthquakes?" *Earthquake Information Bulletin* 10 (1978).

Shepard, Edward M. "The New Madrid Earthquake." *The Journal of Geology* 13 (1905).

Shepherd, William R. "Papers Bearing on James Wilkinson's Relations with Spain, 1787–1816." *American Historical Review* 9 (July 1904).

———. "Wilkinson and the Beginnings of the Spanish Conspiracy." *American Historical Review* 9 (Apr. 1904).

Shinn, Charles Howard. "Spanish Plots in the Old Southwest." *Overland Monthly* 1 (June 1883).

Shoemaker, Floyd C. "New Madrid, Mother of Southeast Missouri." *Missouri Historical Review* 49 (July 1955).

Simpson, C. "Reminiscences of Early Pittsburgh." *Western Pennsylvania Historical Magazine* 4 (1921).

Stevens, Jill. "December 3, 1990—The Earthquake That Didn't Happen." *Natural Hazards Observer* 40 (Mar. 1991).

Sugden, John. "Early Pan-Indianism: Tecumseh's Tour of the Indian Country, 1811–1812." *American Indian Quarterly* 10 (Fall 1986).

———. "The Southern Indians in the War of 1812." *Florida Historical Quarterly* 60 (Jan. 1982).

Swem, E. G. "A Letter from New Madrid, 1789." *Mississippi Valley Historical Review* 5 (Dec. 1918).

"Unpublished Letters Relative to the Battle of New Orleans." *Louisiana Historical Society Publications* 9 (1917).

Van Ravenswaay, Charles. "New Madrid Reminiscences." *Missouri Historical Society Bulletin* 4 (Jan. 1948).

Viitanen, Wayne. "Folklore and Fakelore of an Earthquake." *Kentucky Folklore Record* 19 (1973).

———. "The Winter the Mississippi Ran Backwards." *Register of the Kentucky Historical Society* 71 (Jan. 1973).

West, Elizabeth Howard, ed. "A Prelude to the Creek War of 1813–1814." *Florida Historical Quarterly* 18 (Apr. 1940).

Whickar, J. Wesley, ed. "Shabonee's Account of Tippecanoe." *Indiana Magazine of History* 17 (Dec. 1921).

Whitaker, Arthur Preston. "James Wilkinson's First Descent to New Orleans in 1787." *Hispanic American Historical Review* 8 (Feb. 1927).

———, ed. "Harry Innes and the Spanish Intrigue." *Mississippi Valley Historical Review* 15 (Sep. 1928).

White, Edgar. "Missouri History Not Found in Textbooks." *Missouri Historical Review* 20 (1926).

Wilkeson, Samuel. "Early Recollections of the West." *The American Pioneer* 2 (1843).

Witherell, B. F. H. "Reminiscences of the North-West." *Third Annual Report and Collections of the State Historical Society of Wisconsin, for the Year 1856* (1857).

Books and Pamphlets

(Note: Editions in brackets indicate facsimile reprints used.)

Albach, James R. *Annals of the West.* Pittsburgh: W. S. Haven, 1856.

Alliot, Paul. *Historical and Political Reflections on Louisiana.* New York: bound manuscript, 1804. In *Louisiana Under the Rule of Spain, France, and the United States, 1785–1897*. Robertson, James Alexander, ed. and trans. Cleveland, Ohio: A. H. Clark, 1911 [Freeport, N.Y.: Books for Libraries Press, 1969].

Ambler, Charles Henry. *Transportation in the Ohio Valley*. Glendale, Calif.: Arthur H. Clark, 1932.

American State Papers, Indian Affairs. Washington: Gales & Seaton, 1832.

Anburey, Thomas. *Travels Through the Interior Parts of America*. London: W. Lane, 1789 [New York: The New York Times, 1969].

Annals of Congress, 12th Congress, 1st Session. Washington: Gales & Seaton, 1834–56.

Anon. *An Account of the Earthquakes*. Philadelphia: Robert Smith, Jun.[Junior], 1812.

Anon. *American Husbandry*. London: J. Bew, 1775.

Anon. *Henderson: A Guide to Audubon's Home Town in Kentucky*. Northport, N.Y.: Bacon, Percy & Daggett, no date.

Anon. *The History of Madison County, Ohio*. Chicago: W. H. Beers, 1883.

Anon. *History of Southeast Missouri*. Chicago: Goodspeed, 1888 [Cape Girardeau, Mo.: Ramfre Press, 1955].

Anon. *Tales of Chivalry and Romance*. Edinburgh: Robertson, 1826.

Ashe, Thomas. *Travels in America, Performed in 1806*. Pittsburgh: Cramer & Spear, 1808.

Audubon, John James, and John Bachman. *The Viviparous Quadrupeds of North America*. New York: J. J. Audubon, 1845–48.

Audubon, Maria R, ed. *Audubon and His Journals*. Gloucester, Mass.: Peter Smith, 1972.

Bagnall, Norma Hayes. *On Shaky Ground*. Columbia and London: Univ. of Missouri Press, 1996.

Baily, Francis. *Journal of a Tour in Unsettled Parts of North America, in 1796 & 1797*. London: Baily Brothers, 1856 [Carbondale: Southern Illinois Univ. Press 1969].

Baldwin, Leland D. *The Keelboat Age on Western Waters*. Pittsburgh: Univ. of Pittsburgh Press, 1941.

———. *Pittsburgh*. Pittsburgh: Univ. of Pittsburgh Press, 1938.

Barry, John M. *Rising Tide*. New York: Simon & Schuster, 1997.

Bassett, John Spencer. *The Correspondence of Andrew Jackson*. Washington: Carnegie Institution of Washington, 1926–35.

———. *The Life of Andrew Jackson*. Garden City, N.Y.: Doubleday, Page, 1911.

Bausman, Joseph H. *History of Beaver County*. New York: Knickerbocker Press, 1904.

Beck, Lewis Caleb. *Gazetteer of the States of Illinois and Missouri*. Albany: C. R. & G. Webster, 1823.

Bemis, Samuel Flagg. *Pinckney's Treaty*. New Haven: Yale Univ. Press, 1960.

Betts, Edwin Morris, and James Adam Bear, Jr., eds. *The Family Letters of Thomas Jefferson*. Columbia: Univ. of Missouri Press, 1966.

Billon, Frederic Louis. *Annals of St. Louis in Its Early Days Under the French and Spanish Dominations, 1764–1804*. St. Louis: G. I. Jones, 1886 [New York: Arno Press and The New York Times, 1971].

Bodley, Temple. *History of Kentucky*. Chicago: S. J. Clarke, 1928.

———, ed. *Littell's Political Transactions in and Concerning Kentucky*. Louisville: J. P. Morton, 1926 [New York: Arno Press and The New York Times, 1971].

Bolt, Bruce A. *Earthquakes*. New York: W. H. Freeman, 1993.

———, and K. E. Bullen. *An Introduction to the Theory of Seismology*. Cambridge: Cambridge Univ. Press, 1985.

Boyd, Julian P., ed. *The Papers of Thomas Jefferson*. Princeton: Princeton Univ. Press, 1950.

Brackenridge, H. M. *Recollections of Persons and Places in the West*. Philadelphia: J. B. Lippincott, 1868.

———. *Views of Louisiana*. Pittsburgh: Cramer, Spear & Eichbaum, 1814.

Bradbury, John. *Travels in the Interior of America*. London: Sherwood, Neely, and Jones, 1819 [reprinted in Reuben Gold Thwaites, ed. *Early Western Travels*, Vol. 5. Cleveland: Arthur H. Clark, 1905; facsimile reprint, Lincoln and London: Univ. of Nebraska Press, 1986].

Bradford, Gamaliel. *Damaged Souls*. Boston and New York: Houghton Mifflin, 1923.

Brown, Samuel R. *Views of the Campaigns of the North-Western Army*. Troy, N.Y.: Francis Adancourt, 1814.

———. *The Western Gazetteer; or Emigrant's Directory*. Auburn, N.Y.: H. C. Southwick, 1817 [New York: Arno Press and The New York Times, 1971].

Brunson, Alfred, Rev. *A Western Pioneer*. Cincinnati: Hitchcok & Walden, 1872.

Burnaby, Andrew. *Travels Through the Middle Settlements in North-America*. London: T. Payne, 1765 [Ithaca, N.Y.: Great Seal Books, 1960].

Burton, Arthur G., and Leonard C. Faber. *Missouri: The Sesquicentennial of Statehood*. Washington: U.S. Gov't. Printing Office, 1971.

Butler, Mann. *A History of the Commonwealth of Kentucky*. Louisville: Wilcox, Dickerman, 1834.

Campbell, Maria. *Revolutionary Services and Civil Life of General William Hull*. New York and Philadelphia: Appleton, 1848.

Campbell, Robert Allen. *Campbell's Gazetteer of Missouri*. St. Louis: R. A. Campbell, 1934–1962.

Cappon, Lester J. *The Adams–Jefferson Letters*. Chapel Hill: Univ. of North Carolina Press, 1959.

Carr, Lucien. *Missouri*. Boston and New York: Houghton Mifflin, 1888.

Carter, Clarence Edwin. *The Territorial Papers of the United States*. Washington: U.S. Gov't. Printing Office, 1973.

Carter, Edward C., and Thomas E. Jeffrey, eds. *The Papers of Benjamin Henry Latrobe*. Clifton, N.J.: James T. White, 1976.

Casseday, Ben. *The History of Louisville*. Louisville: Hull & Brother, 1852.

Catterall, Helen Tunnicliff. *Judicial Cases Concerning American Slavery and the Negro*. New York: Octagon, 1968.

Caughey, John Walton. *McGillivray of the Creeks*. Norman: Univ. of Oklahoma Press, 1938.

Chambers, George F. *The Story of the Comets*. Oxford: Clarendon Press, 1909.

Channing, Steven A. *Kentucky*. New York: W. W. Norton and Nashville: American Assoc. for State and Local History, 1977.

Chastellux, François Jean, Marquis de. *Travels in North-America, in the Years 1780, 1781, and 1782*. Translated from the French by an English Gentleman. London: G. G. J. & J. Robinson, 1787 [Chapel Hill: Univ. of North Carolina Press, 1963].

Chevalier, Michel. *Society, Manners and Politics in the United States.* Thomas Gamaliel Bradford, trans. Boston: Weeks, Jordan, 1839 [Garden City, N.Y.: Doubleday, 1961].

Cist, Charles. *Cincinnati Miscellany.* Cincinnati: C. Clark, 1845–1846 [New York: Arno Press and The New York Times, 1971].

Claiborne, J. F. H. *Life and Times of Gen. Sam Dale, The Mississippi Partisan.* New York: Harper & Brothers, 1860.

Clark, Daniel. *Proofs of the Corruption of Gen. James Wilkinson.* Philadelphia: Wm. Hall, Jun. & Geo. W. Pierie, 1809 [New York: Arno Press and The New York Times, 1971].

Clark, Thomas Dionysius. *The Rampaging Frontier.* Bloomington: Indiana Univ. Press, 1964.

Clark, William, and Meriwether Lewis. *The History of the Lewis and Clark Expedition.* Elliott Coues, ed. New York: Dover, 1965.

Cleaves, Freeman. *Old Tippecanoe: William Henry Harrison and His Time.* New York: C. Scribner's Sons, 1939.

Coffin, William F. *1812; The War, and Its Moral.* Montreal: John Lovell, 1864.

Collot, Georges-Henri-Victor. *A Journey in North America.* Paris: A. Bertrand, 1826 [Firenze: O. Lange, 1924].

Combs, Leslie. *Col. Wm. Dudley's Defeat Opposite Fort Meigs.* Cincinnati: Spiller & Gates, 1869.

Cotterill, R. S. *The Southern Indians.* Norman: Univ. of Oklahoma Press, 1954.

Coxe, Daniel. *A Description of the English Province of Carolana.* London: O. Payne, 1741 [Gainesville: University Presses of Florida, 1976].

Cramer, Zadok. *The Navigator.* Eighth edition. Pittsburgh: Cramer, Spear & Eichbaum, 1814 [Ann Arbor: University Microfilms, 1966].

Craven, Avery O. *Soil Exhaustion as a Factor in the Agricultural History of Virginia and Maryland, 1606–1860.* Urbana: Univ. of Illinois Press, 1926.

Cruikshank, E. A., ed. *Documents Relating to the Invasion of Canada and the Surrender of Detroit, 1812.* Ottawa: Gov't. Printing Bureau, 1912.

Cuming, F. *Sketches of a Tour to the Western Country.* Pittsburgh: Cramer, Spear & Eichbaum, 1810 [reprinted in Reuben Gold Thwaites, ed. *Early Western Travels: 1748–1846,* Vol. 4. Cleveland: Arthur H. Clark, 1905; facsimile reprint, Lincoln and London: Univ. of Nebraska Press, 1986].

Cummings, Samuel. *The Western Pilot.* Cincinnati: N. & G. Guilford, 1847 [Cincinnati: Young & Klein, 1978].

Cutler, William Parker, and Julia Perkins Cutler. *Life, Journals and Correspondence of Rev. Manasseh Cutler, LL.D.* Cincinnati: R. Clarke, 1888 [Athens: Ohio Univ. Press, 1987].

Dangerfield, George. *Chancellor Robert R. Livingston of New York, 1746–1813.* New York: Harcourt, Brace, 1960.

Davis, George H. *Active Tectonics and Society: A Plan for Integrative Science.* No location given: The Committee, 1994.

Davison, Charles. *Great Earthquakes.* London: T. Murby, 1936.

Dawson, Moses. *A Historical Narrative of the Civil and Military Services of Major-General William H. Harrison.* Cincinnati: M. Dawson, 1824.

de Hault Delassus, Charles. *An Official Account of the Situation, Soil, Produce, &c. of that part of Louisiana which lies between the mouth of the Missouri and New Madrid, or L'Anse a la Graise, and on the west side of the Mississippi.* No location given: Francis Valle, 1796. (In Library of Congress Rare Book Room.)

de Montulé, Édouard. *Travels in America, 1816–1817.* Translated from the original French of 1821 by Edward D. Seeber. Bloomington: Indiana Univ. Press, 1950.

Denny, Ebenezer. *Military Journal of Major Ebenezer Denny.* Philadelphia: J. B. Lippincott, 1859 [Arno Press and The New York Times, 1971].

Devens, R. M. *Our First Century.* Springfield, Mass.: C. A. Nichols, 1877.

Dohan, Mary Helen. *Mr. Roosevelt's Steamboat.* New York: Dodd, Mead, 1981.

Donovan, Frank. *River Boats of America.* New York: Crowell, 1966.

Douglass, Robert Sidney. *History of Southeast Missouri.* New York and Chicago: Lewis, 1912 [Cape Girardeau, Mo.: Ramfre Press, 1961].

Dow, Lorenzo. *History of Cosmopolite.* Philadelphia: Joseph Rakestraw, 1815.

Dowd, Gregory Evans. *A Spirited Resistance: The North American Indian Struggle for Unity, 1745–1815.* Baltimore and London: Johns Hopkins Univ. Press, 1992.

Drake, Benjamin. *Life of Tecumseh.* Cincinnati: E. Morgan, 1841 [Arno Press and The New York Times, 1969].

Drake, Daniel. *Natural and Statistical View, or Picture of Cincinnati and the Miami Country.* Cincinnati: Looker & Wallace, 1815.

Drinnon, Richard. *White Savage: The Case of John Dunn Hunter.* New York: Schocken, 1972.

Du Roi, August Wilhelm. *Journal of Du Roi the Elder.* Translated from the original German in the Library of Congress by Charlotte S. J. Epping. Philadelphia: University of Pennsylvania and New York: D. Appleton, 1911.

Edgar, Matilda Ridout, Lady. *General Brock.* London, T. C. & E. C. Jack, 1905.

Edmunds, R. David. *The Shawnee Prophet.* Lincoln and London: Univ. of Nebraska Press, 1985.

———. *Tecumseh and the Quest for Indian Leadership.* Boston and Toronto: Little, Brown, 1984.

Esarey, Logan, ed. *Messages and Letters of William Henry Harrison.* Indianapolis: Indiana Historical Commission, 1922.

Evans, Estwick. *Evans's Pedestrious Tour of Four Thousand Miles—1818.* Cleveland: Arthur H. Clark, 1904.

Farley, John E. *Earthquake Fears, Predictions, and Preparations in Mid-America.* Carbondale: Southern Illinois Univ. Press, 1998.

Fischer, David Hackett. *Albion's Seed.* New York: Oxford Univ. Press, 1989.

Flexner, James Thomas. *Steamboats Come True.* New York: Viking, 1944.

Flint, Timothy. *A Condensed Geography and History of the Western States.* Cincinnati: William M. Farnsworth, 1828 [Gainesville, Fl.: Scholars' Facsimiles and Reprints, 1970].

———. *Recollections of the Last Ten Years.* Boston: Cummings, Hilliard, 1826 [New York and London: Johnson Reprint Corp., 1968].

Foley, William E. *The Genesis of Missouri.* Columbia: Univ. of Missouri Press, 1989.

————. *A History of Missouri.* Columbia: Univ. of Missouri Press, 1971.

Ford, Paul Leicester, ed. *The Works of Thomas Jefferson.* New York: G. P. Putnam's Sons, 1904–1905.

————. *The Writings of Thomas Jefferson.* New York: G. P. Putnam's Sons, 1892–99.

Forman, Samuel S. *Narrative of a Journey Down the Ohio and Mississippi in 1789–90.* Cincinnati: Robert Clarke, 1888 [New York: Arno Press and The New York Times, 1971].

Fortier, Alcée. *A History of Louisiana.* New York: Goupil, 1904.

Foster, J. W. *The Mississippi Valley.* Chicago: S. C. Griggs; London: Trubner, 1869.

Foster, James. ed. *War on the Detroit: The Chronicles of Verchères de Boucherville.* Chicago: Lakeside Press, 1940.

Frazier, Harriet C. *Slavery and Crime in Missouri, 1773–1865.* Jefferson, N.C., and London: McFarland, 2001.

Fredriksen, John C. *War of 1812 Eyewitness Accounts.* Westport, Conn., and London: Greenwood Press, 1997.

Fuller, Myron L. *The New Madrid Earthquake.* U.S.G.S. Bulletin 494. Washington: Gov't. Printing Office, 1912 [Cape Girardeau, Mo.: Center for Earthquake Studies, 1989].

Galloway, William A. *Old Chillicothe.* Xenia, Ohio: Buckeye Press, 1934.

Gayarré, Charles. *History of Louisiana.* New Orleans: A. Hawkins, 1885.

Gipson, Lawrence Henry, ed. *The Moravian Indian Mission on White River.* Indianapolis: Indiana Historical Bureau, 1938.

Gleig, G. R. *A Narrative of the Campaigns of the British Army at Washington, Baltimore, and New Orleans.* Philadelphia: M. Carey & Sons, 1821.

————. *A Subaltern in America.* Philadelphia: E. L. Carey & A. Hart, and Baltimore: Carey & Hart, 1833.

Goodell, William. *The American Slave Code in Theory and Practice.* London: Clarke, Beeton, 1853[?].

Gould, E. W. *Fifty Years on the Mississippi.* Columbus, Ohio: Long's College Book Co., 1951.

Graydon, Alexander. *Memoirs of His Own Time.* Philadelphia: Lindsay & Blakiston, 1846.

Green, Thomas Marshall. *The Spanish Conspiracy.* Cincinnati: R. Clarke, 1891 [Gloucester, Mass.: P. Smith 1967].

Griffith, Benjamin W., Jr. *McIntosh and Weatherford, Creek Indian Leaders.* Tuscaloosa and London: Univ. of Alabama Press, 1988.

Griffith, Lucille. *History of Alabama, 1540–1900.* Northport, Ala.: Colonial Press, 1962.

Guild, Jo. C. *Old Times in Tennessee.* Nashville: Tavel, Eastman & Howell, 1878.

Halbert, H. S., and T. H. Ball. *The Creek War of 1813 and 1814.* Chicago: Donohue & Henneberry, and Montgomery, Ala.: White, Woodruff, & Fowler, 1895 [University: Univ. of Alabama Press, 1969].

Hall, James. *Letters from the West.* London: Henry Colburn, 1828 [Gainesville, Fla.: Scholars' Facsimiles and Reprints, 1967].

————. *Notes on the Western States.* Philadelphia: Harrison Hall, 1838.

Halstead, Murat. *The World on Fire.* No location given: International Publishing Society, 1902.

Hamilton, Robert M., and Arch C. Johnston. *Tecumseh's Prophecy: Preparing for the Next New Madrid Earthquake.* U.S. Geological Survey Circular 1066. Denver: Dept. of the Interior, USGS, 1990.

Hamlin, Talbot. *Benjamin Henry Latrobe.* New York: Oxford Univ. Press, 1955.

Harper, Frank C. *Pittsburgh.* New York, Comet Press Books, 1957.

Hartley, Joseph R. *The Economic Effects of Ohio River Navigation.* Bloomington: School of Business, Indiana Univ., 1959.

Harvey, Henry. *History of the Shawnee Indians.* Cincinnati: Morgan, 1855.

Hatch, William Stanley. *A Chapter of the History of the War of 1812 in the Northwest.* Cincinnati: Miami Printing and Publishing, 1872.

Hay, Thomas Robson, and M. R. Werner. *The Admirable Trumpeter.* Garden City, N.Y.: Doubleday, Doran, 1941.

Haywood, John. *The Natural and Aboriginal History of Tennessee.* Nashville: G. Wilson, 1823.

Heckewelder, John. *History, Manners, and Customs of the Indian Nations Who Once Inhabited Pennsylvania and the Neighboring States.* Philadelphia: A. Small, 1819 [Salem, N.H.: Ayer, 1991].

———. *A Narrative of the Mission of the United Brethren Among the Delaware and Mohegan Indians.* Philadelphia: McCarty & Davis, 1820 [New York: Arno Press and The New York Times, 1971].

Hickey, Donald R. *The War of 1812.* Urbana and Chicago: Univ. of Illinois Press, 1989.

Hill, Roscoe R. *Descriptive Catalogue of the Documents Relating to the History of the United States in the Papeles Procedentes de Cuba.* Washington, D.C.: Carnegie Institution of Washington, 1916 [New York: Kraus Reprint Corp., 1965].

Hindus, Michael Stephen. *Prison and Plantation.* Chapel Hill: Univ. of North Carolina Press, 1980.

Horsman, Reginald. *The Causes of the War of 1812.* Philadelphia: Univ. of Pennsylvania Press, 1962.

———. *Expansion and American Indian Policy, 1783–1812.* East Lansing: Michigan St. Univ. Press, 1967.

———. *The War of 1812.* New York: Alfred A. Knopf, 1969.

Houck, Louis. *A History of Missouri.* Chicago: R. R. Donnelley, 1908 [New York: Arno Press and The New York Times, 1971].

———. *The Spanish Regime in Missouri.* Chicago: R. R. Donnelley, 1909 [New York: Arno Press and The New York Times, 1971].

Hough, Susan Elizabeth. *Earthshaking Science: What We Know (and Don't Know) About Earthquakes.* Princeton: Princeton Univ. Press, 2002.

Howe, Henry. *Historical Collections of Ohio.* Cincinnati: State of Ohio, 1888.

———. *Historical Collections of the Great West.* Cincinnati: Henry Howe, 1852.

Hubbard-Brown, Janet. *The Shawnee.* New York and Philadelphia: Chelsea House, 1995.

Hulbert, Archer Butler. *The Ohio River: A Course of Empire.* New York and London: G. P. Putnam's Sons, 1906.

Hunt, Galliard, ed. *The Writings of James Madison*. New York and London: G. P. Putnam's Sons, 1900.

Hunter, John Dunn. *Memoirs of a Captivity Among the Indians of North America*. London: Longman, Hurst, Rees, Orme & Brown, 1823 [New York: Schocken, 1973].

Hunter, Louis C. *Steamboats on the Western Rivers*. Cambridge: Harvard Univ. Press, 1949.

Indians of Ohio, Indiana, Illinois, Southern Michigan and Southern Wisconsin. Indian Claims Commission Findings. New York and London: Garland, 1974.

Ireland, Robert M. *The County Courts in Antebellum Kentucky*. Lexington: Univ. Press of Kentucky, 1972.

Jacobs, James Ripley. *Tarnished Warrior*. New York: Macmillan, 1938.

James, Edwin. *Account of an Expedition from Pittsburgh to the Rocky Mountains*. Philadelphia: H. C. Carey & I. Lea, 1823.

James, James Alton. *The Life of George Rogers Clark*. Chicago: Univ. of Chicago Press, 1928.

James, William. *A Full and Correct Account of the Chief Naval Occurences of the Late War*. London: T. Egerton, 1817.

Jefferson, Thomas. *Notes on the State of Virginia*. William Peden, ed. Chapel Hill: Univ. of North Carolina Press, 1955.

Jordan, Winthrop D. *White over Black*. Chapel Hill: Univ. of North Carolina Press, 1968.

Journal of the House of Representatives of the Commonwealth of Kentucky, 1809. Frankfort: William Gerard, 1810.

Kennedy, Roger G. *Hidden Cities*. New York: Free Press, 1994.

———. *Mr. Jefferson's Lost Cause*. New York: Oxford Univ. Press, 2003.

Kinnaird, Lawrence. *Spain in the Mississippi Valley, 1765–1794*. Washington: U.S. Gov't. Printing Office, 1946–49.

Klinck, Carl F. *Tecumseh: Fact and Fiction in Early Records*. Englewood Cliffs, N.J.: Prentice Hall, 1961.

———, and James J. Talman. *The Journal of Major John Norton, 1816*. Toronto: Champlain Society, 1970.

Knopf, Richard C., ed. *Anthony Wayne, A Name in Arms*. Pittsburgh: Univ. of Pittsburgh Press, 1959.

Knox, Ray, and David Stewart. *The Earthquake America Forgot*. Marble Hill, Mo.: Gutenberg-Richter, 1995.

Kukla, Jon. *A Wilderness So Immense*. New York: Alfred A. Knopf, 2003.

La Rochefoucauld-Liancourt, Duke de. *Travels Through the United States of North America*. London: H. Phillips, 1799.

Latour, Arsène Lacarrière. *Historical Memoir of the War in West Florida and Louisiana in 1814–15*. Philadelphia: J. Conrad, 1816 [Gainesville: Historic New Orleans Collection and Univ. Press of Florida, 1999].

Latrobe, Charles J. *The Rambler in North America, 1822–23* London: R. B. Seeley & W. Burnside, 1835 [New York: Johnson Reprint Corp., 1970].

Latrobe, J. H. B. *The First Steamboat Voyage on the Western Waters*. Baltimore: John Murphy, 1871.

———. *A Lost Chapter in the History of the Steamboat*. Baltimore: John Murphy, 1871.

Law, Judge. *The Colonial History of Vincennes.* Vincennes, Ind.: Harvey, Mason, 1858.

Leahy, Ethel Carter. *Who's Who on the Ohio River and Its Tributaries.* Cincinnati: Leahy, 1931.

Lewis, William. *Genealogy of the Lewis Family in America.* Louisville: Courier-Journal Job Printing Co., 1893.

Littell, William. *The Statute Law of Kentucky.* Frankfort: Johnston & Pleasants, 1810.

———, and Jacob Swigert. *A Digest of the Statute Law of Kentucky.* Frankfort: Kendall & Russell, 1822.

Lloyd, James T. *Lloyd's Steamboat Directory.* Cincinnati: J. T. Lloyd, 1856.

Logsdon, David R. *"I Was There!" in the New Madrid Earthquakes of 1811–12.* Nashville: Kettle Mills Press, 1990.

Longford, ed. *Pakenham Letters: 1800 to 1815.* London: John and Edward Bumpus, 1914.

Lossing, Benson J. *The Pictorial Field Book of the War of 1812.* New York: Harper & Bros., 1868.

Lyell, Charles, Sir. *A Second Visit to the United States of North America.* London: John Murray, 1849.

Madison, James. *Letters and Other Writings of James Madison.* Philadelphia: J. B. Lippincott, 1865.

Malone, Dumas. *Jefferson, the Virginian.* Boston: Little, Brown, 1948.

Marshall, Humphrey. *The History of Kentucky.* Frankfort: Henry Gore, 1812.

McAfee, Robert Breckinridge. *History of the Late War in the Western Country.* Lexington, Ky.: Worsley & Smith, 1816 [No location given: Readex Microprint Corp., 1966].

McCollough, Alameda, ed. *The Battle of Tippecanoe.* Lafayette, Ind.: Tippecanoe County Historical Association, 1973.

McKenney, Thomas L., and James Hall. *The Indian Tribes of North America.* Edinburgh: John Grant, 1934.

McMurtrie, Henry. *Sketches of Louisville and Its Environs.* Louisville: S. Penn, 1819.

McRaven, William Henry. *Nashville, Athens of the South.* Chapel Hill: Scheer & Jervis, 1949.

Melish, John. *Travels Through the United States of America.* Philadelphia: John Melish, 1815.

Merrill, Boynton, Jr. *Jefferson's Nephews.* Princeton: Princeton Univ. Press, 1976.

Michaux, François André. *Travels to the Westward of the Allegany Mountains.* B. Lambert, trans. London: J. Mawman, 1805.

Miller, Nathan. *The Founding Finaglers.* New York: D. McKay, 1976.

Monette, John W. *History of the Discovery and Settlement of the Valley of the Mississippi.* New York: Harper & Brothers, 1846 [New York: Arno Press and The New York Times, 1971].

Mooney, James. *The Ghost-Dance Religion and the Sioux Outbreak of 1890.* Fourteenth annual report of the Bureau of Ethnology to the Secretary of the Smithsonian Institution, 1892–93, Part 2. Washington: U.S. Gov't. Printing Office, 1896.

Morison, Samuel Eliot. *The Oxford History of the American People.* New York: Oxford Univ. Press, 1965.

Morris, Thomas. *Southern Slavery and the Law, 1619–1860.* Chapel Hill: Univ. of North Carolina Press, 1996.

Morrison, John H. *History of American Steam Navigation.* New York: W. F. Sametz, 1903 [New York: Stephen Daye Press, 1958].

Moser, Harold D., et al., eds. *The Papers of Andrew Jackson.* Knoxville: Univ. of Tennessee Press, 1980.

Moulton, Gary E., ed. *The Papers of Chief John Ross.* Norman: Univ. of Oklahoma Press, 1985.

Mueller, Myrl Rhine. *Lost in the Annals.* Little Rock: J & B Quality Book Bindery, 1990.

Musick, John R. *Stories of Missouri.* New York: American Book Co., 1897.

Newton, J. H., G. G. Nicholas, and A. G. Sprankle. *History of the Pan-handle.* Wheeling: J. A. Caldwell, 1879 [Evansville, Ind.: Unigraphic, 1973].

Nobles, Gregory H. *American Frontiers.* New York: Hill & Wang, 1997.

Nolte, Vincent. *Fifty Years in Both Hemispheres.* New York: Redfield, 1854.

North, Sterling. *The First Steamboat on the Mississippi.* Boston: Houghton Mifflin, 1962.

Nutall, Thomas. *A Journal of Travels into the Arkansas Territory During the Year 1819.* Philadelphia: T. H. Palmer, 1821 [Norman: Univ. of Oklahoma Press, 1980].

Officer, Charles, and Jake Page. *The Big One.* Boston and New York: Houghton Mifflin, 2004.

Olmstead, Earl P. *Blackcoats Among the Delaware.* Kent, Oh., and London: Kent State Univ. Press, 1991.

Owsley, Frank Lawrence, Jr. *Struggle for the Gulf Borderlands.* Gainesville: Univ. Presses of Florida, 1981.

Padover, Saul K., ed. *A Jefferson Profile as Revealed in His Letters.* New York: John Day, 1956.

Palmer, John. *Journal of Travels in the United States of North America.* London: Sherwood, Neely & Jones, 1818.

Palmer, William P. *Calendar of Virginia State Papers.* Richmond: no publisher given, 1795 [New York: Kraus Reprint Corp., 1968].

Penick, James Lal, Jr. *The New Madrid Earthquakes.* Columbia and London: Univ. of Missouri Press, 1981.

Pickett, Albert James. *History of Alabama.* Charleston: Walker & James, 1851 [New York: Arno Press and The New York Times, 1971].

Pierce, William Leigh. *An Account of the Great Earthquakes.* Newburyport, Mass.: Herald Office, 1812.

———. *The Year: A Poem in Three Cantoes.* New York: David Longworth, 1813.

Pierson, Rev. Hamilton Wilcox. *Jefferson at Monticello: The Private Life of Thomas Jefferson.* In *Jefferson at Monticello,* James. A. Bear, Jr., ed. Charlottesville: Univ. of Virginia Press, 1967.

Pirtle, Alfred. *The Battle of Tippecanoe.* Louisville: J. P. Morton, 1900.

Pope, John. *A Tour Through the Southern and Western Territories of the United States of North-America.* Richmond: J. Dixon, 1792 [Gainesville: Univ. Presses of Florida, 1979].

Posey, Walter Brownlow. *The Baptist Church in the Lower Mississippi Valley, 1776–1845.* Lexington: Univ. of Kentucky Press, 1957.

Pound, Merritt B. *Benjamin Hawkins: Indian Agent.* Athens: Univ. of Georgia Press, 1951.

Preble, George Henry. *A Chronological History of the Origin and Development of Steam Navigation.* Philadelphia: L. R. Hamersly, 1883.

Press, Frank, and Raymond Siever. *Understanding EARTH.* New York: W. H. Freeman, 1994.

Proctor, George. *The Lucubrations of Humphrey Ravelin, Esq.* London: G. and W. B. Whitaker, 1823.

Prucha, Paul. *American Indian Policy in the Formative Years.* Cambridge: Harvard Univ. Press, 1962.

Purcell, Martha Grassham. *Lucy Jefferson Lewis.* Kentucky: no publisher given, 1924.

Quaife, Milo Milton, ed. *The John Askin Papers.* Detroit: Detroit Library Commission, 1928.

Quick, Herbert, and Edward Quick. *Mississippi Steamboatin'.* New York: Holt, 1926.

Randolph, Sarah N. *The Domestic Life of Thomas Jefferson.* New York: Harper & Bros., 1871 [Cambridge, Mass.: University Press, 1939].

Remini, Robert Vincent. *Andrew Jackson and the Course of American Empire.* New York: Harper & Row, 1977.

———. *The Battle of New Orleans.* New York: Viking, 1999.

Report of the Debates and Proceedings of the Convention for the Revision of the Constitution of the State of Kentucky, 1849. Frankfort: A. G. Hodges, 1849.

Reynolds, John. *My Own Times.* Belleville, Ill.: B. H. Perryman & H. L. Davison, 1855.

Richardson, Major. *The Canadian Brothers.* Toronto and Buffalo: Univ. of Toronto Press, 1976.

———. *War of 1812.* No location or publisher given, 1842 [Toronto: Coles Publishing, 1974].

Robert, Joseph C. *The Story of Tobacco in America.* New York: Alfred A. Knopf, 1949.

Roberts, James. *The Narrative of James Roberts.* Hattiesburg: Book Farm, 1945.

Roosevelt, Theodore. *The Winning of the West.* New York: G. P. Putnam's Sons, 1896.

Ross, James. *Life and Times of Elder Reuben Ross.* Philadelphia: Grant, Faires & Rodgers, 1882[?].

Rothert, Otto A. *A History of Muhlenberg County.* Louisville: Morton, 1913.

———. *The Outlaws of Cave-in-Rock.* Cleveland: A. H. Clark, 1924 [Carbondale and Edwardsville: Southern Illinois Univ. Press, 1996].

Royall, Anne Newport. *Letters from Alabama, 1817–1822.* University: Univ. of Alabama Press, 1969.

Rozier, Firmin A. *Rozier's History of the Early Settlement of the Mississippi Valley.* St. Louis: G. A. Pierrot & Son, 1890.

Ruter, P. S. *Reminiscences of a Virginia Physician.* Louisville: Ben Casseday, 1849.

Rutland, Robert A., et al., eds. *The Papers of James Madison.* Charlottesville: Univ. Press of Virginia, 1984.

Savelle, Max. *George Morgan: Colony Builder.* New York: Columbia Univ. Press, 1932 [New York: AMS Press, 1967].

Schachner, Nathan. *Thomas Jefferson: A Biography*. New York: Appleton-Century-Crofts, 1951.

Schoepf, Johann David. *Travels in the Confederation*. Alfred J. Morrison, ed. and trans. Philadelphia: Campbell, 1911.

Schoolcraft, Henry Rowe. *Transallegania, or, The Groans of Missouri*. New York: J. Seymour, 1820.

———. *Travels in the Central Portions of the Mississippi Valley*. New York: J. & J. Harper, 1825 [Millwood, N.Y.: Kraus Reprint Co., 1975].

Schultz, Christian. *Travels on an Inland Voyage*. New York: Isaac Reilly, 1810.

Scott, Winfield. *Memoirs of Lieut.-General Scott, LL.D.* New York: Sheldon, 1864 [Freeport, N.Y.: Books for Libraries Press, 1970].

Shea, John Gilmary. *Early Voyages Up and Down the Mississippi*. Albany: J. Munsell, 1861.

Shearer, Peter M. *Introduction to Seismology*. Cambridge and New York: Cambridge Univ. Press, 1999.

Sheehan, Bernard W. *Seeds of Extinction: Jeffersonian Philanthropy and the American Indian*. Chapel Hill: Univ. of North Carolina Press, 1973.

Shields, Joseph D. *Natchez: Its Early History*. Louisville: J. P. Morgan, 1930.

Shrum, Edison E. *The Real New Madrid Earthquakes*. Scott County, Mo.[?]: Scott County Historical Society, 1989.

Slotkin, Richard. *Regeneration Through Violence. The Mythology of the American Frontier*. Middleton, Conn: Wesleyan Univ. Press, 1973.

Smith, G. C. Moore, ed. *The Autobiography of Lieutenant-General Sir Harry Smith*. London: J. Murray, 1902.

Smith, Z. F. *The History of Kentucky from its Earliest Discovery and Settlement, to the Present Date*. Louisville: Courier-Journal Job Printing Co., 1886.

Smith, James, ed. *The Posthumous Works of James M'Gready*. Louisville: Worsley, 1831.

Smyth-Davis, Mary F. *History of Dunklin County, Mo., 1845–1895*. St. Louis: Nixon-Jones, 1896.

Snively, William. *Satan's Ferryman*. New York: F. Ungar, 1968.

Spence, William et al. *Responses to Iben Browning's Prediction of a 1990 New Madrid, Missouri, Earthquake*. U.S. Geological Survey Circular 1083. Washington: U.S. Gov't. Printing Office: 1993.

Stampp, Kenneth M. *The Peculiar Institution*. New York: Vintage, 1956.

Starling, Edmund L. *History of Henderson County, Kentucky*. Henderson: no publisher given, 1887 [Evansville, Ind.: Unigraphic, 1965].

Stoddard, Amos. *Sketches, Historical and Descriptive, of Louisiana*. Philadelphia: Mathew Carey, 1812.

Strickland, W. P. *Pioneers of the West*. New York: Carlton & Phillips; Boston: J. P. Magee, 1856.

———, ed. *Autobiography of Peter Cartwright, the Backwoods Preacher*. New York: Carlton & Porter, 1857.

———, ed. *Autobiography of Rev. James B. Finley*. Cincinnati: R. P. Thompson, 1856.

Strickland, William, Sir. *Journal of a Tour in the United States of America, 1794–1795*. London: W. Bulmer, 1801 [New York: New-York Historical Society, 1971].

Sugden, John. *Tecumseh: A Life.* New York: Henry Holt, 1997.

Tanner, John. *The Falcon: A Narrative of the Captivity and Adventures of John Tanner.* New York: Penguin, 1994.

Tarkington, Joseph. *Autobiography of Rev. Joseph Tarkington.* Cincinnati: Curts & Jennings, 1899.

Taylor, John. *Arator.* Georgetown and Columbia, Va.: J. M. & J. B. Carter, 1813.

Thompson, Wilson. *The Autobiography of Elder Wilson Thompson.* Cincinnati: Moore, Wilstach & Baldwin, 1867 [Springfield, Ohio: Edgar T. Aleshire and Cincinnati: Lasserre Bradley, Jr., 1962].

Thornbrough, Gayle, ed. *The Correspondence of John Badollet and Albert Gallatin, 1804–1836.* Indianapolis: Indiana Historical Society, 1963.

———. *Letter Book of the Indian Agency at Fort Wayne, 1809–1815.* Indianapolis: Indiana Historical Society, 1961.

Thorpe, Francis Newton. *The Federal and State Constitutions, Colonial Charters, and Other Organic Laws of the States.* Washington: U.S. Government Printing Office, 1909.

Tributsch, Helmut. *When the Snakes Awake.* Paul Langner, trans. Cambridge, Mass., and London: MIT Press, 1982.

Trowbridge, C. C. *Shawnese Traditions.* Ann Arbor: Univ. of Michigan Press: 1939.

Tucker, Glenn. *Tecumseh: Vision of Glory.* Indianapolis: Bobbs-Merrill, 1956.

Tupper, Ferdinand Brock. *The Life and Correspondence of Major-General Isaac Brock, K.B.* London: Simkin, Marshall, 1847.

Tushnet, Mark V. *The American Law of Slavery.* Princeton: Princeton Univ. Press, 1981.

———. *Slave Law in the American South.* Lawrence: Univ. Press of Kansas, 2003.

Van Every, Dale. *Ark of Empire.* New York: William Morrow, 1963.

———. *The Final Challenge.* New York: William Morrow, 1964.

Van Horne, ed. *The Correspondence and Miscellaneous Papers of Benjamin Henry Latrobe.* New Haven: Yale Univ. Press, 1984–1988.

Van Tramp, John C. *Prairie and Rocky Mountain Adventures, or, Life in the West.* Columbus, Ohio: Segner & Condit, 1870.

Verhoeff, Mary. *The Kentucky River Navigation.* Louisville: J. P. Morton, 1917.

Von Humboldt, Alexander. *The Travels and Researches of Alexander von Humboldt.* Edinburgh: Oliver & Boyd, and London: Simpkin & Marshall, 1833.

Walker, Adam. *A Journal of Two Campaigns.* Keene, N.H.: Sentinel Press, 1816.

Warren, Robert Penn. *Brother to Dragons.* New York: Random House, 1953.

Watts, William C. *Chronicles of a Kentucky Settlement.* New York: G. P. Putnam, 1897.

Weems, John Edward. *Men Without Countries.* Boston: Houghton Mifflin, 1969.

Weld, Isaac. *Travels Through the States of North America and the Provinces of Upper & Lower Canada During the Years 1795, 1796 & 1797.* London, Printed for J. Stockdale, 1800 [New York: A. M. Kelley, 1970].

Weld, Theodore D., comp. *American Slavery As It Is.* New York: American Anti-Slavery Society, 1839 [New York: Arno Press and The New York Times, 1968].

Wertenbaker, Thomas J. *The Planters of Colonial Virginia.* Princeton: Princeton Univ. Press, 1922.

Wetmore, Alphonso. *Gazetteer of the State of Missouri.* St. Louis: C. Keemle, 1837.

Wheeler, J. D. *A Practical Treatise on the Law of Slavery*. New York: Negro Universities Press, 1968.

Whitaker, Arthur Preston. *The Spanish-American Frontier: 1783–1795*. Boston and New York: Houghton Mifflin, 1927.

White, Richard. *The Middle Ground: Indians, Empires, and Republics in the Great Lakes Region, 1650–1815*. Cambridge and New York: Cambridge Univ. Press, 1991.

Whittemore, Henry. *Fulfilment of Three Remarkable Prophecies in the History of The Great Empire State Relating to the Development of Steam Navigation . . . and Railroad Transportation, 1808–1908*. No location or publisher given, 1909.

Wilkinson, James. *Memoirs of My Own Times*. Philadelphia: Abraham Small, 1816.

Williams, Samuel Cole. *Beginnings of West Tennessee*. Johnson City, Tenn.: Watauga Press, 1930.

Williams, Joseph S. *Old Times in West Tennessee*. Memphis: W. G. Cheeney, 1873.

Wood, William Charles Henry. *Select British Documents of the Canadian War of 1812*. Toronto: Champlain Society, 1920–1928 [New York: Greenwood Press, 1968].

Woodward, Thomas Simpson. *Woodward's Reminiscences of the Creek, or Miscogee Indians*. Tuscaloosa: no publisher given, 1859 [Tuscaloosa: Alabama Book Store, and Birmingham: Birmingham Book Exchange, 1939].

Acknowledgments

MANY PEOPLE helped me with this project, of course, and if I've forgotten to mention anyone here, I sincerely apologize. First of all, I have to thank Bill Cooper. If he hadn't brought the New Madrid earthquakes to my attention some years ago, there would have been no book.

A number of friends read the original proposal and had valuable ideas: Amy Clark, Larry Greer, Joe Grossman, Ian Martin, Dave Masiel, and James Rodewald all made significant contributions. Grace Bedoian, the best-kept secret in proofreading, read the galley proof of the book in her typically meticulous fashion.

Several historians, writers, and researchers offered assistance. Boynton Merrill, Jr., was extremely generous with his time, knowledge, and resources relating to the Lewis brothers affair, as was Mary Helen Dohan on the subject of the Roosevelts and their steamboat. They also both read the appropriate sections of the manuscript for accuracy. Herb Goltz shared insights about Tecumseh and the pan-tribal movement. Mark Tushnet helped on the topic of slave murders. My son Ben offered worthwhile suggestions about the section on agriculture.

As a result of my conversations with Jack Forbes on the sensitive matter of terminology regarding North America's indigenous peoples, I came up with the distinction of identifying them as Native Americans when referring to them from their own perspective, as opposed to calling them Indians when viewed from the perspective of white people. As much as possible, I tried to stick to that approach.

More than a few scientists contributed geological and seismological expertise. Arch Johnston, Buddy Schweig, and Ron Street spent hours explaining both the basic principles and the fine points of their fields, as well as the specifics of the New Madrid quakes. Joan Gomberg, Bruce Kutter, Eldridge Moores, Bill Thomas, and Alec Winters were also more than gracious with their assistance. Arch, Buddy, and Alec all read early versions of the earthquake chapters for accuracy.

Bill Porter of Ingram Barge Co. bent over backwards to arrange my passage on two of the company's boats on the Ohio River, and the crews of the *Michael J. Grainger* and the *Alvin C. Johnson* made me feel warmly welcome. Captains "Chevy" Chevront and Michael Fowler, and pilots Mike Murphy and Jeff Perle answered my many questions, generously sharing their comprehensive knowledge of the river. Cooks Alicia Bivens and Billie Joyce Earhart kept me very well fed, and Les Grimm showed me every kindness when I disembarked at Paducah.

Marion Hayes spent an afternoon driving me around the Blytheville, Arkansas, area pointing out surviving surface evidence of the New Madrid earthquakes, and also dug a trench with his backhoe to expose subterranean evidence of the quakes.

Arnie Fieldman shlepped around Washington, D.C., more than once, digging up documents I'd missed in my work at the Library of Congress and the National Archives.

Wayne Viitanen kindly allowed me to photocopy his Ph.D. dissertation, and David Logdson sent me a photocopy of his out-of-print pamphlet.

I was extremely fortunate to be able to work with Meg Hehner, whose maps grace the text.

I originally intended to personally thank all the librarians and archivists who helped me along the way, but the list grew rather too long. I would be remiss, however, if I failed to express my gratitude to the following librarians at Shields Library at the University of California, Davis: John Skarstad of Special Collections, and Gary Clark, Ling Liu, and Jason Newborn of Interlibrary Loan. I have no doubt there were times they wanted to hide when they saw me coming, but they nonetheless processed my endless requests without so much as a grumble.

Fred Chase and Celia Knight could not have been more conscientious or painstaking in their copyediting and proofreading of the manuscript. The book jacket design by Terry Rohrbach of Base Art Co. is everything I could have hoped for.

Alex Smithline is not only a good agent, but he's also a mensch—a combination of qualities not always found in one person.

If there's a better editor in this business than Bruce Nichols, I can't imagine who that might be. He understood from the beginning what I had in mind, and his enthusiasm for the concept was a heartening validation. That this book is a coherent whole is in no small part due to his clarity and guidance.

Many friends and relatives maintained their interest in the project throughout the time I was working on the manuscript, most notably my parents, Ben and Edna, whose support was unwavering.

And of course, Marti—what would I ever do without her?

J. F.

Index

About the Author

JAY FELDMAN is a widely published freelance writer. His work has appeared in *Sports Illustrated, Newsweek, Smithsonian* magazine, *Gourmet, The New York Times,* and a broad variety of other national, regional, and local publications. He has also written for television (the highly acclaimed but short-lived CBS series *Brooklyn Bridge*), film, and the stage. He lives in Davis, California.

His Web site is www.jfeldman.com.

Printed in the United States
By Bookmasters